# Expansion and Global Interaction, 1200–1700

# Expansion and Global Interaction, 1200–1700

## David R. Ringrose

*University of California, San Diego*

Michael Adas
Series Editor

*Rutgers University at New Brunswick*

New York   Boston   San Francisco
London   Toronto   Sydney   Tokyo   Singapore   Madrid
Mexico City   Munich   Paris   Cape Town   Hong Kong   Montreal

Publisher: Priscilla McGeehon
Executive Marketing Manager: Sue Westmoreland
Production Manager: Mark Naccarelli
Project Coordination, Text Design, and Electronic Page Makeup: Nesbitt Graphics
Cover Designer/Manager: Nancy Danahy
Cover Photo: PlanetArt
Art Studio: Mapping Specialists Limited
Photo Researcher: Julie Tesser
Print Buyer: Roy Pickering
Printer and Binder: The Maple-Vail Book Manufacturing Group
Cover Printer: The Lehigh Press, Inc.

For permission to use copyrighted material, grateful acknowledgment is made to the copyright holders on p. 209–213, which are hereby made part of this copyright page.

Library of Congress Cataloging-in-Publication Data

Ringrose, David R.
    Expansion and global interaction, 1200–1700/David R. Ringrose.
        p.    cm.
    Includes bibliographical references and index.
    ISBN 0-321-01125-2 (alk. paper)
    1. Europe—History—To 1490.   2. Europe—Territorial expansion.
    3. Colonization—History.   4. Imperialsim—Historiography.
    5. Mongols—History   6. Asia—History.
    I Title.
D116.R56 2000
940—dc21                                                     00-029640

Please visit our website at http://www.awl.com/history

ISBN 0-321-01125-2

5 6 7 8 9 10—MA—03 02 01 00

# Contents

# *Maps*

# Illustrations

# Readings

# Series Editor's Preface

In a number of ways that distinguish it from all preceding historical epochs, the post-1500 era has proved highly problematic for those attempting to write about or teach history that is genuinely global in its coverage and perspectives. The "rise of Europe," from admittedly modest beginnings in the mid-1400s, to what would ultimately be a position of world dominance by the late-1800s, has resulted in a heavy emphasis on developments in Europe itself in these centuries. Historians dealing with European overseas ventures, from Africa to China and the Americas to the "East Indies," have tended traditionally to portray the unprecedented cross-cultural interaction that resulted from overwhelmingly western perspectives and in accord with periodizations and historical agendas dictated by events and processes in Europe. The responses of non-European peoples have usually been depicted as largely reactive to the incursions and schemes of the Europeans. Until the last couple of decades, most historians have neglected to stress that until well into the eighteenth century European merchants, adventurers, and missionaries played marginal roles in areas like Africa, India, and China; that rather than dominate these areas, they struggled to fit successfully into preexisting patterns of commercial exchange or political hegemony. Few of the mainly European and American scholars who studied the post-1500 processes of overseas expansion gave serious attention to conditions within the societies the Europeans encountered and the ways in which these shaped the means, motives, and outcomes of Asian, African, or Amerindian responses to the intruders from the West as well as the nature of the repercussions of European ventures in these areas.

Aside from area specialists who reached limited audiences, until recently little serious attention was given to historical developments within non-European societies, much less to ongoing interregional exchanges and important new cross-cultural initiatives that had little to do with western contacts and influences. In a reversal of the actual trends of global exchange until at least the late 1700s, ideas, inventions, and trade goods were seen to be diffused from Europe to the rest of the world. In this view, Europe had become the dynamic engine of the interregional interactions and cross-cultural encounters that were increasingly viewed as definitive for early modern and modern world history.

In light of these trends, David Ringrose's wide-ranging contribution to the Longman's World History Series represents a superb synthesis of the rapidly growing historical literature focused on regional and local studies throughout the globe in the early modern era. At the same time, *Expansion and Global Interaction, 1200–1700*, marks a new departure in comparative work on the unprecedented interregional expansion and cross-cultural interaction that were among the defining processes of world history in the centuries from roughly the thirteenth onward. The decentering of our understanding of these processes is signalled in Ringrose's opening chapter, which focusses not on Europe and the forces behind its overseas ventures that one has come to expect, but on the Mongol imperium and its enduring influences on the nomadic peoples and agrarian empires that stretched across the vast Eurasian land mass. When he turns to the Mediterranean in Chapter 2, Ringrose centers his account of key themes in the centuries-long struggle for control of this critical region on both the Ottomans and Spanish, rather than Iberia exclusively. The latter area has been the starting point for virtually all of the more traditional histories of the age of expansion as well as the more recent work of scholars pursuing the world systems' approach to global history. His account of the slave trade begins in Africa; the chapter on the conquest of the Americas with the Inca and Aztec empires; and the sections on South and East Asia with the Mughal, Safavid, and Ming dynasties, and the consolidation of Tokugawa Shogunate in Japan.

Ringrose's approach is all the more remarkable because he has made his career as a distinguished historian of European, particularly Spanish, economic history. Not only has he broken from the Eurocentric expansion of Iberia mode, which, given his background, he could well be expected to adopt, he has also mastered the considerable secondary and published primary literature on the history of the other major centers of global power and expansionism from the thirteenth to the seventeenth centuries. Thus, *Expansion and Global Interaction* exemplifies a broader trend of reorientation within the historical profession—a trend that is making for more genuinely world perspectives on some of the key events and processes in recent human experience. Ringrose's attention to the varying social, economic, and political dynamics within different regions allows us to understand the expansive tendencies of African, Asian, or Amerindian peoples on their own terms. It also provides a meaningful context for studying the impact of European intrusions of varying kinds from trade and exploration to conquest and Christian missionary proselytization. To have accomplished all of these tasks in a single, rather slim, volume is a considerable achievement in itself. To have done so through a cogent, highly readable narrative that captures the heightened sense of transglobal questing, curiosity, and ambition for wealth and power that mark these centuries of expansion and cross-cultural interaction makes this a work that deserves the widest possible readership.

*Michael Adas, Series Editor and Abraham Voorhees, Professor of History*
*Rutgers University at New Brunswick*
*New Brunswick, New Jersey*

# Author's Preface

An extraterrestrial explorer surveying our world in the 1600s would have encountered some puzzling paradoxes and might well have made some very wrong predictions about developments in the next three centuries. The most striking feature such a visitor would see was the dominating presence of three immense empires, China, India, and the Ottoman Empire. Each of them contained many scores of millions of people, ruled territories that extended across thousands of miles, and housed diverse and sophisticated commercial and industrial communities. The Ottoman Empire had already endured for almost three centuries. It not only controlled large parts of three continents but was still pushing outward in the Mediterranean and the Balkans. The Mughal Empire of India was newer, but had just unified the entire Indian sub-continent and stretched from Iran to Burma. China had just been reorganized by victorious Manchu invaders and, as of the time of American independence, was the largest and most powerful empire the world had ever seen. Our alien observer might easily have predicted that Eurasia and Africa would before long be dominated by these three great empires. A closer look would also have shown our observer a fourth large empire, one that covered most of North and South America. This empire, however, looked quite unlike the other three. Despite its enormous geographical extent, it counted well under ten million people scattered across ten thousand miles of nearly empty landscape. This American empire of the seventeenth century was also distinctive in that, by Asian standards, it had a rudimentary economy and little industry, and was dominated by export-oriented mining. The third oddity of this empire was that it was loosely governed from a distant and small country located on the far western edge of Eurasia. Our alien visitor might understandably have seen this as an unstable arrangement with little relevance beyond its own borders.

Another obvious feature that an other worldly visitor would have noticed is a long coastal fringe stretching from Scandinavia to South Africa. This western edge of Eurasia and Africa was characterized by a mosaic of turbulent and warring societies and kingdoms, none of them very large. The last thing an alien would have predicted is that by 1900 a large part of the American area of the world would be populated by people from the southern (or African) part of that chaotic coastal fringe, while governments in its northern (or European) portion would dominate the Asian empires which seemed so impressive in 1650–1700. Such an observer would be more likely to note the presence of small numbers of such Europeans in every corner of the Asian and Indian Ocean world. In such places, the local authorities of the seventeenth century usually saw these Europeans both as political and military nuisances and (on occasion) as commercial and economic assets.

Thus the more plausible predictions of our alien visitor in 1700 would seem greatly mistaken from the viewpoint of 1900, or even 1950, when Europeans governed most of the world. From the perspective of the twenty-first century that we are now entering, however, those hypothetical predictions about the global balance of power may well turn out to be reasonably accurate. This prediction could also prove quite wrong, but it remains that such a view of the future is an intriguing continuation of the global distribution of human creativity that has marked world history for most of the last three thousand years. In that context, 200 years of European supremacy would appear as a fairly brief anomaly.

This book looks at developments around the world between 1200 and 1700 from that perspective. Without a doubt, Europe was an increasingly significant part of the global landscape in this era. Contrary to the older historiography of European expansion, however, Europeans were far from dominant before 1700 anywhere except in parts of America. Even the infamous African slave trade would not have been possible without the ongoing participation of a network of independent African states. Elsewhere, Europeans sometimes seized direct control and established bases in small countries even weaker than they themselves. Yet their contacts with Japan, China, Siam, Burma, India, Persia, and the Ottoman Empire generally took place on terms set by the governments of those societies. Much of the history of this era, therefore, is the story of the dynamism of the world in general. The case of Europe was but one example of expansiveness.

At the same time, however, Europeans were unique in ways that became significant during the nineteenth and twentieth centuries. It was Europeans who organized the massive forced migration of Africans across the Atlantic, in the process creating a wholly new Afro-Euro-Atlantic society totally dependent on markets and capitalism. It was Europeans who extracted thousands of tons of silver from America so that European merchants had something to sell that appealed to Asian markets. Equally important for the future, Europeans were everywhere by 1700. This meant that, however tenuous their situation in some places, they were better positioned than any other society to exploit changing market and investment opportunities on a global scale. In the three centuries after 1650 they were to exploit this advantage ruthlessly. Nevertheless, it is hard to see how, given the information technologies of 2000 C.E. and after, such an advantage can remain the property of any one culture in the future. Thus the world of 1650–1700 points to two distinct futures. In one future, the era 1750–1950, Europeans came to exploit the tenuous advantages that they had achieved as of 1650 in order to impose their goals on much of the world. In the second future, which we are just entering, we may see other large and dynamic cultures reestablish the equilibrium typical of the long-term history of the world. It is well worth remembering that Japan has the second largest and richest national economy in the world and that China, Taiwan, Korea, and India all know how to make their own cars, trucks, rockets, and computers. Moreover, China, India, and Pakistan all know how to build nuclear weapons. Our clothes and radios are made in China and India, we drive cars from Japan and Korea, and we fly in commuter airliners made in Brazil and Indonesia. Perhaps a broader view of the dynamism of the world before 1700 will make it easier to understand how such shifts could come so rapidly after World War II.

This book grew out of an unique experiment in General Education at the University of California, San Diego. A group of faculty, under the direction and inspiration of Professor James Lyon, undertook to create a core course for an undergraduate college that emphasized world and international affairs. Appropriately, that college is now named after Eleanor Roosevelt. The core course, The Making of the Modern World, became a six quarter interdisciplinary program. It was structured around a sequence of chronological periods, but was meant to highlight aspects of the past that explain the human landscape confronted by the modern participant.

More directly, this little book is the result of several years of some-times frustrating experience teaching the segment of this course that dealt with the period 1200–1700. Such an enterprise is a bit like shooting at a moving target from a moving platform. Not only did the interests and preparation of the intended audience (California freshmen and sopho-mores) change. The end of the Cold War changed the world around us dramatically, and with it our perspective on the Western role within it. Hopefully this essay has kept pace with enough of those changes to re-main interesting. In a more personal vein, this book reflects the contribu-tions of others involved in The Making of the Modern World, notably Kathryn Ringrose, Donald Abbott, Richard Madsen, Stefan Tanaka, Hassan Kayali, and Christena Turner—some of whom may be unaware of their contributions to my thinking. My turn towards world history is partly due to Professor Jack Owens of Idaho State University. Jack trapped me into an awkward but stimulating session at the American Historical Association Convention a few years ago. I am also indebted to a sizeable list of anony-mous reviewers who critiqued the manuscript prior to publication. Some of them irritated me a bit, but all of them offered thoughtful and useful com-ments. I also owe a debt to Addison Wesley Longman, which continued to express interest in the project as the company worked through the process of absorbing the division of HarperCollins which had originally taken up the project. In that connection I would like to acknowledge the efforts of Pam Gordon, Abigail Ruth, and Priscilla McGeehon, who managed the re-view process and patiently prodded me to deliver the goods in a timely way. Finally, I want to acknowledge the encouragement and support of Michael Adas, a longtime friend and former colleague. Mike seized upon my loose ramblings about a book like this and challenged me to write them down in a coherent form.

# Introduction

This book begins its examination of the world around 1200 C.E. Before that time, world history is most easily told as parallel histories of distinct regions and civilizations. Although those civilizations were often in contact and borrowed religious traditions such as Buddhism, Christianity, and Islam, their individual historical narratives were largely self-contained. This was changing by 1200, and from that time it gets increasingly difficult to understand local and regional histories without considering the context of global or transcontinental interactions. Earlier, empires and civilizations had often encountered one another usually exchanging luxuries or exotic curiosities. The spread of Islam, Christianity, and Buddhism means that such contacts were far from incidental, but by 1200 the rate of interaction was accelerating.

After 1200, empires and civilizations expanded on a much greater geographic scale, reaching across oceans and continents to make permanent incursions into each other's territory. They invaded each other, exchanged ruling elites, imposed religion and language, borrowed technology, political concepts, and administrative techniques, and became economically interdependent. It is true that such encounters had happened before 1200; in fact, many of the religious and commercial links of later centuries had long since been forged. Beginning around 1200, however, these developments took on a more pronounced intercontinental and even global quality.

This new dynamism greatly complicates the telling of world history after 1200. Empires and cultures continued to be moved largely by their own internal dynamics, but historical outcomes can no longer be explained without attention to the impact of political, cultural, economic, and religious expansion that brought widely separated parts of the world into intimate and permanent contact.

The globalization of history was propelled by three large-scale and interrelated processes. One was the climatic cycle. A global warming trend lasted from about 800 C.E. until about 1200 C.E., and was followed by a pronounced cooling trend that lasted until after 1700. This phenomenon helped to mobilize a second, very different factor.

Around the world, settled civilizations lived uneasily with neighboring nomad societies, societies that had learned how to live in the inhospitable deserts and grasslands that often bounded settled agricultural societies. Those deserts and grasslands were very sensitive to the changes

1

in annual rainfall brought by long-term changes in climate, and the era between 1100 and 1400 saw an intensification of nomadic migrations into settled agricultural areas everywhere from China to Mexico. This population shift produced a number of mobile, militarized societies. The leaders of these warrior societies were adept at lightning invasions of established countries in which they seized control at the center and made themselves into new ruling elites. In several cases the military elites proved adept at constructing major empires.

The third factor, which became prominent in the mid-1300s and reappeared after 1500, was disease. Indeed, one sign that major cultures had previously had little contact was the fact that major epidemic diseases common for centuries in some regions had been unknown in others. The most dramatic was the bubonic or black plague, which swept across most of Europe and Asia beginning about 1330. It often killed over half of the people in large cities, came back periodically once established, and reduced the population of whole continents by 30 percent in one generation. The plague disrupted social hierarchies, eroded the tax systems of large governments, and created political and demographic vacuums—the classic formula for internal upheaval in any society. In the Middle East and sub-Saharan Africa such political and demographic vacuums invited further nomadic invasions from Central Asia and the Atlas Mountains.

Epidemic disease later had an impact in Africa and America. In Africa, tropical diseases protected indigenous society for centuries from serious European invasion. Sub-Saharan Africans had developed immunity to diseases that killed most Europeans within a year of their arrival. The opposite pattern appeared in the Americas. There, Europeans brought with them a series of epidemic diseases. Over centuries Europeans had developed immunity to most of them, but the Amerindians had no immunity and died by the millions. This is a crucial part of any explanation of why such small numbers of Europeans were able to overturn major American empires in 1520 (Mexico) and 1530 (Peru). Climate, nomads, and disease help explain how the process of interaction got started, but they tell us much less about the outcomes.

If climate, nomadism, and disease deserve more attention in our understanding of world history, another factor has often been given too much attention. It is easy to turn the history of European expansion, which also begins a little before 1200, into a history of a world within which Europeans overshadowed and oppressed the societies they encountered. This assumption reflects the worldview of the 1800s, when Europeans and western technology did intrude heavily on the rest of the world. But in 1700 that was far in the future. Most of the "great" European colonial empires of the 1500s and 1600s were great only from a European perspective. Admittedly, Spain's conquest of Mexico and Peru compares with other major examples of empire building. From an Indian, Ottoman, or Chinese perspective, however, the European presence was not particularly significant until after 1700.

In practice, until 1600 most European expansion started as small, highly speculative ventures by men who were marginal to European society, or who were being displaced from the Mediterranean by Ottoman Turkish expansion. In two cases (Mexico and Peru) these daring and ruthless adventurers actually conquered great empires, but in both they were given unique openings by local crises and by devastating ecological accidents involving European disease. The story of the Spanish conquest of the great Amerindian empires as presented in the first weeks of many American history surveys has conditioned us to a misleading view of how much Europeans actually accomplished when they first took up residence in other parts of the world.

This is why the story of the expulsion of the Europeans from the Balkans and much of the Mediterranean by the Turks, and of the Europeans reactive expansion into the Indian Ocean and East Asia, is instructive. Throughout the "age of expansion," especially 1400–1600, developments in the Mediterranean were shaped by the Ottoman Empire. At the same time, the Atlantic plantations and the slave trade depended on the cooperation of African governments, while commercial, cultural, and geopolitical affairs in India, the Far East, and the western Pacific were shaped primarily by the Indian (Mughal) or Chinese Empires. While Europeans created far-flung commercial empires backed by the use of force, and while those "empires" were important to the warlord states that we call European kingdoms, before about 1700 their activities had surprisingly little impact on the mainstream course of events in Africa and Asia. For the most part Europeans elaborated upon age-old trade patterns built by others, and they were able to stay in Asia and Africa largely because they served local needs. Europe was increasingly important for the Afro-Asian world after 1750, but before 1700 Afro-Asia was much more important to Europe than Europe was to Africa or Asia.

In 1700, such developments were still secondary features on the world horizon. What they reflected, however, were important differences between the various forms of expansion under way between 1200 and 1700. European expansion, driven largely by a combination of politics and market-driven profit seeking, emphasized different values and goals from the military expansion of Ottoman, Mughal, or (in Iran) Safavid empire building, Chinese cultural expansion, or Japanese unification. Except possibly in Spanish America, the results of that difference were not apparent until after 1700. At the same time, certain new features had entered the picture of world history, some of which help to explain the period of European ascendancy between about 1800 and 1950. In 1700, Asia and Africa were more important to Europe than Europe was to those places, but the Europeans had created for themselves a strategically important situation just as population had begun to expand all around the world. Thus, this little book may help with understanding both the European ascendancy between 1800 and 1950 and the fact that other parts of the world were able to reassert a degree of balance in the later twentieth century.

Finally, world expansion between 1200 and 1700 offers a helpful perspective on the world since 1950. As we will see, before 1700 China was the most important single factor in stimulating global interaction, while Europe was a secondary but emergent force. As of the beginning of the twenty-first century, the Europeanized West is dominant, but China and its Asian neighbors have become a potent emerging force. The dynamism and potential significance of this new trend needs to be seen in the light of Asia's global significance for several centuries before 1700.

# 1
## THE GLOBALIZATION OF HISTORY

# Climate, Nomads, Mongols

## DEFINING EXPANSION

In 1258 the Mongol army under Chinggis Khan's grandson Hulegu captured and pillaged the city of Baghdad. In the process they murdered the Caliph, ruthlessly slaughtered most of the city's population, and destroyed the political and religious center of the Muslim Middle East. This bloody event, and the subsequent Mongol conquest of southern China, constituted one of the most spectacular examples of imperial expansion in history. Starting in 1206 with a small confederation of nomadic tribes on the northern edge of China, Chinggis Khan and his successors conquered an empire that eventually included Ukraine, Russia, Iraq, Iran, China, Korea, Vietnam, and most of the lands between. Unique in history, this loosely organized empire was assembled in three short generations, without the aid of modern communications, modern transportation, or modern weaponry. It was done by a people easily stereotyped as uncivilized nomadic barbarians but who, in fact, were building upon centuries of interaction between nomadic and agricultural communities across Asia.

The Mongol empire did not last long compared with other empires, but it helped to set the stage for a new phase in world history. Through the next five centuries societies and empires converted, conquered, absorbed, and influenced each other with an intensity and on a geographic scale never seen before. Religious traditions, commercial communities, and political empires expanded far beyond their centuries-old geographic confines. As they expanded, they began a cumulative process of contact, of economic interconnection, and of cultural conflict and assimilation that still continues. Expansion, whether imperial or cultural, was hardly new in 1200 C.E., but from that time it acquired a complexity, geographic scope, and permanence that, excepting the rise of Islam after 700 C.E., is hard to find in earlier episodes.

By 1700 this chaotic expansion had created a world of cultural, religious, and commercial interdependence in which decisions in Rome affected politics in Beijing; the mining industry in Peru affected commerce in Spain, Japan, and India; and sugar prices in the Caribbean influenced trade and politics in Holland, Africa, and the Ottoman Empire. The stage had been set for the imperialism and industrialization of the modern era. This new wave of expasion began in many places at about the same time— in Africa, Europe, the Americas, and South and Southeast Asia.

The Mongol example, however, had a dramatic quality and geographic scope that allows it to appear as a factor in much of subsequent Eurasian history (see Map 1.1). In its brief but spectacular existence the Mongol empire incorporated virtually every element of the cascade of political, commercial, and cultural expansion that marks the age of global expansiveness. We will come back to the Mongols later. For now it is useful to summarize the four kinds of expansion that define the way that the word is used throughout this book

## POLITICAL AND MILITARY EXPANSION

The most common way of presenting expansion is in terms of the extension of political control. As a system of government, the Mongol empire is an example of a distinctive type of such political empire building. It was the most spectacular of several cases of political expansion characterized by roving militarized elites who moved quickly and brutally to establish themselves as rulers of more settled societies, societies often far outside their homelands and with different cultures. This type of military aggression is different from the local wars over dynastic rights that became common inside Europe, but has parallels in the rise of the Incas in Peru, the Spanish occupation of America, and the Turkish conquest of the Balkans, as well as the Mongols themselves. The institutional facades through which these warrior empires governed varied greatly. They ranged from the Mongols' tribal confederation headed by Chinggis Khan and his heirs, to the redistributive autocracy of the Inca, to the dynastic monarchies of Europe. Whatever the form of authority, this kind of political expansion was spearheaded by small, militarized elites with remarkable cohesion and mobility. Where such incidents differ, and where the story of political expansion becomes complicated, is in the ability of these military elites to transform conquest into durable empire—something the Mongols themselves failed to do.

## CULTURAL EXPANSION

Across most of Asia and the Middle East the Mongol empire also provided a framework for cultural expansion, which is much harder to describe succinctly. As peoples came into closer contact, they borrowed (or were forced to accept) values and material goods from the societies they

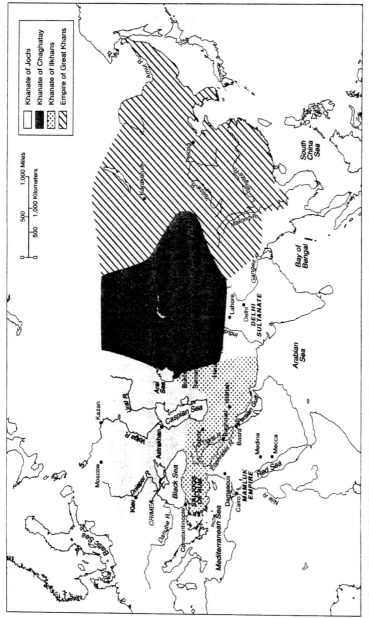

**MAP 1.1 THE MONGOL EMPIRES IN THE THIRTEENTH CENTURY.**
*On the death of Chinggis Khan, his four heirs each assumed administrative authority over a part of the Mongol conquests and expanded on them. By the late 1200s this gave a single ruling system to an empire that stretched from Moscow to Korea and from Turkey to Vietnam.*

7

encountered. These cultural exchanges varied tremendously from one contact to another, ranging from selective borrowing to the imposition of one culture on another. Sometimes the process followed military conquest, but it also happened in gradual, peaceful ways. In western Asia, for example, the Mongols long retained many of the values of their nomadic tribal origins, yet they quickly adopted the Muslim religion of the peoples they encountered. In some cases, as with the Spaniards in America, the conquering elite imposed its own religion and language on the people they conquered, even as the Amerindians held on to many elements of their own culture. Elsewhere, as with most invaders of China and the Norse Vikings who occupied Northern France, the conquerors not only adopted the local religion, but were assimilated by the culture of the society they had invaded. After 1200 this kind of cultural expansion became more frequent. Nevertheless, even where religion and language were imposed upon conquered societies, as with Catholicism and Spanish in the Americas, the long-term result was a new cultural configuration, as in contemporary Latin America.

## RELIGIOUS EXPANSION

The Mongol empire also offered a context for the conscious, even aggressive, expansion of particular religions. The Mongols themselves were pragmatic about religion if the peoples that they conquered were willing to accept their new political obligations. They were well aware that it was easier to rule a conquered country if the new rulers adopted the religion that justified political authority among its people. By providing a common legal tradition and safe communications throughout Asia, the Mongol empire facilitated the spread of religion systems. Among the great religions, Islam was probably the biggest beneficiary of this situation, but under Mongol rule Buddhism also made great strides and Christian missionaries visited many parts of central Asia and China.

Beyond the Mongol empire, the missionizing urge of Christianity was seen in the Crusades that began in 1095 and, after 1492, in the Christianization of America as well as in remarkable missions to Africa, India, China, and Japan. Islam, meanwhile, continued to spread across sub-Saharan Africa, Southeast Asia, Indonesia, Anatolia, and into the Balkans. In the period 1430–1530 the same process of aggressive religious expansion could be seen in the spread of the imperial cult in the Inca empire. Thus the global reach of Islam, Christianity, and Buddhism in 1700 constituted one of the major expansive phenomena of the preceding four centuries. Although religious expansion often coincided with cultural expansion, the two are not coterminous. The Islam of Southeast Asia, for example, and the Christianity that developed in black Africa were heavily influenced by local culture.

## ECONOMIC EXPANSION

The Mongol empire also provided a framework for economic expansion. This expansion had two complementary aspects, neither of which was like the economic imperialism of the nineteenth century. By incorporating the unruly warrior nomads of a vast part of Eurasia into a single political system, the Mongols gave their subject societies relatively stable conditions and markets. This encouraged prosperity and demographic expansion in many of the agricultural societies under Mongol rule. At the same time, the size of the empire made much safer the trade routes between China, the Middle East, India, and Europe. Goods and information crossed the Eurasian land mass with a regularity never before observed. The expansion of trade was obvious within the Mongol empire, but it did not depend solely on the stable institutions of that empire.

Trade had its own organizing mechanisms and expanded everywhere in Africa, Asia, and Europe. Just as political expansion was carried out by specialized military elites, long-distance trade was conducted by specialized commercial societies. These mercantile cultures founded strings of colonies along important trade routes. Tied together over long distances by language, family connections, and familiar business practices, such commercial societies facilitated long-distance trade between separate and distinctive societies and economies. The conditions created by the Mongol empire provided an unprecedented opportunity for this type of commerce. Such trade reached from China to England and West Africa. At various times and places this specialized commercial role was played by Arabs, the Gujeratis of western India, Greeks, Jews, Chinese, Malays, Armenians, Italians, and a number of African societies, to name only a few.

Thus the Mongol empire encouraged all four expansive urges (political, cultural, religious, and economic), but each form of expansion had its own geography, internal dynamic, and inner logic. Any given example of conquest or cultural interaction inevitably included elements of all four, but the mixture varied greatly from one case to another. Indeed, the Mongol empire itself was the result of such processes; to understand its real significance, we must examine the forces that made it possible and see those forces as applicable to more than just the Mongol example. After all, the period of Mongol greatness in Asia (ca. 1206–1360) also included bursts of expansion in Africa and Europe and successful resistance against the Mongols in India and the Middle East. The interactions that took place between distinctive societies can only be understood if we remain aware of the complexities of the expansion that caused them.

## NOMADS AND FARMERS

Before the Mongols and the thirteenth century, world history is more easily told as the history of separate civilizations and religious traditions. China, India, Sub-Saharan Africa, the Mediterranean/Middle East, and the Americas each contained distinctive cultures marked by their own stories of creation, religious systems, and political traditions. Separation obviously did not mean total isolation, and, except for the lack of contact between America and Africa–Eurasia, early civilizations long were in touch with each other. Trade, ideas, and information moved throughout

the Afro-Eurasian world and between North and South America. Sometimes, as with the spread of Buddhism, Islam, and Christianity, the results
were quite dramatic. Before about 1000 C.E., most contacts between civilizations were relatively sporadic and easily disrupted. By 1200, however,
it is becoming much harder to write world history as a series of parallel
and separate narratives.

At the same time, there was a common factor that shaped history almost everywhere, a factor that relates not only to the rise of the Mongols
but to the creation of several large empires by other communities of nomadic warriors around the world. This factor was the unstable equilibrium between settled farming societies and nomadic hunting and herding
ones. When civilizations are defined in terms of customs, technology, language, and ethnicity, rather than in terms of political boundaries, we discover that every large civilization has spread across a variety of climate
zones and ecological systems, producing a variety of subcultures adapted
to specific environments. These subcultures included nomadic tribes with
economies based on grazing and hunting, peasant societies based on sub-
sistence cereal farming, and urbanized communities that depended upon
commercial agriculture and capital-intensive irrigation.

As a result, every large civilization experienced an ongoing internal
tension between town-based farmers and nomadic, pastoral communities
of the mountains, grasslands, and deserts. The pastoral subcultures were
adapted to the exploitation of dry prairies and the livestock and game that
grazed upon them. This imposed a mobile, nomadic way of life that per-
petuated the values and attitudes of the hunter and warrior. Such subcultures did little regular farming and were limited in their ability to accumulate fixed capital goods. They understood the technologies of settled
societies, but used them in ways that fitted their nomadic lifestyle. By
contrast, farming subcultures were fixed to the landscape. This allowed
them to make long-term investments in fields, irrigation, storage facilities,
and urban centers. They could support cities, a specialized governing
class, and complex religious institutions. They developed manufacturing
industries that required fixed equipment and served stable markets. Most
markets were local, but many industries depended on exchanges with nomadic neighbors and on long-distance trade.

The relationship between nomadic and farming subcultures within a
particular civilization is often presented as a conflict between two separate worlds. Although this idea has some validity, the situation is better
understood if we think of it as a system of mutual dependence, almost a
symbiotic relationship. Despite recurrent conflict, relations between nomadic or pastoral peoples and farming communities involved trade or
barter based on the differences between their respective economies.
Farming villages and larger cities traded food grains, dried fruit and nuts,
cloth, metals, and manufactures to nomadic herders in return for horses,
cattle, sheep, wool, hides, yarn, and other animal products. The towns
also supplied trade goods and markets for city-based merchants who travelled in long-distance caravans. The pastoral nomads, however, knew the

overland trade routes, supplied and organized the necessary mules, horses, camels, and supplies, and provided the trail guides and protection essential to any cross-country trek. The rulers of farming societies sometimes organized effective infantry armies, as in the Roman and Han Empires, but such armies are expensive to maintain. Nomads could provide fast-moving mounted warriors for hire. Therefore, it was routine for settled governments to use armies of hired nomadic warriors to protect them from their neighbors and from attack by other nomadic marauders.

If interdependence between nomads and farmers was common, it was also unstable. If something changed the relationship between pastoral nomads and the grazing lands upon which they depended, or if the balance between usable farmland and the population supported by farming was upset, the precarious nomad–farmer equilibrium was disrupted. As a result, nomadic warriors sometimes invaded settled cities by force, pillaging and seizing political control. If annual grazing migrations were disrupted, whole nomadic tribes were forced to seek new pasture lands. This pattern was a background factor in several areas. In Europe it was represented by the barbarian invasions of the third through sixth centuries and by the Viking, Muslim, and Hunnic invasions between 700 and 1000 C.E. It is also exemplified by the Muslim tribesmen who erupted from Arabia in the seventh century. Such migrations were also important in the history of the central Asian plains long before the Mongol invasions, and, as we will see, similar processes took place in Africa and America. Thus the nomad–farmer frontiers around the world offer part of the explanation for the growing restlessness of the world's peoples after 1200 C.E.

## CLIMATE AND NOMADIC MIGRATIONS

The broad lines of nomadic mobilization, and its acceleration after about 1200, were almost certainly affected by long-term shifts in global climate. This relationship remains speculative because it is hard to document in ways that are comfortable for conventional historians, but the nomad–farmer frontier was extremely sensitive to climatic changes, and the chronological correlations are strong. We have good evidence that between about 300 and 800 C.E. the world experienced a cooling trend, which was followed by a better defined period of warming from 800 C.E. until about 1200 C.E. This was followed by a well-documented cooling trend that lasted until about 1700 C.E. and is referred to as "the little Ice Age" by European historians.

The interaction between nomads and farmers, when confronted by destabilizing climatic shifts, set the stage for the breakup of several great empires between 300 and 800 C.E. Climatic warming sustained the expansion of both nomadic and farming societies between 800 and 1200 C.E. Thereafter, climatic change encouraged the recurrent invasion of settled societies by militarized nomadic elites and former nomads and thus shaped subsequent world history.

The logic behind this generalization is easier to see if we look at the geography of the nomad–farmer frontier. (See Map 1.2.) For various reasons the frontier is more obvious in the Old World than in the New. It ran along an immense belt of prairies, deserts, and mountains that were hostile to farmers and sensitive to climatic and demographic change. In Africa, Europe, and Asia, this frontier follows a massive belt of mountains that starts with the Atlas Mountains of Morocco in Africa and the rugged sierras of nearby Spain. This mountain chain runs across Southern Europe, forming the Pyrenees, Alps, and Balkan ranges before crossing into Asia Minor and the Middle East. There it includes the Taurus and Zagros ranges and the rugged mountains of the Caucasus. This huge mountain barrier then culminates in the immense massif of the Himalayan Mountains, which extends from Iran and Afghanistan through South Central Asia and Tibet, separating China from India, Burma, and Vietnam.

South of this mountain world in Africa and the Middle East, and north of it in Asia, we find a huge band of deserts and prairies. In Africa and Arabia these arid plains include the vast deserts of the Sahara and Arabia. As one moves south into Africa, however, the Sahara gradually turns into grassland and then into reliably watered farmland. In the Middle East, the Iranian Plateau offers a similar open plain, but in most of Asia these vast prairies and deserts stretch north of the mountainous east–west spine of the continent. North of the Black Sea and east of the Caspian Sea, prairies and deserts stretch for thousands of miles north of the Himalayas and China into Mongolia and Manchuria. Scattered through the dry plains are the oasis-like river valleys of Egypt, the Holy Land, Mesopotamia, Iran, Afghanistan, and south-central Asia. Adjacent to the mountain ranges and vast semiarid plains are the watered, fertile lowlands of China, Southeast Asia, India, Africa, and Europe. These oases and watered lowlands supported the civilizations and empires that fill most of world history, but it must be remembered that they lived in a complex relationship with their nomadic neighbors.

A similar contrast can be found between the fertile valleys of central Mexico and the drier plains and deserts that stretch northward into what is now the southwestern United States. There the dry-land societies, without domestic livestock, were less pastoral and more dependent on hunting and food gathering, but the interaction between nomadic plains communities and settled farming ones was similar. In the Andes the pattern was made more complex by the mosaic of small-scale ecologies created by the extreme variations in altitude found in the Andean highlands. Even there, however, the tension between the values of a hunter–warrior society and settled farmers was constant. It is well illustrated by the fifteenth-century Inca conquest of the urbanized Chimu empire on the coast of Peru, with its settled agriculture and advanced irrigation systems.

Changing climate affected the unstable equilibrium along the nomad–farmer frontier in locally different ways. The changes were driven by two patterns. Generally speaking, a cooling trend allows glaciers to ex-

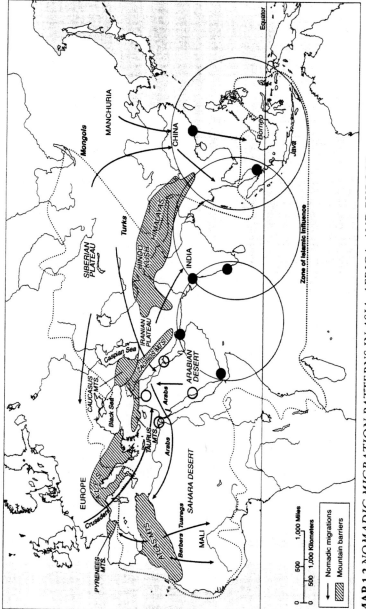

**MAP 1.2** *NOMADIC MIGRATION PATTERNS IN ASIA, AFRICA, AND EUROPE.*
*This map provides a schematic picture of the main mountain barriers and areas of origin of the more important nomadic migrants mentioned in the text. They were drawn to the agricultural zones in China, Southeast Asia, India, Iran, the Fertile Crescent, Egypt, Europe, and West Africa.*

13

pand and move down into mountain valleys and brings cold weather to lower altitudes and latitudes. Reduced energy in the hemispheric weather pattern weakens the northern jet streams and the prevailing winds and monsoons in tropical zones. As a result, the moisture that the winds pick up from the ocean is not carried as far inland and rainfall becomes less reliable, causing drier weather and greater extremes of hot and cold in the continental interiors. A long-term warming trend reverses the process and makes life possible at higher altitudes and in more northerly locations. It also brings more, and more regular, rainfall into the plains and deserts of Central Asia, Africa, central Europe, and central and southwestern North America. These changes inevitably affect the equilibrium between nomadic communities and their urbanized, agricultural counterparts.

Thus it is not surprising that the cooling period that began around 300 C.E. coincided with the disintegration of several empires: the Han Empire in China, the Roman Empire in the Mediterranean, and the polity that built the immense ceremonial center at Teoteohuacan in Mexico. A bit later it caught up with the Ghanian empire in Africa, the city kingdoms in Mayan Central America, and the Gupta Empire in India, which collapsed under the pressure of Hunnic nomads around 500 C.E. The only notable survivors from this pattern were the Byzantine Empire and Sassanian Persia, both of which had the advantage of being located at the crossroads of age-old trade and urban networks. Elsewhere, complex governments gave way with the decline of internal tax revenue and invasion by "barbarian" nomads whose traditional homelands could no longer sustain them.

The warming trend that began around 800 C.E. provides a more immediate background to the expansion that began in the 1200s. Archaeology shows that between 800 and about 1250 farming expanded into the highland valleys of Norway and Scotland, and even achieved toeholds in Iceland and Greenland. Sailors, fishermen, and settlers moved around the Northern Atlantic more safely, without being blocked by Arctic ice. On a global scale, a variety of larger political and cultural systems began to consolidate. The warming period between 800 and 1200 C.E. encouraged the expansion of agriculture and the growth of cities in the farming cultures of China, India, the Middle East, sub-Saharan Africa, Europe, and the Americas. This did not always result in large political empires, but it produced a variety of structures that transcended the boundaries of small political states. The era corresponds with the dynamic Song Dynasty, which ruled much of China between 960 and 1279. It saw the emergence of an interdependent but politically disunited South and Southeast Asian world. While that area produced such splendors as Angkor Wat in modern Cambodia, it also created the most complex long-distance trading economy the world had ever seen, with regular commerce from Africa and Arabia to China. Concurrently we can point to the rise of trading cities and new polities in the Mali Empire in west Africa, the Ethiopian conquest of Axum in east Africa, the Toltec political system in Mexico, and the Anazazi and Cahokian cultures in North America. In Europe this era saw the emergence of a series of uniquely autonomous universities and a distinctive urban culture oriented to trade and manufacturing. A politically disunited Europe was giving rise to a society that included important niches for both capitalism and learning.

Global warming after 800 C.E. also encouraged the expansion of the militaristic nomadic societies which lived all along the world's nomad–farmer border zone. In the European world the Norwegian and Danish Vikings spread across the Atlantic, captured parts of England, Ireland, and France, and established themselves in Sicily. The Swedes (Varangians), meanwhile, travelled along the Russian rivers, reaching the Black Sea and Persia, and at one point provided the palace guard for the Byzantine Emperor in Constantinople. From 1095 C.E. the European military class, partly derived from Viking conquerors, acted as nomadic invaders in the Holy Land during what Europeans called the Crusades. After about 1050, therefore, Europe itself escaped the wave of nomadic invasions that hit China and the Middle East in the next three centuries. Similar nomads from the Atlas Mountains of Morocco and the North African plains disrupted the Ghanian Empire in Africa before themselves building the empire of Mali.

The most dramatic development coinciding with the era of global warming after 800 was the rise of Islam. (See Map 1.3.) In the middle of the seventh century the prophet Mohammed appeared in Arabia. His initial followers, who came from the nomadic world of the Arabian Desert, were already moving into the politically disunited Fertile Crescent (modern Iraq, Syria, Lebanon, and the Holy Land). They brought an appealing new faith and a series of fast-moving nomadic warrior armies that co-opted local elites while imposing themselves as overlords wherever they went. By 1000 C.E., Islam had spread from Spain to northern India. The Muslim practice of co-opting local ruling groups into their ruling class meant that local elites usually converted to Islam soon after conquest. The broad mass of local populations, however, converted to Islam more gradually, and even today countries like Egypt, Iraq, and Syria have large Christian populations.

The first centuries of Islam (700–1258 C.E.) saw an attempt to combine religion and political power in a single government ruled by the Caliph in Baghdad. By 1000, however, the power of Baghdad and its Abbasid Caliphs was limited and independent Islamic centers had emerged in Iran, Egypt, North Africa, and Spain. The most important long-term split within Islam involved Iran and much of Iraq, where a dispute over the proper line of succession after Mohammed laid the basis for the distinctive Shiite Muslim tradition. This was reinforced by the strength and depth of Persian culture, which, while accepting Arabic as the language of religion, continued to use the Persian language for political and cultural purposes and as the everyday language. The result after 1000 was a collection of autonomous Islamic states loosely presided over by the Abbasid Caliph in Baghdad and uniquely tied together by common religion and a

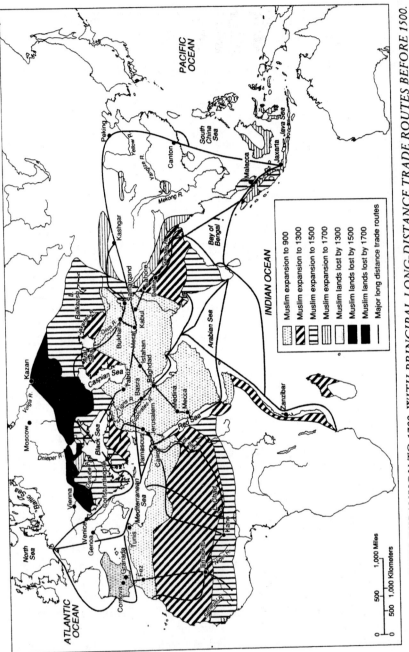

MAP 1.3 *ISLAMIC EXPANSION TO 1700, WITH PRINCIPAL LONG-DISTANCE TRADE ROUTES BEFORE 1500.*

16

---

READING 1.1

*Two brief descriptions of Baghdad by outsiders come from Jewish travellers of this era. The first is from the writings of Benjamin of Tudela, a Jewish traveller from Navarre (now part of Spain), who wrote between 1165 and 1173; the second is by the Rabbi Petachia of Ratisbon in Germany, who travelled between 1170–1187.*

Thence it is two days to Baghdad, the great city and royal residence of the Caliph Al Abbasi of the family of Mohammed. He is at the head of the Mohammedan religion, and all the kings of Islam obey him; he occupies a similar position to that held by the Pope over the Christians. He has a palace in Baghdad three miles in extent, wherein is a great park with all varieties of trees. . . . He is truthful and trusty, speaking peace to all men. The men of Islam see him but once in the year. The pilgrims that come from distant lands to go unto Mecca which is in the land of Al Yemen [sic], are anxious to see his face, and they assemble before the palace . . .

---

common language for religion and law. Although political power was dispersed in Islam, Baghdad remained its cultural center and one of the great Islamic cities of the era. (See Readings 1.1 and 1.2.)

## TURKS AND MONGOLS, NOMADS AND EMPIRES

In this context the story of the Mongols, with which we began, becomes easier to understand. The nomadic and pastoral world of Central Asia included two large groups of culturally similar tribes. To the East, on the northern edge of China, were several tribes generically referred to as the Mongols. Speaking similar languages, their culture was interconnected with that of China and their history one of perennial trade and conflict with the Chinese. The second large group lived west of China in the Eurasian interior. They, too, were a problem for the Chinese, often moving into China from Turkestan. The Turkic tribes, however, also tended to move south and west towards Russia, Europe, the Iranian plateau, and India.

In the east, the expansiveness of the nomads meant that the remarkable Song recovery was never able to restore imperial authority to northern China. Northwest of the main part of China, a group of Tibetan nomads seized control of several Chinese provinces and in 1038 assumed the

---

READING 1.2

Baghdad is a metropolis. It is the seat of the Caliph or sultan. This is the great king who rules and governs nations. Baghdad is very large, more than a day's journey from end to end. To go round it is more than three days' journey.

---

Published in *Jewish Travellers in the Middle Ages: 19 Firsthand Accounts*, Elkan Nathan Adler (ed.) (New York: Dover, 1987), excerpts from pp. 43–45 and pp. 69–70.

Chinese title of Hsi-Hsia Empire. North and East of central China, between 900 and 960 C.E., the Khitans of Manchuria conquered part of the old empire, resisting the Song Empire until after 1100. At that point the Jurchen warriors of Manchuria not only took control of the Khitans, but captured Song territory north of the Yangtze River and created the nomad-controlled Jin (Qin) Empire. Thus, even before the Mongol conquest, large parts of China were ruled by nomadic, militarized warrior elites.

Such was the context when Chinggis Khan's first major campaign conquered the Hsi-Hsia empire in 1207 (see Illustration 1.1). By 1227 he had also captured the Qin empire and had become expert in the use of Chinese siege and artillery techniques. This set the stage for an attack on

**ILLUSTRATION 1.1**
*CHINGGIS KHAN, FOUNDER OF THE MONGOL EMPIRE.*

*Source:* Reproduced in various places. The best I have found is in Adam T. Kessler, *Empires Beyond the Great Wall: The Heritage of Genghis Khan* (Los Angeles: Natural History Museum of Los Angeles, 1993), frontispiece: Portrait of Genghis Khan in his sixties. Painting by a Chinese artist on stretched silk. Courtesy of the National Palace Museum, Taipei, Taiwan, Republic of China.

the heartland of the Chinese Empire. Meanwhile, the conquered nomadic military elites were absorbed into the Mongol military machine and helped shape the political history of an expanding share of the world. Only when the Mongols confronted the highly organized and wealthy Song Empire of southern China was their progress slowed. It took forty-five years of battles and sieges before the Mongols, under Chinggis Khan's grandson, Kubilai Khan, completed the conquest of China in 1279.

In India, Muslim traders were present on the coasts soon after the Caliphate was established in Baghdad. India then saw important raids by nomadic (in this case Turkish and Muslim) warriors in the north around 1000 C.E. Unlike China, however, Indian geography and the strength of indigenous Hindu states meant that it took much longer to impose control by a militarized Muslim elite over all of India, and Muslim control of the southern half of the subcontinent was always tenuous. It was just after 1000, when nomadic warriors were imposing themselves on northern China, that the first raids by the Turkic tribesmen of Mahmud of Ghazni, who was building a kingdom in mountainous Afghanistan, began a twenty-year series of raids on Indian cities.

At first these were loot and run invasions, but the Hindu elites of northern India were unable to organize a resistance to the nomadic incursions. Around 1200, therefore, just as Chinggis Khan was starting the Mongol conquest of China, a Turkic tribe imposed itself upon northern India, creating the Muslim Sultanate of Delhi in 1206. (See Reading 1.3.) The religious fanaticism of these Muslim invaders was the beginning of the recurrent bitter relations between Muslims and Hindus still seen in modern India. They ruled much of northern India with varying degrees of effectiveness for the next 300 years. This Sultanate of Delhi successfully repelled the Mongols when the latter invaded India in the mid-1200s, but the Sultanate lost much of its cohesion after 1400.

In Western Asia recurrent nomadic expansion was taking place on an even greater geographic scale. From 800 C.E. onwards several Turkic peoples gradually filtered into Russia, Eastern Europe, Iran, and the Middle East. In 896 the pressure that they exerted on the steppe peoples of southern Russia forced the Huns to invade the Danube plain in what is now Hungary. Using Hungary as their base, the Huns raided central Europe for the next half-century. At one point, around 950, they got as far as the borders of France before they were stopped. While this was taking place in Europe, other Turkic peoples were having an even more dramatic impact on the Middle East.

In Iran, the rulers of various Persian states were becoming both Muslim and urbanized. As a result they increasingly relied on mercenary or slave troops, most of whom were recruited from Turkic tribes entering the Middle East. Thus it is hardly surprising that in the mid-800s the various contenders for succession to the Caliphate in Baghdad were using Turkish slave soldiers, first as body guards and then as troops for whole armies. (See Reading 1.4.) Referred to as *mameluks* because of their status as slaves, these soldiers became powerful participants in the politics of the

## READING 1.3

*Muslim Turks first conquered northern India in 1175, establishing the Sultanate of Delhi. Ruling by military force, these Muslims were hostile to the native Hindus and, unlike previous invaders, maintained their Muslim cultural identity. One of the more prominent Sultans was Ala-ud-din Khilji, who ruled between 1296 and 1316. Some of the policies and attitudes of this fierce warrior are summed up by the Indian historian Zia-ud-din Barni, who lived during his reign.*

The Sultan next directed his attention to the means of preventing rebellion, and first he took steps for seizing upon property. He ordered that, wherever there was a village held by proprietary right, in free gift, or as a religious endowment, it should by one stroke of the pen be brought back under the exchequer. The people were pressed and amerced [subjected to fines], money was exacted from them on every kind of pretence. . . . Secondly he provided so carefully for the acquisition of intelligence, that no action of good or bad men was concealed from him. No one could stir without his knowledge, and whatever happened in the houses of nobles, great men, and officials, was communicated to the Sultan by his reporters. . . . Thirdly he prohibited wine-drinking and wine-selling, as also the use of beer and intoxicating drugs. . . . Fourthly, the Sultan gave commands that noblemen and great men should not visit each other's houses, or give feasts, or hold meetings. They were forbidden to form alliances without consent from the throne, and they were also prohibited from allowing people to resort to their houses. . . .

After the promulgation of these interdicts, the Sultan requested the wise men to supply some rules and regulations for grinding down the Hindus, and for depriving them of that wealth and property which fosters disaffection and rebellion. . . . The Hindu was to be so reduced as to be left unable to keep a horse to ride on, to carry arms, to wear fine clothes, or to enjoy any of the luxuries of life. . . . No Hindu could hold up his head, and in their houses no sign of gold or silver or of any superfluity was to be seen. These things, which nourish insubordination and rebellion, were no longer to be found. . . . Blows, confinement in the stocks, imprisonment and chains were all employed to enforce payment [of the tribute]. . . .

---

Excerpted from H. M. Elliot and John Dowson (eds.), *The History of India as Told by Its Own Historians* (London: Trubner & Co., 1871), vol. III, pp. 179–83, 191–195, as given in William McNeill and Jean Sedlar (eds.), *China, India, and Japan: The Middle Period* (New York: Oxford University Press, 1971), pp. 147–153.

Caliphate and played an important role in the decline of its central authority. By 1000, therefore, the military establishments of the Muslim power centers in the Middle East had all been infiltrated by recently nomadic Turkish warriors.

This set the stage for an invasion in 1055 by a larger and better organized nomad force known as the Seljuk Turks. Converted to Islam in the late 900s while living north of Iran, the Seljuks had developed the capacity to organize large tribal coalitions. They also had stratified elites and well-developed royal governing institutions. Moving rapidly through Iran into the Middle East, the Seljuks used these skills effectively. They co-opted the Turkish mercenaries already present in the area and, by 1100, had

READING 1.4

*As early as the 800s the Turks were used in the armies of various Muslim rulers, including the Abbasid Caliphs at Baghdad. In the following, the historian Abu al-Jahiz (776–869 C.E.) compares the Turkish mercenaries of his time with their main competitors, the Kharijites of Iran.*

. . . Turks are as good as the Kharijites [Iranians] with the lance, and in addition, if a thousand of their horsemen are hard-pressed they will loose all their arrows in a single volley and bring down a thousand enemy horsemen. No body of men can stand up against such a test. . . . The Turk will hit from his saddle an animal, a bird, a target, a man, a crouching animal, a marker post or a bird of prey stooping on its quarry . . . [Engaging in combat] the Turk does not wheel round like the Khurasani, indeed if he turns his horse's head it is deadly poison and certain death, for he aims his arrow as accurately behind him as he does in front of him. . . . As for their ability to stand up trotting, sustained galloping, long night rides and cross-country journeys, it is truly extraordinary. . . . When the Turk travels with horsemen of other races, he covers twenty miles to their ten, leaving them and circling around to right and left, up on to the high ground and down to the bottom of the gullies, shooting all the while at anything that runs, crawls, flies or stands still. . . . But your Turk, though he has covered twice the distance and dislocated his shoulders with shooting, has only to catch sight of a gazelle or an onager near the halting-place, or put up a fox or a hare, and he is off again at a gallop as though he had only just mounted.

---

Excerpted from Charles Pellat (ed.), *The Life and Works of Jahiz*, trans. D. M. Hawkes (Berkeley: University of California Press, 1969), as presented in William H. McNeill and Marilyn Waldman (eds.), *The Islamic World* (Chicago: University of Chicago Press, 1983), pp. 113–116.

built an empire that included most of Iran, Iraq, Syria, the Caucasus, and the eastern two thirds of modern Turkey. One can still visit the huge stone caravansaries that the Seljuks built every twenty miles along the caravan routes from the Mediterranean coast to central Asia. The Seljuk Sultans nominally acknowledged the religious authority of the Caliph at Baghdad, but the title of Sultan carried an assumption of political autonomy that ignored the Caliph's pretensions to secular authority. The Seljuks in fact controlled a major empire based on their capabilities as an aggressive and fast-moving warrior elite. The Caliphate in Baghdad continued to function, but was politically weak. The Caliphs maintained a semblance of political autonomy thanks to the Turkish slave soldiers that they had recruited. Also referred to as *mameluks,* these slave soldiers provided a degree of stability in Egypt and parts of the Middle East outside of Seljuk control.

When the Mongols burst into the Middle East in the middle of the 1200s, therefore, the stage was set for them to build their empire with remarkable speed. (See Readings 1.5 and 1.6.) The entire region was controlled by political structures in which military elites had learned how to move rapidly into the center of an esablished state and replace the existing government. Indeed, many Middle Eastern governments were already

## READING 1.5

*The Mongols first erupted into Iran, India, and the Middle East about 1220 C.E. The speed and scope of their conquests was immediately seen as awesome. The following summary looks for ways to convey the unprecedented nature of the invasion. It was written by the Iranian historian Ibn Al-Athir sometime between 1220 and his death in 1233.*

. . . Nay, it is unlikely that mankind will see the like of this calamity, . . . these [Tatars] [Mongolian warriors] spared none, slaying women and men and children, ripping open pregnant women and killing unborn babes. . . . For these were a people who emerged from the confines of China, and attacked the cities of Turkistan . . . and thence advanced on the cities of Transoxiana, such as Samarqand. . . . one division then passed on into Khurasan, . . . even to the limits of Iraq. . . . Another division, distinct from that mentioned above, marched on Ghazna and its dependencies, and those parts of India, Sistan and Kirman which border thereon. . . . Now this is a thing the like of which ear hath not heard; for Alexander, concerning whom historians agree that he conquered the world, did not do so with such swiftness . . . But these Tatars conquered most of the habitable globe, and the best, the most flourishing and most populous part thereof, and that whereof the inhabitants were the most advanced in character and conduct, in about a year; nor did any country escape their devastations which did not fearfully expect them and dread their arrival. . . .

Excerpted from Edward G. Browne (ed.), *A Literary History of Persia* (Cambridge: Cambridge University Press, 1902), vol. 2, pp. 427–431, as presented in McNeill and Waldman, *The Islamic World*, pp. 248–253.

controlled by the descendants of the Turkish warriors who had been drawn into regional politics a generation or two before. Furthermore, the Mongols had incorporated into their armies numerous Turkish tribes as they swept ruthlessly across Asia and into Iran. Once the Seljuks had been defeated in a series of key battles, many elements of the defeated Seljuk army were integrated into the growing Mongol system.

The Mongol invasion dismantled the empire of the Seljuk Turks at the same time that it destroyed the Caliphate in Baghdad. This laid the basis for a reorganization of political power in the Middle East. The Mongols were finally stopped in the Middle East after the capture of Baghdad when, in 1260, they were defeated by the dead Caliph's Turkish slave troops (*mameluks*) who had previously run Egypt and the Holy Land on behalf of the Caliph. After containing the Mongols, these Turkish warriors consolidated what came to be known as the Mameluk Empire. It was based in Egypt, and included the Holy Land, the Muslim pilgrimage shrines in Arabia, and parts of Syria. The *mameluks* also reestablished the Caliphate in their own capital, Cairo, making it the religious center of Islam. These former slave troops of the defunct Caliphate in Baghdad ruled an empire that lasted 250 years. Its ultimate fate was to be absorbed in 1517 by larger and longer-lived empire with similar nomadic origins, that of the Ottoman Turks.

READING 1.6

*The Mongols often dealt mildly with cities that surrendered promptly, but their treatment of any place that resisted struck terror into the hearts of those who heard descriptions of their behavior. This is illustrated by an account of the treatment of the Persian city of Merv, which resisted the Mongol attack. It comes from the Muslim historian 'Ala-ad-Din Juvaini, and was written approximately 1260.*

Mujir-al-Mulk [governor of Merv] saw no way out save surrender and submission. . . . The Mongols now entered the town and drove all the inhabitants, nobles and commoners, out on to the plain. For four days and nights the people continued to come out of the town; the Mongols detained them all, separating the women from the men. . . . The Mongols ordered that apart from four hundred artisans whom they specified and selected from amongst the men and some children, girls and boys, whom they bore off into captivity, the whole population, including the women and children, should be killed, and no one, whether woman or man, be spared. The people of Merv were then distributed among the soldiers and levies, and, in short, to each man was allotted the execution of three or four hundred persons. . . . So many had been killed by nightfall that the mountains became hillocks [compared with the piles of corpses], and the plain was soaked with the blood of the mighty.

. . . When the army departed, those that had sought refuge in holes and cavities came out again, and there were gathered together some five thousand persons. A party of Mongols belonging to the rearguard then arrived and wished to have their share of the slaughter . . . and in this way cast into the well of annihilation most of those that had previously escaped. Then they proceeded along the road to Nishapur and slew all they found of those who had turned back from the plain and fled from the Mongols when half way out to meet them. . . .

Excerpted from John Boyle (ed. and trans.), *The History of the World Conqueror by 'Ala-ad-Din 'Ata-Malik Juvaini, Translated from the text of Mirza Muhammad Qazvini* (Manchester: Manchester University Press, 1958), vol. i, p. 23–34, 153, 159–164, 201–207, as reproduced in McNeill and Waldman, *The Islamic World*, pp. 264–266.

While the warmer, moister climate between 800 and 1200 may have contributed to the expansion of the nomadic societies of Asia into China, Russia, and the Middle East, other responses to the climatic shift were also under way. Among them were the rise of the Mali Empire in west Africa and the consolidation of a rather different and chronically disunited culture in the far western (or European) corner of Eurasia.

During the 600s the broad belt of arable land south of the Sahara saw the emergence of several African kingdoms along the caravan routes between west Africa and the Sudan and Egypt. The most prominent was the Empire of Ghana, which controlled the west African gold mines and, in the 1000s, could field an army of 100,000 troops. The improving climate, however, set in motion two processes that undermined the empire of Ghana. Better farming conditions all across Africa strengthened neighboring African states. At the same time, the Berber nomads of North Africa had converted to Islam and fused into a nomadic people called the

Almoravids. By the mid–1000s the Almoravids were aggressivly raiding west Africa and in 1076 they seized control of the Empire of Ghana, weakening its position in the region.

In practice, Islam entered west Africa by two routes. It moved along trade routes from east to west as Muslim merchants travelled through the region. Aside from its religious aspects, Islam brought with it written record keeping, a more sophisticated accounting system, and Arabic as a common language. All three have obvious value for long-distance trade. At the same time the Almoravids brought a more puritanical form of Islam, which became the religion of the ruling elite in Ghana. This increased the friction between the new nomadic ruling elite and the non-Muslim societies that they controlled. In this the pattern was similar to that of northern India.

By 1200 most of the commercial and ruling elites of west Africa had converted to Islam. They also adopted practices that reinforced African concept of kingship. In this context several provinces in the western part of the disintegrating Empire of Ghana rebelled under the leadership of the legendary King (Mansa) Sundiata. (See Reading 1.7.) By the time that Sundiata died in 1260, he had created an empire that stretched a thousand miles from the Atlantic Ocean to Timbuktu and even farther east. The Mali Empire did for west Africa what the Mongols did for Asia. It provided a political framework with a consistent legal tradition and consistent commercial conditions throughout west Africa. This in turn stimulated the gold trade, the caravan routes north across the Sahara to the Mediterranean, and trade east across central Africa to the Sudan and the Middle East. As we will see, the real goal of the first Iberian expansion into the Atlantic was to contact this Mali economy without having to depend on African middlemen.

## EUROPE AND THE CRUSADES

The rise of the Mali Empire was paralleled by a very different form of expansion in western Europe. Thanks to a series of barbarian invasions and the concurrent disintegration of the Roman Empire in the third through sixth centuries, western Europe became a disorganized patchwork of competing states. In that environment, Charlemagne (ruled 768–814) and his successors briefly created a fragile empire and fought desperately to ward off invasions by Muslims, Vikings, and Huns. The climatic warming after 800 facilitated this struggle, and by 1000 C.E. the invaders had been driven off or assimilated. New ways of organizing agriculture had laid the basis for population growth, cavalry armies, development of regional monarchs, and a growing volume of maritime trade that was being carried on by Europeans themselves.

This dynamic new European culture was marked by three distinctive traits. For one, from the northern Balkans to England, Europe sub-

---

READING 1.7

*The founding epic of the Mali Empire recounts the life of its first emperor, Sundiata. Sundiata was dispossesed as a child by a competing chieftain, and after a long struggle, returned to claim his heritage and build an empire.*

[Driven from his homeland by the evil Soumaoro, Sundiata ultimately defeated Soumaoro and destroyed his capital city. His warriors say] . . . Which of us alone would have dared face Soumaoro? . . . What family was not dishonored by Soumaoro? . . . But it was in the midst of so many calamities that our destiny suddenly changed. A new sun arose in the east . . . A man came to us. He had heard our groans and came to our aid, like a father when he sees his son in tears. Here is that man. Maghan Sundiata, the man with two names foretold by the soothsayers. . . . With a strong hand Kamandjan stuck his spear in the ground in front of the dais and said, "Sundiata, here is my spear, it is yours."

. . . Thereafter, one by one, the twelve kings of the bright savanna country got up and proclaimed Sundiata "Mansa" in their turn. Twelve royal spears were stuck in the ground in front of the dais. Sundiata had become emperor . . . Balla Fasseke, the grand master of ceremonies, took the floor again following the crowd's ovation. "Sundiata, Maghan Sundiata, king of the Mali, in the name of the twelve kings of the 'Bright Country,' I salute you as 'Mansa.'"

In their new-found peace the villages knew prosperity again, for with Sundiata happiness had come into everyone's home. Vast fields of millet, rice, cotton, indigo, and fonio surrounded the villages. Whoever worked always had something to live on. . . . You could go from village to village without fearing brigands. . . . New villages and new towns sprang up in Mali and elsewhere. "Dyulas," or traders, became numerous and during the reign of Sundiata the world knew happiness. . . . [Some rulers] are feared because they have power, but they know how to use it and they are loved because they love justice. Sundiata belonged to this group. He was feared, but loved as well. He was the father of Mali and gave the world peace.

---

Excerpted from *Sundiata*, D. T. Niane, ed., G. D. Pickett, trans. (Harlow: Longman, 1965), in Oliver A. Johnson, *Sources of World Civilization, vol. I, to 1500* (Englewood Cliffs, Prentice-Hall, 1994), pp. 429–324.

---

scribed to a single version of Catholic Christianity. The supervision of this Church was increasingly organized around the papacy in Rome in a way that the analogous Muslim Caliphates never thought to achieve. Not only was this wing of Christianity well organized, but it was also aggressive about its obligation to maintain access to the Holy Land from which Christianity had come. It was also committed to bringing the Word of God to non-Christians. The same Church stimulated the rise of European universities, a development that played a major role in reshaping the entire European worldview.

A second trait of European culture was its political disunity. By 1000, Europe's ruling elites were no longer nomadic, but they were the product of the assimilation of such nomads into post-Roman society. Confronted by external pressures, they had remained militarized and highly mobile. In this context a number of regional kingdoms and principalities emerged—including Castile, Portugal, Aragon, France, and England—but seen from a distance the pattern was one of competing regional warlords.

The third important European trait was the rise of a vigorous network of trading communities after about 1000. Within these commercial societies the most prominent people were the merchants, who controlled several cities in Italy. Although this new commercial society was similar to those of the Chinese, Gujaratis, Africans, or Arabs, it was distinctive in a particular way. Europe's merchant towns lived inside a culture that had religious leaders who aspired to control political authority in a disunited and even anarchic civilization. This encouraged Europe's merchant communities to develop their own political institutions. Those institutions gave them a political autonomy that permitted more experimentation with capitalist institutions and commercial relationships than might have been possible in a united European empire.

Thus, a culture that was on the defensive against invaders in the 800s and 900s, itself became actively expansive. By the early 1000s, Italian port towns were organizing trading and raiding ventures against Muslim North Africa, and Europe's Mediterranean merchants had started to build a trade network that stretched from Morocco to the Black Sea. At the same time, religious controversy had led to the separation of the Latin Church of Rome from the Orthodox Church of Byzantium (1058). Concurrently the Middle East was being invaded by the Seljuk Turks in the 1000s and 1100s. Indeed, the disruption of the pilgrim trade to the Holy Land created by the Seljuk invasion played an important role in triggering the European invasion of the Middle East.

Political and religious forces in European culture reacted to the unstable situation in the Middle East by forming an army of nomadic invaders. Beginning in 1095, the Crusades brought European invaders and sporadic European control to Egypt, the Holy Land, and southern Turkey. Most of the Crusaders reached the Holy Land by marching through the Byzantine Empire. In 1204, the Fourth Crusade conquered the (Christian!) Byzantine Empire, looted Constantinople, and briefly brought the Greek-speaking Aegean under western European rule. After 1200, however, European control became precarious. Soon after the Mongol invasion was stopped and the Mameluk Empire was consolidated in 1260, Europe's military forces were ejected from the Holy Land by their Muslim counterparts.

This did not end European activity in the Middle East, but it did change its character. While European political expansion found other targets, Europe's commercial communities continued to insert themselves into the Middle East. Emerging city-states like Venice, Genoa, and Barcelona established merchant colonies in most Near Eastern ports. In the tradition of mercantile diasporas, these colonies were enclaves that used the law and language of their home countries while developing local commercial contacts and opening trade with African and Asian merchants

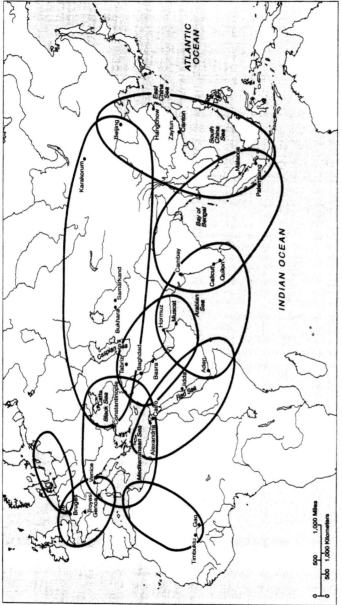

**MAP 1.4** *AFRO-EURASIAN TRADE CIRCUITS PRIOR TO 1500.*

*Within each of these circuits, trade was conducted by distinct groups of merchant communities, often organized as trade diasporas. European arrival in Asia added an additional circuit that looped around Africa, but the underlying structure of this system did not change dramatically until the later 1600s, when the expanding wealth of the Atlantic world increased the relative importance of the emerging European elements.*

from farther afield. At the same time, some city-states seized control of islands like Crete and Chios, creating commercially oriented mini-empires. Thus Europe expanded its activity in the Middle East despite the military failure of the Crusades, the split between Catholic and Orthodox Christianity, and the failure to convert the Muslims to Christianity.

By the 1200s, therefore, much of the world had experienced the installation of militarized elites subscribing to values derived from the lifestyle of the plains and deserts of Africa, Asia, and America. Such mobile military elites were not new to world history, but, in the three centuries before 1300, they imposed themselves on more parts of the globe than ever before. At the same time, major religions had expanded their influence across Africa, Europe, and Asia. Sometimes this happened as a result of political imperialism, sometimes in conjunction with commercial networks that reached from England to China and Japan. (See Map 1.4.) This surge of expansion was not unique to any particular civilization, but reflected an era of prosperity and relatively good farming and grazing conditions that coincided with the global warming that stretched from 800 to about 1200 C.E.

# 2

# THE STRUGGLE FOR THE
# MEDITERRANEAN, 1300–1700

## BACKGROUNDS AND COMMON
## DENOMINATORS

The era between 1300 and 1700 appears in many textbooks as the story of European expansion, organized around European arrivals in other parts of the world. This Eurocentric approach reflects the nineteenth and early twentieth century assumption that western civilization was superior to that of anyone else and was bound to control the outcome of contact with other societies. That assumption is no longer so obvious, and it is increasingly clear that, before 1700, European contacts with other cultures often ended as standoffs or as cultural transactions rather than in conquest or domination. Spain's role in America is the main exception, and even there the survival of Spanish control often rested on cultural compromises and transactions. Each of the world's expanding societies had unique traits as well as much in common with Europe, and western historians long understated the importance of non-European developments during the era in question. Because they ignored other examples of expansion, they often misunderstood the choices made by Europeans themselves.

Rather than tracking European expansion, therefore, we will look at five large arenas around the world and at the interaction between the types of expansion at work in each. We will concentrate upon five historical settings: the Mediterranean basin (including the Balkans and much of the Near East), the tropical Atlantic (including the Caribbean and West Africa), the American mainland of Mexico and Peru, the Indian Ocean from Indonesia to Africa and Arabia, and the Asia of China, Japan, and the western Pacific. This chapter examines the Mediterranean basin; later chapters deal with the other cases.

The Mediterranean basin stretches from Spain and Morocco in the west to the Black Sea and the Middle East. It includes southern Europe, North Africa, the Balkans, and Anatolia and extends into Iran, itself a perennial bridge between the Mediterranean and central Asia. Since the time of Mohammed in the seventh century the Mediterranean basin has been shared and fought over by Muslims and Christians. By 1300, most of the northern coast of the Mediterranean, from Spain to Constantinople, and most of the islands, were in Christian hands, while the southern coast from Morocco to southern Turkey was Islamic. In 1300 the two largest political features in the region were the Mameluk Empire and the Mongols. Based in Egypt, the Mameluk Empire was ruled by a military elite that had originated as the Turkic slave soldiers (*mameluks*) of the Caliph in Baghdad. When the Mongols destroyed the Caliphate, these mameluks set up their own empire with its capital in Cairo in 1260. It controlled both the Christian Holy Land and the Muslim Holy Places in western Arabia, the latter being both a major political obligation and a source of prestige in the Islamic world. The rest of the Middle East, including the Caucasus and eastern Turkey, was part of the unstable Ilkanate, one of the four sections into which the Mongol Empire had been subdivided. Christian or Muslim, the rest of the Mediterranean basin was a mosaic of small and midsized political centers: the remains of the Byzantine Empire, Christian kingdoms in the Balkans; an assortment of Italian city-states and principalities; emerging kingdoms in France, Aragon, and Castile; and several Muslim states in North Africa, the largest of which was the Sultanate of Morocco.

Overall, the most intriguing form of expansion in the Mediterranean as of 1300 was neither political nor religious. It was the remarkable growth of mercantile "mini-empires" created by city-states on Europe's southern coast. The most prominent examples were Venice and Genoa. None of the cities that ran these "empires" had large armies, or populations much larger than 100,000 people. As we saw earlier, the Crusaders who brought European control to the Holy Land had been expelled before 1300. In place of the military and political links with the Near East created by the Crusaders, we find networks of European trade routes, commercial consulates with extraterritorial rights, and island colonies oriented toward export agriculture. The two largest (and competing) of these commercial "empires" were Genoa and Venice. Genoa maintained extensive Aegean and Black Sea connections, including a colony at Kaffa on the Crimean Peninsula. Venice sought to monopolize the Asian spices that reached the Mediterranean via the Red Sea and maintained trading enclaves in the Mameluk Empire. Smaller cities like Pisa, Ragusa, Marseilles, and Barcelona also had commercial contacts across the Mediterranean. Individually, and as "mini-empires," these trading networks were another variation on the age-old pattern of long distance trade based on strings of colonies settled by trading societies with common languages and commercial techniques.

Nothing in the situation of 1300 suggested that by the 1520s the Mediterranean would be the scene of a titanic struggle between two immense empires: the Ottoman Turks and the Habsburg rulers of Spain. The Ottoman Empire was created by a tiny tribe of Turkish warriors who had settled in west-central Turkey; the Habsburg–Spanish Empire was the result of a series of peculiarly European marriages between ruling families which brought together a collection of territories centered in the Kingdom of Castile.

Until about 1450 the Spanish and Turkish Empires had separate historical narratives, but four common denominators. One was ongoing interaction with the commercial system of the Italian city-states. Muslim and Byzantine merchants in the East depended on Europeans for safe, efficient shipping and the distribution of Asian goods in Europe. The small Iberian kingdoms that were to become Spain depended on the Italians for finance and for ships to move their armies. Merchants in Seville and Barcelona relied on Italian commercial credit and banking facilities. Italian businessmen, with their commercial mini-empires, had made themselves indispensable at both ends of the Mediterranean.

A second common denominator was interaction between political expansion and religious expansion. In Islam, empire and religion were linked in complex ways. The formal goal of Islam was to place the world under Muslim rule. This goal did not require conversion of conquered peoples, only their recognition of Muslim political authority. The concept helped to legitimize wars of conquest in the minds of Muslim leaders, even though it did not require active missionary work. This way of legitimizing political authority was combined with a parallel belief by Turkic military elites. Their nomadic heritage told them that conquest justified itself. The simple fact that they had prevailed established them as legitimate rulers regardless of the religious beliefs of their subjects. Thus religion helped justify Muslim conquests, but was not required to establish the legitimacy of rule. This left room for working arrangements for religious minorities without anxiety about their lack of conformity to Islam.

In Europe, however, rulers held authority as trustees ordained by God. European monarchs supported the Catholic Church because they needed its sanction to present themselves as legitimate. For this to work, however, the subjects of a Christian ruler also had to be Christian, otherwise the ruler could not be sure that they acknowledged his legitimacy. At the same time, the Catholic Church encouraged conversion of all peoples (for the sake of their souls) and authorized religious orders like the Franciscans, the Dominicans, and, after 1540, the Jesuits, all of which were dedicated to converting unbelievers. European rulers who endorsed conquest, therefore, also sought help from missionaries. Both Franciscans and Dominicans are documented in Tunis by the 1230s, and Franciscans participated in the first Canary Island ventures in the mid-1300s. By the late 1500s the Jesuits were engaged in similar efforts to convert India, China, and Japan. Missionaries appear in the vanguard of every European conquest from the thirteenth to the eighteenth centuries. Thus political and religious expansion were linked together in both the Spanish and Turkish Empires, but in different ways.

A third factor common to both empires, and the one most difficult to evaluate, was the growing frequency of unstable weather that accompanied a worldwide climatic cooling trend after about 1250. The impact of the "little ice age" that is noticeable by 1300 is hard to evaluate outside of Europe because of limited research. We know that Europe began to experience wet, unstable weather in a way that correlates with a reduction in the amount of energy driving the hemispheric weather pattern. Europe, which had a dense population by 1250 thanks to improved farming techniques and favorable weather, was confronted with a series of unusually cold, wet years and mediocre crops beginning in 1307. Food reserves were depleted everywhere. Then, in 1315–1317, the weather was so bad that crops failed totally in England and much of western Europe, with major crop failures as far east as Hungary and Greece. One estimate says that 15 percent of Europe's population died of starvation. This crisis was followed by a similar failure in 1328 and by generally unpredictable weather.

The problem of bad weather was not unique to Europe, but evidence from other areas is more tenuous. Eastern Europe and central Asia experienced colder winters and hotter, drier summers. In India annual rainfall declined steadily through the 1300s, and in sub-Saharan Africa important lakes were drying up by 1330—evidence of declining rainfall. China, meanwhile, experienced the same stormy, unstable weather and floods that afflicted Europe. All of these clues suggest that reduced atmospheric energy had weakened prevailing winds. As a result, less moisture was being carried into the inland areas of the continents.

The fourth common denominator arrived in Europe when the bubonic plague hit Italy in 1347. The plague probably originated in India centuries earlier, and first visited the Mediterranean in the 500s C.E. During the Middle Ages the plague bacillus, which was carried by fleas living on rats, became endemic in the rodent population of central Asia. When the Mongol Empire opened up trans-Asian trade routes, one unintended result was that nomadic livestock spread the plague across Eurasia. There is evidence of plague epidemics in China beginning in the 1330s, and by 1400 China's population had declined 30 percent. Deteriorating weather and population decline corresponded with the declining effectiveness of Mongol rule in China and the emergence of regional warlords.

Plague-infected fleas reached the Black Sea in 1346. In that year, as they were laying siege to the Genoese colony of Kaffa on the Crimean peninsula, the Mongols catapulted the bodies of plague victims into the besieged town. The disease was carried on Genoese ships to Italy and within a few years the plague raged across Europe and the Middle East. (See Reading 2.1.) Because the primary hosts for the plague were rats and fleas, humans were slow to develop resistance to the disease. As a result, Europe experienced gradually diminishing waves of epidemics well into the seventeenth century. Vigorous quarantines by public authorities eventually stopped epidemics from spreading, and the last major European outbreak of the plague struck the French port of Marseilles in 1720. As in China, by 1400 the plague had cut Europe's population by 25 percent to 30 percent.

We know that the same plague also swept through the Middle East. Although hard to estimate, mortality rates in Muslim countries may have been even higher than in Europe. The reasons for the higher rates are not

---

READING 2.1

*One of the more effective reports of the plague comes from the eyewitness account by the Italian Matteo Villani, who saw the epidemic of 1348 and wrote this Description of the Plague in Florence:*

In the year of Christ's Incarnation for our salvation 1346 . . . there arose . . . in the parts of the Orient that lie closest to Cathay and northern India and in the ports and other provinces surrounding the coastal ones, a pestilence [that struck] men of all conditions and ages and both sexes. They began to spit blood and to die, some immediately, some within two or three days, though a good many took longer to die. And it happened that those who served these sick people, catching that sickness or infected with that same corruption, immediately became sick and died in a similar manner. Most of them had a swelling in the groin, many had swellings in their armpits, right and left, and others had swellings in other parts of their bodies; in almost every instance some singular swelling was evident in the infected body. This pestilence came intermittently, and passing from one nation to the next, before the end of one year, it had struck all of that third part of the world that is called Asia. Toward the end of this time, it reached the nations of the Great Sea [the Mediterranean], the shores of the Tyrrhenian Sea, Syria and Turkey down into Egypt and to the shores of the Red Sea and, to the North, to Russia and Greece, Armenia, and the other nearby countries. During that time . . . Sicily was totally enveloped by this mortal pestilence. Next, the ports of Africa and its eastern provinces, . . . Sardinia and Corsica and the other islands of this sea. On the other side, which is called Europe, it reached in like manner the nearby lands to the West, attacking the south more fiercely than the northern parts. . . . By 1349 it had extended all the way west to the shores of the Oceanic Sea of Europe, Africa, Ireland, the island of England and Scotland . . . In our city . . . and the district of Florence three out of five persons or more died, of both sexes and all ages, among the lowly, the middling, and the great alike.

Throughout the entire world, the human race lost like numbers and in like fashion. . . . There were in fact provinces of the Levant [Middle East] where even more died. . . . We heard from Genoese merchants . . . that some time before this pestilence somewhere in upper Asia there either emerged from the earth or fell from the skies a great fire, a fire which spread westward, consuming a vast land and offering no refuge. And a good many people said that the smell of this fire generated the corruptible matter of the general pestilence. But this we cannot ascertain. . . .

---

Taken from F. G. Dragomanni (ed.), *Matteo Villani, Cronica* (Florence, 1846), trans. Lydia Cochrane, as given in Julius Kirshner and Karl F. Morrison (eds.), *Readings in Western Civilization*, vol. 4, *Medieval Europe* (Chicago: University of Chicago Press, 1986), pp. 447–451.

---

clear, but governments like that of the Ottoman Empire did not consider public health to be their responsibility. Without quarantines, epidemics lasted longer and spread farther in the Muslim world, a situation that some historians believe explains the supposed economic passivity of the Middle East after about 1400.

Plague and bad weather destabilized central governments everywhere. Supply systems, heavily dependent on human labor, broke down.

Local communities lacked manpower for the harvests and resisted paying taxes to distant rulers. In the Middle East, the Mongol Ilkhanate collapsed, while Europe experienced rebellion, civil wars, and international conflicts. The result was an international power vacuum throughout the Mediterranean basin—a situation ripe for action by the more agile actors on the scene.

## ASSEMBLING THE SPANISH "EMPIRE" IN EUROPE

At the western end of the Mediterranean a loosely organized, militarized society was laying the foundation for what came to be called Spain. Emerging from Asturias in the northwestern corner of Iberia, by the 1100s a small warrior tribe had captured the center of the peninsula from its Muslim rulers and created the Kingdom of Castile. Although far from the Holy Land, this off-and-on military expansion was cast as a Crusade against the Muslim infidels who had occupied Spanish soil (and had done so for 300 years). As early as 1080 the Castilians had captured Toledo in central Spain, and by 1250 they controlled the southern parts of the peninsula except for the Muslim Kingdom of Granada.

The era of the bubonic plague (1346 and after) saw a long civil war among the great families of Castile, but in 1390 a new dynasty, the Trastámara family, had consolidated power. By 1400, the Kingdom of Castile was an important country in a disunited Europe. It is more important to note, however, that as Castile expanded, its kings prevented the Castilian nobility from converting conquered Muslim states into institutionally distinct kingdoms. This meant that parliamentary, bureaucratic, and clan politics throughout Castile were focused on a single royal court in Toledo. The leverage that this gave astute rulers who sought to increase royal authority was crucial in the development of the Spanish empire.

Alongside the rise of Castile, the kings of Aragon (who were also the Counts of Barcelona) exploited the political fragmentation of the Mediterranean to create an island empire. Building upon the county of Catalonia and the tiny Kingdom of Aragon, the Aragonese kings assembled the "empire" referred to as the Crown of Aragon. In the process, the military elite of Aragon and the commercial elite of Barcelona established a Spanish presence in the Mediterranean that lasted until the end of the 1700s. As in Castile, this process began before the advent of the plague and was sometimes advertised as a Crusade. Landed, royal, and commercial interests combined to conquer the Muslim island kingdoms of Mallorca and Menorca, impose Aragonese rule in Sicily, and conquer the island of Sardinia. This overseas expansion was augmented by the conquest of Valencia on the mainland and the extension of Aragonese authority as far as Tunisia and the Duchy of Athens. In 1443 this ambitious campaign added the Kingdom of Naples to the Aragonese empire, bringing southern Italy under Spanish rule.

**ILLUSTRATION 2.1**
*SEVILLE IN THE 1500s.*
*From the time of its capture by the Christian Castilians in the early 1200s, Seville was a major base for Iberian expansion. By the late 1500s it was a center for both Atlantic and Mediterranean trade. With as many as 150,000 inhabitants, it was one of the great cities of the Christian Mediterranean, although no more than a third the size of Istanbul (Constantinople).*

Source: J. H. Elliott (ed.), *The Spanish World: Civilization and Empire, Europe and the Americas, Past and Present* (New York: Harry Abrams Inc., and London: Thames and Hudson Ltd., 1991), p. 254.

Aragonese exploitation of the Mediterranean power vacuum of the 1300s and 1400s created two risky legacies for the emerging Spanish empire. One was an Aragonese political structure that depended on negotiation and compromise between king and local elites. In contrast to Castile, as Aragon expanded, each conquered territory was organized as an autonomous kingdom with its own law courts, legislature, and coinage. The king of this Aragonese "empire" was not ruler of an enlarged Aragon, in the way that the king of Castile became king of an enlarged Castile. Instead, he became king of Aragon, of Valencia, of Mallorca, of Menorca, of Naples, and so on. The result was a cluster of theoretically distinct kingdoms, each with the same ruler, but with few shared institutions. As a result, the king of Aragon had to negotiate with several regional governments to accumulate resources for any large enterprise. The system worked as long as royal policy paralleled the self-interest of the commercial and military elites who ran the individual kingdoms, and it remained coherent as long as all parties were focused on the western Mediterranean. When the crown passed to kings who wanted to use Aragonese resources to fight more distant battles, however, royal authority in the Crown of Aragon proved weak. One result was a full-scale revolt by Catalonia in

1640, when Philip IV of Spain (1621–1665) tried to force the Aragonese and Catalans to pay for wars in other parts of Europe.

The second risky legacy of the Aragonese empire was a vested interest in the security of the Mediterranean. Future rulers of Aragon, compelled to defend their authority, had to confront any power that threatened Aragon's island kingdoms and commerce. As long as Muslim North Africa was weak and disunited, and the Mameluk Empire was preoccupied with the Mongols and the Ottoman Turks, the Aragonese could compete effectively with the commercial Italian city-states and the dynastic politics of a disunited France. As a loose confederation of ten autonomous kingdoms and counties, spanning a thousand miles of ocean, however, the Crown of Aragon was vulnerable to changes in the Mediterranean balance of power.

While the monarchies of Castile and Aragon were evolving, the European institution of kingship was also changing. The changes look like technicalities from a global perspective, but they are crucial to understanding the Spanish Empire that emerged after 1500. They also laid the institutional bases for many of the European countries we know today. By the 1400s two medieval principles had fused to create a unique form of hereditary monarchy. Acceptance of this hereditary principle made possible formation of a major empire without military conquest. Some parts of the Habsburg–Spanish empire of the early 1500s were acquired by outright conquest, including Navarre, Genoa, and Milan. Much of the empire, however, was assembled through marriage and inheritance. Many of the conflicts involved in this kind of empire building were actually waged to affirm existing jurisdictional claims rather than to achieve outright conquest.

Europe's royal families were part of a landed, military nobility. Although often described as landlords, they usually did not "own" land in the modern sense. Instead, they owned defined *rights* to what the land and its occupants could produce. These rights were originally granted by a lord's king, and included the delegation to the lord of the ruler's right to provide justice and collect taxes. This meant that landed nobles provided local justice in the king's name. Over time, however, the right to income from the land *and* the right to provide local government came to be seen as private property by the lords. A powerful noble, with extensive estates, believed that he owned a package of rights to income and administration that he could transfer to his heirs. Government functions and landed income thus became personal assets that could be sold or given to a subordinate.

Europe's royal families of the 1400s emerged from competing noble clans that sought to gain control of the estates and jurisdictional authority that were the property of whomever was king. In one sense, therefore, what made the king important was the *amount* of income and jurisdictional authority that he owned. The patrimony (lands and jurisdictions) accumulated by a noble (or king) were his property and could be sold, given away, or willed to heirs, much as we distribute property in a modern will. They could *also* be combined through marriage, which allowed the children of such marriages to inherit the estates and jurisdictions owned by both parents. As the idea that governmental jurisdiction was a form of property developed, powerful families also developed the tradition, sometimes codified into law, that all of the properties and jurisdictional rights owned by both parents had to go to the oldest son, and (France excepted) if no son was available, to the oldest daughter. In such a society, two or three generations of careful royal service and strategic marriage choices could create a huge patrimony of scattered lands and rights to political jurisdiction.

Alongside this principle of hereditary dynasticism we find a second fateful development. A European ruler was legitimate only if his jurisdiction was sanctioned by the Catholic Church. The logic was simple. God created the world and it was his. The papacy existed to administer to the spiritual needs of all Christians. Secular rulers existed as trustees to take care of the worldly needs of Christians while they made the transition from birth to Heaven. The papacy was the intermediary that conferred God's sanction upon any new ruler. This assertion of the "equality" between papal–spiritual and imperial–secular authority was the result of a prolonged struggle between two emerging foci of power. They were the papacy (and its far-flung hierarchy) and the emerging feudal kingdoms. This ideology contained a fundamentally static view of the world, in which everyone was born into a divinely ordained place where they were expected to stay. After all, the important goal was to stay right with God and get to Heaven.

The political implications of this way of making government legal were important. It meant that, in theory, the king's most important function was as a judge and mediator who kept society in balance and defended it against outside threats. This was the logic behind the fact that so many European kings fought in the Crusades, since access to the Holy Land for pilgrims was necessary to the proper order of things. The concept of the king as trustee and moderator also subjected him to legal limits. He was authorized to decide legal disputes, but (in theory) he could not unilaterally change the law. Indeed, because property law was crucial to his own patrimony, a king had little choice but to respect legal traditions.

This view of royal authority led to a prolonged struggle with the papacy over the ultimate source of sovereignty in Europe. Medieval ideology made kings trustees under divine authority. For centuries the papacy sought to use this idea to subordinate secular rulers to papal discipline and to establish the rule that no king was legitimate without papal approval. This ran counter to the interests of most regional kings, who sought either to control the papacy or to establish royal control over those parts of the Church within their own domain. The Crusades themselves (begun 1095) were part of this struggle, since they represent one aspect of the evolving papal claim to be leader of Christianity against the heathen. The nature of the debate can be seen in Readings 2.2, 2.3, and 2.4.

## READING 2.2

*The complex relationship between religious and political authority plagued dynastic rulers in Europe for centuries. They needed religious legitimation, but sought to avoid control by the papacy. It was a debate that had been going on for centuries. This selection, from the* Bull Unam Sanctam *of Boniface VIII in the 1300s, both defines the principle of church superiority and reflects Boniface's frustration in dealing with European kings.*

... In this Church and in its power are two swords, to wit, a spiritual and a temporal, and this we are taught by the words of the Gospel ... Both, therefore, the spiritual and material swords, are in the power of the Church, the latter indeed to be used *for* the Church, the former *by* the Church, the one by the priest, the other by the hand of kings and soldiers, but by the will and sufferance of the priest. It is fitting, moreover, that one sword should be under the other, and the temporal authority subject to the spiritual power ...

In *Translations and Reprints from the Original Sources of European History*, Vol. III, No. 6 (Philadelphia: Department of History of the University of Pennsylvania, 1912); excerpted from Oliver A. Johnson (ed.) *Sources of World Civilization*, Vol. I, *To 1500* (Englewood Cliffs: Prentice Hall, 1994), pp. 353–354.

## READING 2.3

*An alternative position can be found in Niccolo Machiaveli's famous essay on* The Prince (1513), *where, among many other things, he offers a section "On Cruelty and Clemency Whether It Is Better to Be Loved or Feared":*

The question arises: is it better to be loved than feared, or vice versa? I don't doubt that every prince would like to be both; but since it is hard to accommodate these qualities, if you have to make a choice, to be feared is much safer than to be loved. For it is a good general rule about men, that they are ungrateful, fickle, liars and deceivers, fearful of danger and greedy for gain. While you serve their welfare, they are all yours, but when the danger is close at hand, they turn against you. People are less concerned with offending a man who makes himself loved than one who makes himself feared: the reason is that love is a link of obligation which men, because they are rotten, will break any time they think doing so serves their advantage; but fear involves dread of punishment, from which they can never escape.

Still, a prince should make himself feared in such a way that, even if he gets no love, he gets no hate either; because it is perfectly possible to be feared and not hated, and this will be the result if only the prince will keep his hands off the property of his subjects or citizens, and off their women. When he does have to shed blood, he should be sure to have a strong justification and manifest cause; but above all, he should not confiscate people's property, because men are quicker to forget the death of a father than the loss of a patrimony.

Returning to the question of being feared or loved, I conclude that since men love at their own inclination but can be made to fear at the inclination of the prince, a shrewd prince will lay his foundations on what is under his own control, not on what is controlled by others. He should simply take pains not to be hated, as I said.

From *The Prince* (1513) as excerpted in Mark Kishlansky (ed.), *Sources of World History*, Vol. I (New York: HarperCollins, 1995), pp. 242–243.

---

READING 2.4

*The problem with the two preceding points of view is that they offered fertile ground for people to justify resisting or ignoring royal jurisdiction. Consider the logic in this excerpt from the essay "Must Subjects Obey Princes Who Issue Orders Counter to the Law of God?" by Philippe Duplessis-Mornay, written in 1579. Duplessis-Mornay (1549–1623) was a French Huguenot (Protestant) who rejected papal authority over kingship. He also held that kings ought not order their subjects to violate God's will, and subjects could legitimately overthrow a king who tried to do so.*

. . . There are, however, many princes nowadays who boast the name of Christ, yet dare to arrogate an immense power that most assuredly does not depend from God. There are also many adulators who worship them as gods on earth, and many others seized by fear, or else coerced by force, who either really believe that obedience is never to be denied to princes or at least wish to seem to believe it. . . .

In short, we see that kings are invested with their kingdoms by God in almost the same manner in which vassals are invested with their fiefs by their superior lords, and that they are deprived of their benefices for the same reasons. Therefore we must on all counts conclude that the former are in an almost identical place as the latter and that all kings are vassals of God. Having said this, our question is easily finished. For if God occupies the place of a superior lord, and the king that of a vassal, who will not declare that one should rather obey the lord than the vassal? If God commands this [one thing], and the king the other [a contradictory thing], who will consider someone refusing to obey the king as a rebel? Who will not on the contrary condemn it as rebellion if he fails to obey God promptly or if he obeys the king instead? . . . Thus we are not only not obliged to obey a king who orders something against the law of God, but we even commit rebellion if we do obey him. . . .

---

From his *A Defense of Liberty Against Tyrants* as presented in Mark Kishlansky (ed.), *Sources of World History*, Vol. II (New York: HarperCollins, 1995), pp. 8–9.

By the 1400s the principles of the proprietary nature of jurisdiction and that of the divinely ordained power to judge and protect had merged. Kings could accumulate property through marriage and inheritance, including the proprietary rights of monarchy. At the same time, a king had to consult and bargain with other elements in society because they also "owned" land and bits of jurisdiction, some of which had been given to them by earlier rulers. Thus European monarchs ruled by divine right, but they got things done only through elaborate consultation with parliaments, district assemblies, town governments, and chartered guilds.

Furthermore, royal authority was not standardized. The privileges of the king varied from one kingdom to another. Thus, when we talk of the king of Aragon ruling over ten different kingdoms, we are talking about an "empire" that was a federation of kingdoms with one thing in common. The same person "owned" the local version of royal jurisdiction and was the arbiter of disputes and coordinator of defense, however they were defined in each kingdom. This is why, when talking about the Aragonese empire, historians see a weak political system in which the king depended upon his political skills to mesh the commercial interests of Barcelona with the land hunger of the nobility and the Church's urge to convert infidels.

Only in the light of divine-right legitimation and jurisdiction as a form of property can we grasp what went on as the Spanish Empire was assembled. Rather than an empire of conquest, it was an empire brought together by negotiated family mergers. This made legal sense to Europeans, but it created empires that, from a military perspective, were strategic and logistic nightmares. Such empires were also open to endless disagreement about royal authority and jurisdiction. The ruler of such an empire often had to defend his "property" (right to rule) and his reputation in places surrounded by unfriendly territory. With those factors in mind, we can summarize the creation of a Spanish empire that was difficult to rule and nearly impossible to defend.

In effect, dynastic monarchy expanded its territorial jurisdiction by marriage and inheritance. The process also involved warfare, but the objectives and rationales of war derived from dynasticism as opposed to open conquest. This is amply illustrated by the rise of what became the Spanish Empire in Europe. By 1390 the Trastámara family in Castile had won a civil war for control of the crown and made Castile important in Atlantic politics. In 1406 the death of Henry III left Castile to Juan II, his six-year-old son, with Fernando de Antequera, Henry's brother and Juan's uncle, as Regent. In 1410, the King of Aragon died without an heir and Fernando de Antequera persuaded the Aragonese parliament (*corts*) to elect him King of Aragon. This put members of the Trastámara family on both thrones. Fernando was succeeded in Aragon by his sons and, in 1479, by his grandson. This was the Ferdinand of Aragon who married Queen Isabella.

In Castile, meanwhile, the young Juan II became king in his own right and was followed in 1454 by his son, Henry IV. Henry was an incompetent politician and soon found himself in a civil war against an alliance of powerful families. He died fighting for the succession of his daughter against his sister, Isabella. Isabella won, thanks to her marriage alliance with Ferdinand of Aragon in 1469. This joined the two branches of the Trastámara family and allowed Isabella to seize the Castilian crown from its legal heiress. It also guaranteed that Isabella's heir would rule *both* Castile and Aragon. By bringing these two kingdoms into the hands of a single ruler, Ferdinand and Isabella created one of the most powerful political entities in western Europe.

This Iberian "merger by marriage" was soon dwarfed by other dynastic mergers. While the Trastámara clan under Isabella was securing its position in Castile and Aragon, a parallel merger took place in northern Europe. Another aristocratic family, the Habsburgs, had built a power base in Austria during the 1400s and had added the title of Holy Roman Emperor. The Holy Roman Empire, successor to the empire created by Charlemagne in 800 C.E., exercised jurisdiction over a region corresponding roughly with modern Germany. The Emperor's power was tenuous, but it brought great prestige and the possibility of creating a stronger government in Germany. At the same time, the dukes of Burgundy had been building another country as rulers of the Low Countries (modern Belgium and the Netherlands). Emperor Ferdinand of Habsburg arranged for the marriage of his son and heir, Maximilian, to Mary, only child of Duke Charles of Burgundy in 1477. When Duke Charles was killed in battle, his patrimony passed to Mary, opening the way for a child of Maximilian and Mary to inherit Germany, Austria, and the Low Countries. In due course Maximilian and Mary produced a son named Philip, who was in line to rule most of northern Europe.

Skilled practitioners of dynastic merger, Ferdinand and Isabella negotiated several marriages between their children and the Habsburgs and the king of Portugal. The most important one was between their daughter, Juana, and young Philip of Habsburg and Burgundy. Juana inherited Castile from Isabella in 1504. Not long after, Philip died and Juana was declared insane. Their oldest son, Charles, was thus destined to inherit all of the royal real estate on both sides of his family.

Following a succession crisis and the death of his royal grandparents, in 1516 Charles became ruler of Austria, Burgundy, Castile, and Aragon. He was sixteen years old. Three years later he engineered his election as Holy Roman Emperor. By the time he was nineteen, Charles of Habsburg–Trastámara had assembled an empire that included more than half of western Europe. Known in history as Charles V, he spent the rest of his life trying to protect the chaotic collection of royal prerogatives he "owned." His claims to legitimacy were challenged both by France and by the Protestant Reformation. At the same time, Charles had to defend Europe from the other great empire of the age, that of the Ottoman Turks.

The last great step in this remarkable process of dynastic empire building came sixty years later. In 1578 King Sebastian I of Portugal invaded Morocco in a quixotic "Crusade" and was slaughtered, along with his entire army. After the brief reign of Sebastian's elderly uncle, the childless Cardinal-Archbishop Henry, Philip II of Spain could argue that he was the closest heir to the Portuguese throne. His case rested on the fact that his father, Charles V, had married the daughter of the king of Portugal in the 1520s, making Philip grandson of that king. A quick military occupation confirmed the claim, leading to the merger of the Spanish empire with Portugal and its colonies.

It is important to note that this "Spanish" empire in Europe was not built primarily by conquest. Its existence depended on the fact that the ruling elites of dozens of kingdoms and provinces accepted the logic of divine sanction, proprietary dynasticism, and inheritance. The ruler of this haphazard empire thus could rarely collect revenue without negotiation, and if he violated local traditions, local elites felt authorized to rebel against him. Royal claims were not always recognized by everyone in a given principality, but they defined the conflicts that arose where such claims were contested. In spite of these limits, Charles frequently assembled large armies and fleets, but he had no central bureaucracy to manage them, and had to carry out complex negotiations to finance every campaign.

It is important to remember that, despite decades of dynastic marriages and mergers, the Habsburg–Spanish Empire in Europe did not actually exist until the 1520s. Charles V had acquired direct authority of most of his realms by 1519, but his authority was not consolidated until after 1521. (See Map 2.1.) Consequently, while his reign is often seen as an attempt to conserve his empire, much of it was also devoted to the more basic task of consolidating his authority.

After 1560 Philip II enjoyed unique extra revenue from another empire in America, but the cost of fighting the Turks, and an endless war to reestablish Habsburg authority in the Low Countries (the Netherlands), bankrupted him three times. What looks like an imposing empire on a map, therefore, was constantly on the verge of coming apart and provided its rulers with surprisingly limited resources. (See Reading 2.5.) By 1715 the Spanish empire in Europe had been dismantled except for the territory of modern Spain. By that time the underlying assumptions about monarchy had come under attack in many parts of Europe, especially England, the Netherlands, France, and Germany. Protestantism had forced a more pragmatic approach to the link between religious orthodoxy and political loyalty. Sovereignty increasingly was seen as residing in the state or the institution of the crown, rather than the wearer of the crown, and dynastic inheritance was often a facade for legitimation of rulers by international settlement.

## THE RISE OF THE OTTOMAN EMPIRE

While the Trastámaras and Habsburgs were methodically exploiting dynastic marriage and civil war to assemble an empire in the West, a very different empire was emerging in the eastern Mediterranean. The Seljuk Turks, as they left central Asia and established their empire in the 1100s, brought with them several small Turkish tribes as allies. Some of these tribes settled on the western edge of the Seljuk Empire in Anatolia, where they formed a buffer zone between the Seljuks and the Byzantine Empire. In 1300 the Byzantines still controlled the northern and western coasts of Anatolia, the Aegean Sea, and the lower Balkans. If the Mongol invasion of the 1200s weakened the Seljuk empire, the Fourth Crusade (1204) did the same thing to Byzantium. In this context, a tiny Turkish state emerged around 1280 when its leader placed its 400 warriors in the service of the Seljuks. His successor, Osman, provided the name of the ruling family of what became the Ottoman Empire.

The Ottomans alternately served as mercenaries for the Byzantines and the Seljuks, expanding their own territory at the expense of both. In the 1320s and 1330s the Ottomans took part in various Aegean wars and raids in Greece and in 1326 they captured the inland city of Bursa, near Constantinople, making it their capital. The death of the Byzantine emperor in 1341 brought a civil war in that empire, and as mercenaries hired

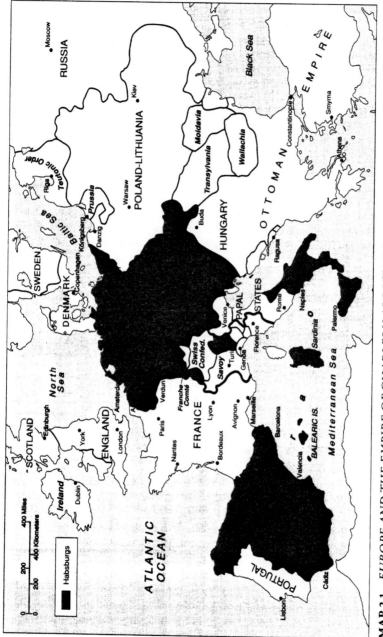

**MAP 2.1** *EUROPE AND THE EMPIRE OF CHARLES V ABOUT 1550.*

*By 1550 control of the entire Habsburg heritage was too complicated for one person, given the lack of common imperial institutions, and Charles V assigned Germany and Austria to his brother Ferdinand.*

READING 2.5

*For over forty years the personality of Philip II of Spain dominated European and Mediterranean affairs. Here is a final epitaph on one of the great practitioners of dynastic empire building, written by the Venetian Ambassador to Philip at the time of his death in 1598:*

September 13, 1598: The king is dead. His Majesty expired at the Escorial this morning at daybreak, after having received all the sacraments of the Church with every sign of devoutness, piety, and religion. . . .

His Majesty lived seventy-one years, three months, and twenty-four days; he reigned forty-two years, ten months, and sixteen days. He was a prince who fought with gold rather than with steel, by his brain rather than by his arms. He has acquired more by sitting still, by negotiation, by diplomacy, than his father did by armies and by war. He was one of the richest princes the world has ever seen, yet he has left the revenues of the kingdom and of the crown burdened with about a million of debts. He owes to his good fortune rather than to the terror of his name the important kingdom of Portugal, with all its territories and treasure; on the other hand he has lost Flanders. In Africa he has gained Peñon, but lost Goletta [near Tunis]. Profoundly religious, he loved peace and quiet. He displayed great calmness, and professed himself unmoved in good or bad fortune alike. He had vast schemes in his head: witness his simultaneous attack on England and on France, while assisting his son-in-law [Emperor of Germany and Arch-Duke of Austria] to acquire Saluzzo, while attempting to expel the French from Italy, while facing the revolution in Flanders [the Low Countries or Netherlands]. . . . He has feigned injuries, and feigned not to feel injuries, but he never lost the opportunity to avenge them. . . .

From the *Calendar of State Papers . . . Venice . . .*, vol. 9, Trans. Horatio F. Brown, presented in James C. Davis, Ed., *Pursuit of Power: Venetian Ambassadors' Reports on Turkey, France, and Spain in the Age of Philip II, 1560–1600* (New York: Harper & Row, 1970), pp. 120–122.

by one of the contenders, the first Ottoman army reached Europe. In 1350 the Ottomans took advantage of Byzantine helplessness during the bubonic plague and invaded Europe as far inland as Bulgaria. By 1354 they had acquired their first permanent European territory, and by 1371 the Ottomans controlled northern Greece. Subsequently they conquered Bulgaria in 1376, Macedonia in 1387, southern Serbia at the battle of Kosovo in 1389, and Albania in 1392. The Byzantine Empire was reduced to its capital city and scattered fragments in the Aegean Sea.

To this point the Ottoman Empire had been organized like other nomadic warrior empires. The impulse for Ottoman expansion came from the warrior ethos of the nomadic tribesmen of central Asia. The sultan's authority depended in part upon the prestige of the original Ottoman tribe, which became the core of an imperial aristocracy. It also rested upon alliances with other Turkish tribes. These tribes acknowledged the sultan's authority in principle, but often acted on their own. Ottoman power thus depended on the shaky loyalty of tribal allies, whose energy was kept in check by sending restless tribes to the frontier, where they had obvious enemies to fight. As of 1400 the Ottomans had conquered a large empire, but its structure had the same weaknesses as its Seljuk and Mongol predecessors—it depended on personal loyalties and on the self-interest of allied warrior tribes. Those tribes made possible the rapid conquests typical of militarized nomads, but the resulting empire was unstable. Any attack by a really powerful enemy could induce allied tribes to switch allegiance.

This fragility surfaced when the last great central Asian warrior, Timurlane, swept through the Middle East and Anatolia. Timurlane has one of the worst reputations for ruthlessness and cruelty of all of history's great conquerors—he is reputed to have left city after city decorated with pyramids of human skulls. Starting in the 1370s from his base in Samarkand, he conquered the Mongol Ilkhanate, reaching the Ottoman city of Ankara in 1402. There Timurlane smashed the Ottoman army and captured their sultan, who died in captivity. Timurlane himself died suddenly in 1405, leaving his empire and that of the Ottomans in disarray. The Ottomans, drawing resources from their European provinces, soon reconquered Anatolia. After a difficult succession crisis, the shrewd Sultan Murad II seized power in 1421. (See Map 2.2.)

Empires that last a long time are successful in part because they shift from rule by conquest and coercion to arrangements that draw conquered local elites into the central government. It was the importance of local elites in European politics, for example, that allowed empire building through dynastic marriage, since those elites benefited from royal authority. A durable imperial government must also professionalize its army and reorient military leaders from tribal allegiance to loyalty to the central government. The state also has to build a bureaucracy staffed by officials loyal to the ruler. This requires a system for recruiting and training officers and administrators whose loyalty to the ruler is stronger than their loyalty to tribe or family.

A stable empire also needs a working relationship between political and religious authority. This is important because legitimation of a ruler usually depends on religious approval. This presented a problem for European rulers. The Protestant Reformation, which began in 1517, challenged the authority of the papacy and thus the legitimacy of rulers who claimed that their authority came from God by way of the pope. Because this concept of divinely sanctioned royal trusteeship required that all subjects subscribe to the religion of the ruler if the ruler was to feel secure about their loyalty, European rulers, Protestant as well as Catholic, tried to suppress religious dissent. This problem was less urgent for the Mongols and Turks, who believed that the right to rule came from conquest. This right of conquest was reinforced by the Muslim obligation to extend the rule of Islam, but that obligation did not imply that religious conformity was necessary for imperial authority to be legitimate.

The Ottomans, whose empire lasted 700 years, illustrate well the transition from conquest to durable imperial institutions. Timurlane's invasion revealed the structural problems of the Ottoman empire of conquest. In response, the sultans of the 1400s created a system for recruiting bureaucrats and commanders in which officials were committed to the

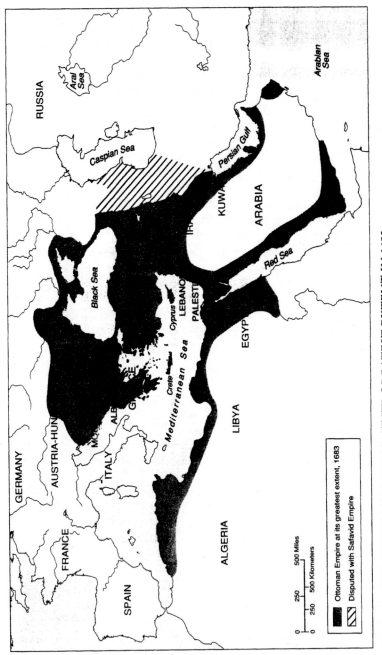

**MAP 2.2** *THE OTTOMAN EMPIRE AT ITS GREATEST EXTENT IN 1683.*
*For over 150 years, this empire was a power in the Mediterranean as far west as Algeria. It reached north to the Austrian border near Vienna, controlled all of the Black Sea, and dominated both the Persian Gulf and the Red Sea.*

Ottoman Empire at its greatest extent, 1683

Disputed with Safavid Empire

500 Miles

250

500 Kilometers

250

0

RUSSIA

Aral Sea

Caspian Sea

Persian Gulf

Arabian Sea

KUWAIT

ARABIA

IR

Red Sea

Black Sea

Cyprus

LEBANO

PALESTI

EGYPT

Crete

Mediterranean Sea

ALB

G

LIBYA

MO

ITALY

AUSTRIA-HUN

GERMANY

FRANCE

ALGERIA

SPAIN

state as the source of their salaries, prestige, and status. The heart of this system was the Janissary Corps, an elite group of soldiers that originated as the sultan's palace guard. Under the new system, the sultan drafted young boys from Christian families and made them legally the slaves of the sultan. Their slave status, however, was very different from the plantation slavery of the American South. As adult administrators, slave status defined these men as the sultan's property. This made it legal for the sultan to punish them without using normal judicial processes. Had these officials been free men, the sultan would have had to use Muslim law courts, making punishment slow and uncertain. Their formal status as slaves encouraged royal officials to be careful not to ignore or contradict royal policy. This system of recruitment was not humane by modern standards, but it did constitute a form of service to the sultan that brought status and, potentially, high office.

The children drafted into royal service were taken to Anatolia and placed in Turkish foster homes, where they were converted to Islam and taught to speak Turkish. They also studied literature, farming, and basic administrative and military skills. Many of these recruits entered the army as apprentices to senior officers and spearheaded the introduction of new military technology such as artillery and muskets. The best recruits graduated to a royal school at one of the sultan's palaces, where they spent two to eight years in further studies. The very best students then graduated to an elite academy in the main palace in Istanbul. There, as imperial pages, they studied the Koran, Arabic, Persian, Turkish, music, calligraphy, and mathematics, along with riding, archery, and weaponry. The top graduates of this academy were candidates for senior positions in the sultan's government and could look toward careers as governors, court officials, ambassadors, admirals, and generals. The less successful graduates of the palace academy entered the sultan's personal cavalry, the most prestigious unit in the army. In this way the sultans created a system that recruited trained officials who depended upon the ruler for income and prestige and who, because of their Christian origins and status as the sultan's "slaves," were not involved in family strategies and provincial politics.

The sultan's government also built an administrative and tax collection system to support the core of a trained army that could be mobilized quickly. Cavalry soldiers were assigned as administrators of *timars*, administrative districts consisting of clusters of villages. The holder of the timar lived in the district, mediated between the village elders and the central government, collected the sultan's taxes, and settled disputes that could not be handled by village institutions. Each soldier–administrator kept part of the taxes he collected to support himself as a cavalryman and his assistants. The timars were grouped into larger *sanjaks* (the equivalent of counties). Each sanjak was governed by a mid-level army officer. The sanjaks in turn were grouped into four or five large provinces. The governors of these provinces had the status of senior generals, and were drawn from the trained officials produced by the palace academy.

Newly conquered areas were incorporated into the imperial system by appointing local leaders as timar holders and sanjak administrators. Thus they administered their own people, but in the Sultan's name. Because the sultan's taxes were well defined and not high, and because local elites were left in place, most conquered peoples found Ottoman authority easy to accept. The demand made by timar holders were usually reasonable and they seem to have dealt fairly with disputes that could not be settled by local institutions. The Ottomans were flexible enough in conquered regions to appoint local leaders as timar holders even when they were not Muslim. For this reason, while conversion to Islam was sometimes slow among the general population, regional elites often converted soon after conquest. Given the behavior of many Balkan warlords, Ottoman rule was easy for Christian communities to accept. The combination of trained officials, a formal administrative hierarchy, autonomy for village government, and co-option of local elites helps explain the durability of the Ottoman empire, even in predominantly Christian areas.

Thus it was that, while the Trastámaras were starting their dynastic mergers, the Ottoman sultans were consolidating their authority and carrying out reforms. Although they built on earlier practices, the reforms institutionalized Ottoman authority and neutralized or marginalized unreliable Turkish tribesmen, many of whom had deserted to Timurlane.

The Ottoman sultans also succeeded in integrating non-Muslim communities into their empire. This achievement was important, since until 1517, less than half of their subjects were Muslim. Islamic belief held that the faithful were obligated to bring the world under Muslim rule, but this did not imply forced conversion. Indeed, since non-Muslim subjects paid an extra tax, governments were not inclined to encourage conversion. This is in sharp contrast to the European approach, which assumed that you were not a loyal subject unless you subscribed to the religion of your ruler. The Spanish conquest of Granada, for example, resulted in the forced baptism of its Muslim population, two bloody rebellions, and ultimately the expulsion of the descendants of those forced converts.

Muslim doctrine held that religions based upon the same biblical tradition as Islam (the Old Testament and much of the New Testament) were entitled to a recognized, if subordinate, position within Islam. These "Peoples of the Book" included Jews and Christians. Muslim India ultimately acknowledged a similar status for Buddhists and Hindus. Since Islam had built its legal system on the *Koran*, which did not apply to other Peoples of the Book, the Ottomans formalized the *millet* system.

Under this system the head of each religious community was co-opted as the intermediary between the government and the community that practiced that religion. Religious communities used their own law for internal affairs and collected taxes as they chose. Their collective obligations to the imperial government were negotiated through the religious head of the community (Patriarch of Constantinople, Head Rabbi). Christian and Jewish communities were free to regulate affairs among their own members, practice their religion openly, and educate their children as they chose.

Jews living in the Ottoman Empire in the 1400s and 1500s frequently wrote to their counterparts in Europe to decribe freedoms that were dramatically different from the growing anti-semitism of Europe. Ottoman authorities welcomed the Jews expelled from Bavaria in the 1480s and from Castile and Aragon in 1492. The sultan's government was remarkably open to such minorities and it was routine to find Jews, Serbs, Albanians, Kurds, and Orthodox Greeks in high government offices, including that of Grand Vizier, Ottoman equivalent of Prime Minister.

From the sultan's viewpoint this system of government had several advantages. It provided reliable tax revenue, it made local elites and religious minorities dependent on the sultan's government, and it supported a large, ready reserve for his army. It also integrated the industrial and financial skills of non-Muslims into the empire and provided the sultan with large military resources. In a crisis, or when staging a major campaign, the cadre of soldier–administrators could be mobilized quickly. In the late 1400s, when Isabella of Castile had difficulty mobilizing 15,000 troops to fight in Granada, the sultan could call up 50,000 soldiers in a matter of weeks. This discrepancy in the ability to mobilize military resources continued. In 1525 France and Spain had a major confrontation and neither army had more than 25,000 troops. With great difficulty Philip II of Spain maintained 75,000 soldiers in the Low Countries in the 1570s. By contrast, in the 1520s Sultan Suleiman the Magnificent sent 150,000 soldiers into the Balkans every year while also campaigning on other fronts. (See Illustration 2.2.) (See Readings 2.6, 2.7.)

The difference in the ability to mobilize manpower shaped the ways in which Spaniards and Turks exploited military technology. Primitive cannon and gunpowder were used throughout Asia and Europe by 1400. Short of manpower, European rulers like Isabella of Castile and Charles V encouraged innovations in hand weapons and mobile cannon as "labor-saving" antipersonnel weapons. By 1525 the arquebus, a primitive shotgun, and field artillery were important in the wars between European monarchs.

The Turks were also alert to such innovations. Turkish museums, and paintings of their Balkan army of the 1520s, show that cannon and muskets were adopted as fast in the Middle East as they were in Europe. The Turks also innovated in gunnery, but took a different direction from the Europeans. The best early cannon were made of bronze. Bronze is an alloy of copper and tin, both of which were expensive. The Turks had little trouble mobilizing huge armies, which reduced their need for labor-saving field artillery, but they were often confronted with long and expensive sieges against cities. Thus their innovations took the form of massive siege cannon that used more expensive metal than European rulers could afford. Twenty feet long and three feet in diameter, some of the guns in the siege of Budapest were so large that they could not be moved. They were brought overland as raw metal and fuel and were cast on the site of the siege. Capable of firing a 1,300-pound ball every two hours, such cannon were useless on the battlefield, but against fortified towns they were devastating. Both European and Ottoman society readily adopted new technology, but each did so in response to its own needs.

**ILLUSTRATION 2.2**
*SULEIMAN THE MAGNIFICENT, OTTOMAN SULTAN, 1520–1566.*
*Suleiman is shown here leaving his palace with an honor guard en route to daily*
*prayers. Detail taken from a woodcut published in 1563.*

Source: Gulru Necipoglu, *Architecture, Ceremonial, and Power: The Topkapi Palace in the Fifteenth and Sixteenth Centuries* (Cambridge: The MIT Press, 1991), p. 24. Described as a detail from an anonymous woodcut in nine sheets, published and engraved by Domenico de' Franceschi, ca. 1563, and taken from William Stirling-Maxwell, *Soliman the Magnificent Going to Mosque. From a series of engravings on wood published by Domenico de'Franceschi at Venice in MDLXII* (Florence and Edinburgh, 1877).

The Ottoman sultans of the 1400s created an imperial government that proved remarkably durable. As with any large organization, it changed over time, reflecting its social and economic context. In the seventeenth and eighteenth centuries the administrative elite and the Janissaries got involved in factional politics and policy at court lost its coherence. Local elites, especially in the Balkans, increasingly reoriented to local constituencies and reverted to Orthodox Christianity. By 1914 and World War I, Serbia, Albania, Greece, Bulgaria, and Romania all were independent.

During the nineteenth century it was customary for Europeans to refer to this empire as "the sick man of Europe" because of its resistance to western modernization and apparent vulnerability to attack. Yet despite its "sickness" the Ottoman Empire governed the Middle East and part of the Balkans until after World War I ended in 1918. Its fifteenth-century rulers built systems for recruiting reliable officials, for effective administration and taxation, for sustaining a huge army, and for integrat-

## READING 2.6

*The Venetians were particularly aware of the military resources of the Ottomans since they had confronted them in numerous wars. One estimate of Turkish military potential is found in the report of the Venetian Ambassador to Istanbul written in 1585 and excerpted here. He also comments on the process of succession when the Sultan dies:*

[Ottoman Sultans] succeed to the throne without any kind of ceremony or election or coronation. According to Turkish law of succession, which resembles most countries' laws in this respect, the oldest son should succeed to the throne as soon as the father dies. But in fact, whichever of the sons can first enter the royal compound in Constantinople is called the sultan and is obeyed by the people and by the army. . . . Because this government is based on force, the brother who overcomes the others is considered the lord of all. . . . This lord has thirty-seven kingdoms covering enormous territory. His dominion extends to the three principal parts of the world, Africa, Asia, and Europe; and since these lands are joined and contiguous with each other, he can travel for a distance of eight thousand miles on a circuit through his empire and hardly need to set foot in another prince's territories.

. . . the security of the Turkish lands depends first on the abundance it has of all the necessities of life. Not only is there enough for the daily needs of her people, but great quantities of foods and other goods are exported. From Constantinople go wool, leather, furs, and cambric; from Greece, cotton and spun thread; from Syria, silk, ginger, spices, cotton, dyes, spun thread, pistachios, muslin, and carpets; from Alexandria, spices, ginger, vegetables, dates, gold and silk edged ribbons, textiles, carpets, sugar and other things; and from the Morea, wheat and other grains. . . .

The security of the empire depends more than anything else on the large numbers of land and sea forces which the Turks keep continually under arms. . . . The sultan always has about 280,000 well-paid men in his service. Of them about 80,000 are paid every three months out of his personal treasury. These include roughly 16,000 janissaries, . . . 12,000 cavalry, . . . and armorers, artillerymen, . . . grooms, servants, pages, doctors, and others. . . . The other 200,000 cavalry are called timariots because they are not paid with money like the others, but are assigned landholdings. Each of them is required to maintain one armed horseman for every 5,000 aspers of income produced by his timar. . . .

The timariots are in no way inferior as fighting men to the soldiers paid every three months with cash, because the timars are not inherited like the fiefs distributed by Christian rulers. Fief-holders [in Christian lands] don't count for much militarily, because it often happens that the owner of a fief is not a soldier and knows nothing about warfare; moreover, fiefs are often inherited by women or minor children. But with the Turks, those who hold timars are sure to be soldiers, since these lands are not assigned to anyone else. As soon as a timariot dies, his timar is immediately given to another soldier, so that this militia is always composed of professional fighting men.

From Alberi, III, 3: 253–322, Davis, *Pursuit of Power* (New York: Harper & Row, 1970), pp. 126–133.

### READING 2.7

*Chislain de Busbecq was a Flemish nobleman who was the Austrian ambassador to the Ottoman Sultan Suleiman the Magnificent in the 1550s. Greatly concerned that European rulers did not take the Ottoman Empire seriously enough, he sent this confidential letter to a fellow diplomat in 1555.*

... The Sultan's head-quarters were crowded by numerous attendants, including many high officials. ... In all that great assembly no single man owed his dignity to anything but his personal merits and bravery; no one is distinguished from the rest by his birth, and honor is paid to each man according to the nature of the duty and offices which he discharges. Thus there is no struggle for precedence, every man having his place assigned to him by virtue of the function which he performs. The Sultan himself assigns to all their duties and offices, and in doing so pays no attention to wealth or the empty claims of rank ... Thus each man is rewarded according to his deserts, and offices are filled by men capable of performing them. In Turkey every man has it in his power to make what he will of the position into which he is born and of his fortune in life. Those who hold the highest posts under the Sultan are very often the sons of shepherds and herdsmen, and, so far from being ashamed of their birth, they make it a subject of boasting. ... Just as they consider that an aptitude for the arts, such as music or mathematics or geometry, is not transmitted to a son and heir, so they hold that character is not hereditary. ... This is why the Turks succeed in all that they attempt and are a dominating race and daily extend the bounds of their rule. Our method is very different; there is no room for merit, but everything depends on birth; considerations of which alone open the way to high official position. On this subject I shall perhaps say more in another place, and you must regard these remarks as intended for your ears only.

... I compare the Turkish system with our own; one army must prevail and the other be destroyed, for certainly both cannot remain unscathed. On their side are the resources of a mighty empire, strength unimpaired, experience and practice in fighting, a veteran soldiery, habituation to victory, endurance of toil, unity, order, discipline, frugality, and watchfulness. On our side is public poverty, private luxury, impaired strength, broken spirit, lack of endurance and training; the soldiers are insubordinate, the officers avaricious; there is contempt for discipline; license, recklessness, drunkenness, and debauchery are rife; and, worst of all, the enemy is accustomed to victory, and we to defeat. Can we doubt what the result will be? Persia alone interposes in our favor; for the [Turkish] enemy, as he hastens to attack [us], must keep an eye on this menace in his rear. ...

From *The Turkish Letters of Ogier Ghiselin de Busbecq, Imperial Ambassador at Constantinople, 1554–1562*, trans. Edward Foster (Oxford: Oxford University Press, 1927), excerpted from Kevin Reilly, *Readings in World Civilizations*, vol. 2 (New York: St. Martins, 1995), pp. 81–85.

ing religious minorities into the empire. Despite internal stresses and gradual disintegration, it lasted until 1921, making it one of the longest-lived regimes in history. By contrast, Spain's American empire lasted only 300 years while her European empire survived barely 200 years and had been dismantled by 1715.

## TOWARD A CONFRONTATION BETWEEN EMPIRES

In the last half of the 1400s Spaniards and Turks, starting at the opposite ends of the Mediterranean, began to impinge upon each other and upon the trading empires of Venice and Genoa. Neither Venice nor Genoa had a strong army, but both could mobilize strong fleets. As the Ottomans took control of the Aegean and Black Seas, their empire absorbed commercial activities that generated taxes and profits for Ottoman notables. Not surprisingly, Ottoman policy increasingly paid attention to commercial matters. Thus the same commercial motives that drew Europeans toward Asia began to shape Ottoman policy in the Mediterranean and the Middle East.

As of 1400, the Genoese were strong in the Aegean and Black Seas, where they met caravans from China, Iran, and India. They did much of their trade in Constantinople, capital of the now tiny Byzantine Empire, and their dealings with the Turks were guarded. The Venetians were more interested in the Mediterranean trade in spices from Asia. Traditionally spices reached the Mediterranean either via the Persian Gulf and Aleppo in Syria, or by way of the Red Sea, Cairo, and Alexandria. The decline of the Ilkhanate and Timurlane's invasion left Iraq and Syria chronically unstable. Thus the safest spice route in the 1400s was through the Red Sea and the Mameluk Empire, by way of Cairo. As capital city, seat of the caliphate, and a major trade center, Cairo had replaced Baghdad as the metropolis of the Middle East. (See Reading 2.8.)

The Venetians therefore supported the Mameluks and often found themselves at war with the Ottomans. For similar reasons, the Genoese did what they could to please the Ottomans, who gave them facilities in the Aegean and the Black Sea that they withheld from Venice. One key to the puzzle was Byzantine Constantinople, which provided both Venice and Genoa with a Christian base for trade in the Black Sea.

This was the context for renewed Ottoman expansion once the empire had been reorganized after 1421. The Turks first moved into Syria and the Balkans. They built a serious navy and defeated the Venetians at sea for the first time in 1430. In 1453 Mehmed II "the Conqueror" conquered Constantinople, adding "Emperor of Rome" to his titles. By 1464 he had conquered Greece, Serbia, and Bosnia. The Genoese had helped defend Constantinople in 1453, prompting the Turks to favor the Venetians, and the Genoese steadily lost ground in the eastern Mediterranean. By 1490 Venice had the upper hand over Genoa and dominated the trade

## READING 2.8

*In 1481 the Jewish traveller Rabbi Meshullam Ben R. Manahem of Volterra (Italy) visited Alexandria and Cairo. Allowing for overstatement, he left this description.*

Alexandria (Egypt) is as big as Florence. It is well built and the city walls are high and fine, but all the city is very dry and it has more ruins than buildings. . . . In Alexandria I saw four large fondaks [warehouses], one for the Franks and another for the Genoese and their Consul and two for the Venetians and their Consul, I also saw the Admiral [Mameluk governor], who had a pigeon and, whenever he wished to send a message to the Sultan, he placed it in the pigeon's mouth or fastened the letter to it and the pigeon took it to Cairo and brought it to the window of the Sultan's house and there was always a man waiting in the window on the look out. . . .

I have seen Misr [Cairo] and inquired about the people to know their ways, and, if I were to write and describe the glory and wealth of the city and the men therein, this book would not suffice, and I swear that if it were possible to place all the cities of Rome, Milan, Padua, and Florence together with four other cities, they would not, the whole lot of them contain the wealth and population of the half of Cairo, and this is true. . . . In Misr [Cairo] there are big fondaks [warehouses], with a street between them, and round the street the houses are shops with two, three, or four doors, which are closed every night, and there are always watchmen there; and in the fondaks there are all kinds of goods, and the merchants and craftsmen sit near their shops, which are very small, and show samples of all their goods; and if you wish to buy from them, a matter of importance, of some value, they bring you into their warehouse, and there you can see the wonderful goods they have, for you could hardly believe that there are one thousand and more warehouses in each fondak; and there is nothing in the world that you do not find in the fondaks in Cairo, even the smallest things. . . . On Friday, the 22nd of June, 1481, I saw the Sultan face to face. He is an old man of 80, but straight as a reed, tall, and good looking, clothed in a white garment. He was riding, and more than two thousand *mameluk* soldiers were with him. . . . Anyone who wishes to see the Sultan can see him easily. He has a fine large fort in the city, and he sits on the front on Mondays and Thursdays openly in the company of the Governor of the city, and his Dragomans at his side, and mameluks all round, more than three hundred to protect him.

---

In Elkan Adler, *Jewish Travelers in the Middle Ages* (New York: Dover Publications, 1987), pp. 159–170.

in Asian goods bound for Europe, a tricky situation that required good relations with the Mameluk Empire. This led the Venetians to start another war with the Ottomans (1499–1503). The growing power of the Ottoman Empire is shown by its response. Within months the Turks mobilized 300 ships and 65,000 sailors and Venice quickly made peace. She became the European agent for Ottoman merchants, and even agreed to protect Turkish merchant ships in Christian waters.

The Genoese, squeezed out of the eastern Mediterranean, had to find other commercial outlets. This coincided with Aragonese activity in the western Mediterranean and encouraged Genoese investment in Atlantic Europe. By the 1480s the Genoese were active in Castilian trade at Seville, the base for Castilian conquest of Muslim Granada. At the same time, both Castile and Portugal hoped to expand their influence in North Africa. The Catalans and Genoese had long traded at Ceuta on the Moroccan coast. In 1415 the Portuguese captured the town, which remains a Spanish province to this day. After Granada was "pacified" (1482–1492), religious conservatives around Queen Isabella were determined to conquer North Africa. Southern Italy was occupied by Spanish troops in 1495 in response to a French invasion, and the North African ports of Melilla and Oran were captured in 1497 and 1509. Spain had projected itself across the Mediterranean more strongly than ever. The Genoese, meanwhile, compensated for their losses in the East by investing in trade at Barcelona, Seville, Lisbon, London, and Antwerp, and became an important lobby supporting Spanish expansion into Africa. The presence of Spaniards in Italy, their capture of Muslim Granada, Melilla, and Oran, plus the ongoing Spanish protectorate over Tunis all were noted by the Turks and Venetians.

Meanwhile, Ottoman attention was also caught by the arrival of European (Portuguese) ships in the Indian Ocean and Red Sea after 1498. This threatened Muslim pilgrim routes as well as the Asian spice trade. Mecca was as important in Muslim politics as the Holy Land had been in Christian politics at the time of the Crusades. The Mameluk Empire was unable to respond to the Europeans in Asian waters, a fact revealed when the Portuguese destroyed their Indian Ocean fleet in 1508. The Mameluk ability to protect pilgrimages to Mecca had been compromised. To complicate matters, 1502–1514 saw the instability of Iran and Iraq exploited by an aggressive new Iranian ruler, Shah Ismail. Under Ismail, the Safavid Turks built a new Iranian empire, capturing Syria and Iraq and threatening southern Anatolia.

Concerned about a possible alliance between Ismail and the Mameluk Empire or the Venetians, the Ottomans began to undermine the Mameluk government. They publicized the idea that the Mameluks had abandoned their responsibility to protect the pilgrimages and suggested that they were unable to guard Mecca and the spice trade from the Portuguese. The Turks "helped" the Mameluks, first by sending shipbuilding supplies to the Mameluk navy base in the Red Sea. Soon they were sending craftsmen and "advisers" to help construct the fleet. Then they sent Turkish troops to protect Turkish personnel. In 1510, the Turks also sent their leading admiral to supervise the situation. When, in 1514, the Mameluk Sultan visited "his" navy base in Suez, he discovered that it was controlled by Turks, and when the new "Mameluk" fleet sailed in 1515 to attack the Portuguese, it was commanded by a Turkish admiral. The new Red Sea fleet was, in fact, built, manned, and commanded by the Ottoman Empire.

To isolate the Mameluks, in 1514 the Ottomans sent an army into Syria and Iraq, where they defeated Shah Ismail. Backed by a large fleet off the Syrian coast, this extended Ottoman power into the Caucasus and the Middle East. (See Reading 2.9.) It not only ended the threat of an alliance between Ismail and the Mameluk Empire, it also removed the buffer zone between the Mameluks and the Ottomans. Victory over the Iranians, the reduction of Venice to the status of marketing agent, and infiltration of the Mameluk empire set the stage for a dramatic example of political expansion.

In 1517, the year after Charles V inherited half of Europe, the Ottoman Sultan Selim "the Grim" invaded the Mameluk Empire by land and sea. Using fast-moving troops in the nomadic tradition, within a few months the Ottomans had conquered Iraq and the Persian Gulf, Syria, the Holy Land, Arabia (including the Muslim Holy sites), and all of Egypt and had gained access to the Indian Ocean. The Caliph of Cairo, religious leader of Sunni Islam, was moved to Istanbul, where he could be supervised by Ottoman officials. In one swift campaign the Turks became rulers of the entire Middle East, Arabia, and Egypt. The entire region from Hungary to Arabia and from Iran to Algeria was now under the control of a well-organized imperial government.

## CONFRONTATION AND STALEMATE

Turkish dominance of the Middle East had serious repercussions for Europe. The Venetians now had no choice but to deal with the Turks if they wanted to trade with the East. In following decades, despite threats of a Muslim conquest of Europe, the Venetians were repeatedly found selling cannon, muskets, gunpowder, and military supplies to the Turks, regardless of papal prohibitions. Given the Portuguese attempt to monopolize European trade in Asian spices, the Venetians had no choice but to collaborate with the Turks.

The new situation brought Turkish power into Spain's backyard. North Africa had long been the site of several Muslim states and an Iberian sphere of influence. Catalan and Genoese merchants had traded there for centuries, dealing with Arab and Jewish merchants whose contacts reached far into the African interior. As of 1515 the Castilians and Portuguese controlled the African ports of Ceuta, Melilla, Oran, and Tunis. With their conquest of Egypt in 1517, however, the Ottomans soon turned North Africa into a Turkish protectorate. Turkish governors, garrisons, and navy bases were installed in ports like Tripoli and Algiers, forcing the Genoese, Spaniards, and Portuguese to seek other ways of trading with Africa.

The sudden expansion of Turkey also changed the situation inside Europe and forced the Spaniards to divide their attention. In the first half of the 1500s, Charles V was simultaneously embroiled in an ongoing war with France over control of Italy and in religious wars in Germany as a result of the Protestant Reformation. In the second half of the century France was disrupted by civil war, but Philip II was confronted by a major and costly revolt in the Low Countries (1565–1608), further compli-

READING 2.9

*A letter, effectively a declaration of war, from the Ottoman Sultan Selim of Turkey to the Shah Ismail of the resurgent Safavid Empire in Persia. Ismail had invaded the area of northern Syria and Iraq and the southern part of modern Turkey, threatening the balance of power between the Ottoman and Mameluk Empires. Selim mounted a major campaign in the region as a pre-lude to taking over the nearby Mameluk Empire based in Egypt. Note the ide-ological component, since the Ottomans were moderate Sunni Muslims while the Safavids were rather intolerant Shi'ite Muslims.*

I, sovereign chief of the Ottomans, master of the heroes of the age, who unites the force and power of Feridun [legendary king of ancient Persia], the majesty and glory of Alexander the Great, the justice and clemency of Chusraw [king of Persia at time of Mohammed's birth]; I, the exterminator of idolaters, de-stroyer of the enemies of the true faith, the terror of the tyrants and pharaohs of the age; I, before whom proud and unjust kings have humbled themselves, and whose hand breaks the strongest scepters; I, the great Sultan-Khan, son of Sultan Bayezid-Khan, son of Sultan Muhammed-Khan [conqueror of Con-stantinople], son of Sultan Murad-Khan, I address myself graciously to you, Amir Isma'il, chief of the troops of Persia, comparable in tyranny to Zahhak and Afrasiab [legendary tyrants in the Persian national epic], and predestined to perish like the last Darius, in order to make known to you that . . . it is He [the Almighty] who has set up Caliphs on earth . . . it is then only by practic-ing the true religion that man will prosper in this world and merit eternal life in the other. As to you, Amir Isma'il, such a recompense will not be your lot; because you have denied the sanctity of the divine laws; because you have de-serted the path of salvation and the sacred commandments; because you have impaired the purity of the dogmas of Islam; because you have dishonored, soiled and destroyed the altars of the Lord, usurped the scepter of the East by unlawful and tyrannical means; because coming forth from the dust, you have raised yourself by odious devices to a place shining with splendor and magnif-icence; because you have opened to Muslims the gates of impiety; because un-der the cloak of the hypocrite, you have sowed everywhere trouble and sedi-tion; because you have raised the standard of irreligion and heresy . . . you have dared . . . to permit the ill-treatment of the *ulama*, the doctors and amirs descended from the Prophet, the repudiation of the Koran, the cursing of the legitimate Caliphs. Now as the first duty of a Muslim and above all of a pious price is to obey the commandment, "O, you faithful who believe, be the ex-ecutors of the decrees of God!" the ulama and our doctors have pronounced sentence of death against you, perjurer and blasphemer, and have imposed on every Muslim the sacred obligation to arm in defense of religion and destroy heresy and impiety in your person and that of all your partisans.

Animated by the spirit of this *fetwa*, conforming to the Koran the code of divine laws, and wishing on one side to strengthen Islam, on the other to liber-ate the lands and peoples who writhe under your yoke, we have resolved to lay aside our imperial robes in order to put on the shield and coat of mail, to raise our ever-victorious banner, to assemble our invincible armies.

From the book *The Muslim World on the Eve of Europe's Expansion*, ed. John J. Saunders, Copyright 1966 Englewood Cliffs, NJ: Prentice-Hall, as found in Mark Kishlansky, et al., *Societies and Cultures in World History*, Vol. B, *1300–1800* (New York: HarperCollins, 1995), p. 456.

cated by repeated interventions by England. This meant that the Turkish threat in both central Europe and the Mediterranean, where Spain's coasts were being raided by North African fleets, stretched Habsburg–Spanish resources to the limit. The Muslim ports in North Africa became Turkish navy bases, threatening Spain's Mediterranean trade and its control of Sicily and Italy. At one point the Turks even joined forces with France, Spain's worst enemy inside Europe.

To make things worse, Turkish resources were immense by sixteenth-century standards. As we have seen, Suleiman the Magnificent (sultan, 1521–1566) routinely fielded 150,000 troops every year and could mobilize 200 to 400 ships. After conquering the Middle East and most of North Africa between 1517 and 1521, the Turks turned their attention northward. (See Illustration 2.3.) In eight years they moved north from Serbia and Bulgaria to conquer Bosnia, Croatia, Romania, Hungary, and Ukraine. Suleiman was finally stopped in 1529 at the siege of Vienna. Despite the refusal of the Protestant German princes to help with the defense of the city, its dogged defenders managed to hold out until bad weather and the refusal of the Janissaries to campaign in the winter forced Suleiman to withdraw. The Turks were stopped in Austria, but for the next 150 years the boundary of the Ottoman Empire was less than 100 miles from Vienna in the heart of Europe.

Sultan Suleiman then shifted his attention elsewhere. The continued rise of the Safavid Empire in Persia forced the Ottomans to protect their eastern boundaries even as they continued to put pressure on Europe. The 1530s and 1540s saw Turkish naval campaigns in the Mediterranean as the Spaniards were evicted from Tunis and other North African ports. Suleiman intervened in European wars and at one point took part in a joint operation with the French Navy against the Spanish coast. The Turkish fleet actually spent a winter in the French base at Toulon, although the joint campaign never amounted to much.

Having captured the Balkans and southern Russia, Suleiman focused his attention on Africa and Italy. In the 1550s and 1560s he expelled the Spaniards from most of their fortified positions on the African coast. In 1565 he mounted a huge siege of Malta, a key point for traffic between the eastern and western Mediterranean and between North Africa and Italy. The siege was broken at the last minute by a combined Spanish, Genoese, and papal fleet. In 1570, however, the Turks captured the island of Cyprus and planned an invasion of Italy. The invasion was only forestalled in 1571 by an almost accidental battle between the Turkish fleet and an armada of Spanish, Genoese, Venetian, and papal ships. The encounter took place off the Turkish port of Naupaktos (Lepanto). (See Illustration 2.4.) The Turkish fleet was destroyed and the invasion of Italy was canceled.

The cancellation of the Italian invasion, however, had less to do with European might than many textbooks imply. The 200 ships and 30,000 men lost at Lepanto were only part of the Turkish navy. Within a

**ILLUSTRATION 2.3**
*TURKISH JANISSARIES IN SERBIA UNDER OTTOMAN RULE.*
*By 1526 all of Serbia and Hungary had been conquered by Suleiman the Magnificent. This 19th-century engraving shows a Turkish garrison returning to its castle in Serbia after a raid. By the 19th century, attitudes toward Turkish control had become negative, and the drawing is in part a hostile caricature. In the first century and a half of Turkish control in the Balkans, their rule was accepted by the general population.*
Source: The Granger Collection, New York.

year the fleet had been replaced, and in 1574 the Turks drove the Spaniards from Tunis, one of their oldest bases in Africa. Much more important for the fate of Europe at that moment was the fact that the Safavid Empire in Iran again invaded the Ottoman empire. The Turks were forced to put the Mediterranean theater on a back burner while dealing with a crisis in the east.

How can we evaluate the outcome of this titanic struggle? The Turks were defeated at Vienna in 1529, Malta in 1565, and Lepanto in 1571. These are hailed as great victories by European historians, and so they are. Yet they did little more than stop the Turks from further expansion. The Ottomans, however, had won in Egypt, Tunis, and Budapest before being distracted by events in Iran. Moreover, they governed a third of Europe for the next 300 years and controlled half the shores of the Mediterranean until the nineteenth century. At best, the European victo-

**ILLUSTRATION 2.4**
*THE BATTLE OF LEPANTO, 1571.*
*The Battle of Lepanto marks the end of Ottoman expansion in the Mediterranean for several decades and was seen in the West as a major victory. This drawing depicts a small section of the battle, which involved over a hundred ships in each fleet.*

Source: James C. David (ed. and trans.), *Pursuit of Power: Venetian Ambassadors' Reports on Spain, Turkey, and France in the Age of Philip II* (New York: Harper & Row, 1970), illustration 30, p. 101. Described there as detail from Camocio, *Isola, famosa porti,* plate 64. From an original in the Free Library of Philadelphia.

ries in the struggle for control of the Mediterranean produced a durable stalemate that left the Ottoman Empire in possession of much of the disputed territory.

As we saw, in the 1300s the Mediterranean basin was the setting for a political power vacuum. Excepting the Mameluk Empire and the Mongol Ilkhanate, at that moment the region was a mosaic of small and weak Muslim and Christian states. This situation was accentuated by the bubonic plague. The most distinctive development at that moment was neither political nor religious; it was an expanding network of trade, investment, and commercial interdependence organized by several European city-states, the most important of which were Venice and Genoa. Characterized by strong navies and tiny armies, the autonomy of these city-states was a by-product of European political fragmentation.

By 1520 the setting had changed dramatically. The Mediterranean was dominated by two huge empires. The climax of this development came with the Ottoman seizure of the Middle East and North Africa in 1517 and the failure of their siege of Vienna in 1529. For the rest of the sixteenth century the Mediterranean saw a struggle that was confirmed as a stalemate at Lepanto in 1571.

The maritime republics of Genoa and Venice confronted this situation in two ways. The Venetians made their peace with the Turks to keep up their trade in Asian spices and eastern Mediterranean commodities. The Genoese retained some eastern connections but looked elsewhere for investment outlets. This explains their growing importance in Barcelona, Seville, Lisbon, London, and Antwerp. They also invested heavily in risky loans to European rulers and provided much of the capital for early African and American ventures organized in Spain and Portugal.

The head-to-head confrontation of large armies and navies along stable frontiers left little room for the less disciplined and more aggressive elements in European society. Europe's land-hungry fighting nobility, its missionary communities, and many of its merchants were forced to seek other outlets. The Ottoman invasion of Europe was halted, but the cost sapped Spanish resources and ultimately made it impossible for the Habsburgs to maintain the dynastic empire they had assembled in Europe. Moreover, Turkish land and sea power made talk of renewing the medieval Crusades look like a sad joke, especially when Venetian, and later Dutch and English, merchants had little difficulty trading in the eastern Mediterranean as long as they shared the profits with their counterparts inside the Ottoman Empire.

If we combine the Genoese search for new investments, the discovery of several islands in the Atlantic, Turkish control of North Africa, and the information available to Europeans about the Mali Empire, it becomes easier to understand why people in Europe were ready to take risks in the Atlantic. Initially the numbers were small. Expeditions counted a few small ships and dozens, occasionally hundreds of men, compared with the 150,000 troops in the Ottomans' Balkan army and the

230 ships they had at Lepanto. The Atlantic ventures reflect in part expansive urges derived from the peculiarities and frustrations of European society. It is also true, however, that a growing number of expeditions went into the Atlantic after 1400 because it became increasingly difficult and costly for Europeans to do business and build careers in the Mediterranean world.

## 3

# A NEW KIND OF SOCIETY

# *Africa, Europe, and the Plantation System*

## THE LURE OF AFRICA

Many older textbooks tell us that the Portuguese sailed down the coast of Africa in search of a sea route to Asia and its valuable spice trade. While there is some truth in that statement, it presents the first phase of European expansion into the Atlantic as more purposeful and organized than it really was. Europeans ventured into the Atlantic in a sporadic and disjointed way, with more immediate and varied goals. By far the most important initial goal was not Asia, but Africa itself. The west African gold trade, which traditionally reached the Mediterranean through Muslim middlemen and north African seaports, was well known in Italy, Catalonia, Castile, and Portugal. The search for access to this African wealth had remarkable unintended consequences throughout the tropical Atlantic. In addition, important people at the Portuguese court were committed to carrying a Christian Crusade into Africa, an aspect of Portuguese activity that often worked at cross purposes with commercial aspirations. Before we describe these activities, however, we must first look at what attracted Europeans to sub-Saharan Africa.

In 1324 Emperor Musa of Mali (ruled 1312–1337) made the pilgrimage to Mecca expected of all good Muslims, travelling across 3,500 miles of central Africa and the Mameluk Empire as he did so. Imperial pilgrimages were hardly everyday events, and prompted a great deal of comment, but there was nothing exceptional about making such a trip. Musa first toured several hundred miles of his own empire, then followed well-known trade routes across several African kingdoms on his way to the Nile River and Mameluk Egypt. At least two of his royal predecessors had made the same trip.

Emperor Musa's pilgrimage was notable not because it happened, but because of the size and wealth of his entourage. Musa arrived in Cairo with several hundred retainers and a caravan of camels that reputedly included a hundred animals loaded with gold bars and bags of gold dust. The quantity of gold that this entourage spent just in Cairo was reported to have disrupted currency exchange rates for months. Such stories spread around the Mediterranean, and their impact is illustrated by pictures in Mallorcan atlases as early as 1320. The impression is unmistakable in the Catalan Atlas of 1375. Its map of Africa was vague about the location of towns south of the Mediterranean coast, but the Mali Empire is clearly identified. It is highlighted by the picture of a handsome black king seated on an ornate throne. He holds a scepter in one hand and a huge gold nugget in the other. (See Illustration 3.1.) The preoccupation with African trade is also suggested by a Catalan merchants' manual of 1385, which actually includes more information about Africa than about Italy. It mentions seventeen north African ports and 200 kinds of merchandise traded there. By that date involvement in Africa was over a century old, as shown by evidence of a Catalan protectorate in Tunis in 1250 and by Catalan colonization of islands off the Tunisian coast.

Mansa (i.e., Emperor) Musa of Mali was, in fact, ruler of a large empire south of the Sahara Desert, an empire that stretched a thousand miles from the Atlantic coast eastward across the grasslands and fertile farmland of the Niger River basin. By the 1300s the ruling elites and merchants of central and western Africa had converted to Islam, and the cities of the region housed important centers of Muslim scholarship. Islam had arrived in part along the east–west trade routes used by Emperor Musa. A more fundamentalist form had also arrived with the nomadic Berbers and Almoravids, who swept south from Morocco to capture some of the kingdoms in the region and disrupt the old Empire of Ghana. Exploiting written Arabic as a tool for record keeping, Musa's predecessors built up an empire similar to those created by nomadic invaders in the Middle East. They co-opted the ruling elites of African kingdoms by employing their members as officials and army officers. At the same time, the Mali emperors linked local religious cults to rituals at the imperial court. Like earlier Muslim conquerors in the Middle East, they also used nomadic cavalry and slave troops to create a professional army that, along with regular administration, made it safe for the undefended merchant to travel throughout the empire. (See Reading 3.1.)

The wealth of the Mali Empire, and west Africa in general, rested on several factors. Its large agricultural society not only paid taxes but provided food, textiles, and metal products for regional trade. The second element was mining, which produced substantial quantities of gold. Always in demand for coinage and jewelry, and itself a way of storing wealth,

**ILLUSTRATION 3.1**
*EARLY CATALAN MAP OF AFRICA AND MALI, LATE 1300s.*
*This map shows north and west Africa as it was known to Italian and Spanish*
*merchants by 1400. It illustrates a Europeanized Emperor (Mansa) Musa of Mali.*
*He is presented with European-style imperial regalia and throne and is shown*
*holding a large gold nugget in his hand while greeting a trade caravan. This*
*neatly summarizes Iberian perceptions of Africa as a major source of gold and*
*trade.*

Source: Peter Stearns, Michael Adas, and Stuart Schwartz, *World Civilizations: The Global
Experience* (New York: HarperCollins, 1992), p. 319. By the Catalan map maker Abraham
Cresques with permission of the British Library.

gold was exported to the Mediterranean and the Middle East in return for
salt, dates, silk, manufactures, and wool cloth. A third source of wealth
was the age-old network of trade routes that connected west Africa and
the rest of the world. The route of Musa's pilgrimage ran east–west, south
of the Sahara, and linked west Africa with Ethiopia, Egypt, and Arabia.
More important trade routes ran north–south between the cities of the
Mali Empire and the Mediterranean ports of Ceuta, Tangiers, Melilla,
Oran, Algiers, Tunis, and Tripoli. (See Map 3.1.) This was the trade that
attracted Italians and Spaniards to Mediterranean Africa as early as the
1200s, and which drew the Portuguese down Africa's coast.

A fourth component of the Mali economy was the slave trade. As in
the Mediterranean and the Middle East, slavery was a routine part of
African society and took various forms. Indeed, because of the nature of
property law in sub-Saharan Africa, it was easier to become wealthy by
owning and controlling labor than by controlling access to land. Slavery
could be found in every part of Africa, and African slaves had been used

READING 3.1

*One of the great world travellers of the 1300s was the Muslim Ibn Battuta,*
*who was a native of Morocco and visited countries from Mali to China and*
*India. Here we have an excerpt of his assessment of the practice of Islam in*
*Mali as of 1353, about the time that Mansa Musa visited Mecca.*

Amongst their good qualities is the small amount of injustice amongst them,
for of all people they are the furthest from it. Among these qualities there is
also the prevalence of peace in their country, the traveller is not afraid in it nor
is he who lives there in fear of the thief or of the robber by violence. Another
of the good habits amongst them is the way they meticulously observe the
times of the prayers and attendance at them, so also it is with regard to their
congregational services and their beating of their children to instill these things
in them. When it is Friday, if a man does not come early to the mosque he will
not find a place to pray because of the numbers of the crowd. Among their
good qualities is their putting on of good white clothes on Friday. If a man
among them has nothing except a tattered shirt, he washes and cleans it and at-
tends the Friday prayer in it. Another of their good qualities is their concern
for learning the sublime Qur'an by heart. They make fetters for the children
when they appear on their part to be falling short of learning it by heart.

   Among the bad things which they do—their serving women, slave women
and little daughters appear before people naked, exposing their private parts.
Also among their bad customs is the way women will go into the presence of
the sultan naked, without any covering; and the nakedness of the sultan's
daughters. Another of their bad customs is their putting of dust and ashes on
their heads as a sign of respect. And another is that many of them eat animals
not ritually slaughtered, and dogs and donkeys.

From *Ibn Battuta in Black Africa,* as presented in Mark Kishlansky, Patrick
Geary, Patricia O'Brien, and R. Bin Wong, *Societies and Cultures in World His-*
*tory, Vol. A, to 1500* (New York: HarperCollins, 1995), p. 215.

in the Middle East for centuries. Before the development of the Euro-Atlantic slave trade, most African slaves started as prisoners of war. Because
they usually were captured from neighboring kingdoms, making escape
easy, war captives were traded to slave markets far from their place of
birth. Most slaves in sub-Saharan Africa had a defined civic status, and in
many places became additional members of the households that acquired
them. They were often given fictive family relationships, married non-
slave members of the community, and sometimes even inherited the family's assets. In many African communities the slave status of such household slaves was not inherited by their children.

   Slavery was thus widespread, and trade in slaves was a routine aspect of Africa's complex commercial system. This generalized slave trade
made it possible for traders from outside of sub-Saharan Africa to buy enslaved war captives and take them to places completely outside the
African context. Thus we hear about groups of young slaves included in
the caravans that crossed the desert to the Mediterranean or Middle East.
Within west Africa, commerce and mining opened the way to much more

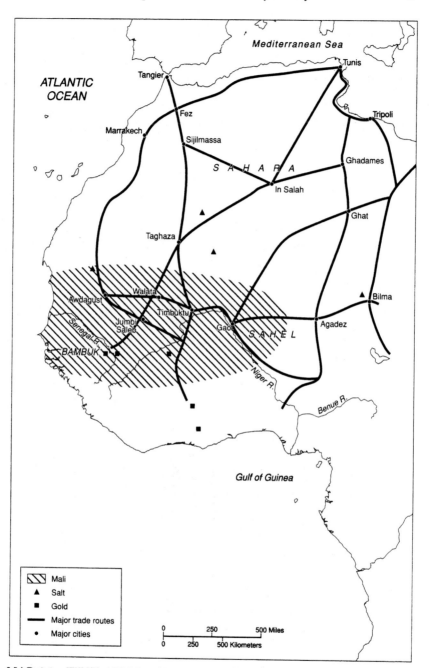

**MAP 3.1**  *WEST AFRICA, THE MALI EMPIRE, AND MAIN AFRICAN TRADE ROUTES BETWEEN 1300 AND 1500.*

oppressive forms of slavery, both in the African gold mines and on royal estates that produced crops for export. Mining is hard, miserable work and has been done with slave populations for millennia. The west African gold mines and royal estates were examples of hard-labor gang slavery similar to that of Roman *latifundia*, the silver mines of classical Athens or Roman Spain, and the Iraqi sugar plantations of the eleventh and twelfth centuries. It was thus different from the more common household slavery of African society.

The heart of the Mali empire and its commercial economy was inland. Its trade was centered on the Saharan "seaports" that serviced the caravan routes across the seas of sand between Mali and its markets. Until the later 1400s, Atlantic Africa was marginal to African trade. Most of the coast was controlled by small kingdoms on the fringe of the geopolitics of fifteenth-century Africa. In this the African coast resembled parts of the Indian Ocean basin (see Chapter 5) and thus provided the Portuguese with experience that proved useful as they penetrated Asia. The Mali Empire itself reached the Atlantic coast in the area of modern Gambia and Senegal. By the end of the 1400s Mali was being successfully challenged by the Songhay Empire, another product of nomadic incursions from Morocco. As the coastal traveller moved south to the Volta, Niger, and Congo deltas he encountered a great variety of small and medium sized kingdoms. Some, like Benin and Congo, were relatively large countries with organized armies and bureaucracies.

It is hardly surprising, therefore, that Genoese, Catalan, Castilian, and Portuguese merchants and adventurers were attracted by the possibility of Atlantic routes that would let them trade with Africa. They did not need the dream of a route to Asia to encourage expansion into African waters. The European intrusion into the Atlantic, while it had a political component, was driven by the haphazard activities of commercial adventurers, soldier–nobles, and missionaries bent on spreading Christianity. Portugal, the country initially most visible in this process, was itself marginal to European politics in the 1400s. Barely avoiding conquest by Castile in 1385, Portugal was a poor land of farmers and cattle herders, with a total population of 750,000 people—not much more than the city of Istanbul in 1600.

## EUROPEAN RESPONSE: AFRICAN CONTACT AND ISLAND "EMPIRES"

The lure of Africa was reinforced by other practical European activities. Commercial fishing found markets in Europe, and the coasts of Africa provided excellent fishing grounds. Lisbon, the Portuguese capital, had a good harbor and had gradually become an important seaport. At first Portugal exported only salt, fish, wine, grain, and forest products to northern Europe for other kinds of food, textiles, and hardware. By 1400, however, the Venetians and Genoese were sending Mediterranean goods by sea to England and the Low Countries through the straits of Gibraltar, and Lisbon became an important supply port for ships in transit. This attracted Genoese merchants to Lisbon, and once there they invested in local trade. Thus, while Portugal was not a wealthy country, Lisbon became a crossroads for Europe's maritime trade and had access to Italian capital seeking investments outside the Mediterranean.

The Castilian city of Seville developed a similar position. Sixty miles upriver from the Atlantic, Seville was a safe port. It was also an export center for Spanish wheat and wool. Wool had become an important raw material in international trade. The wool exports in particular help explain the Genoese presence in Seville, since the Italian textile industry used large amounts of high-quality raw wool. Seville's role was complemented by smaller ports on the coast, including Cadiz and Palos, where Columbus first set sail. Thus the early Atlantic ventures took place, not in isolation, but on the margins of an expanding European trade network.

The physical environment also makes it easier to understand how early Atlantic ventures were logical outgrowths of developments in late medieval Iberia. Prevailing Atlantic winds forced Europeans to develop navigation techniques that allowed them to sail by dead reckoning for long distances out of sight of land. Those skills were supplemented by the ability to calculate latitude and by adoption of the compass, a technology that originated in China and reached Europe by way of the Middle East. Prevailing winds made it easy to sail southwest along the African coast, but they also made a direct return difficult. Atlantic sailors solved this by sailing north from Africa, and cutting across the prevailing winds—a maneuver that took them far out into the Atlantic. As they reached the latitudes that crossed Portugal, they found prevailing west winds that carried them eastward to the mainland. This practice led to the discovery of the Azores Islands in the late 1300s. These uninhabited islands 700 miles out in the Atlantic acquired strategic importance as a supply station long before anyone knew that they sat astride the best route for sailing from America to Europe. By 1400 these activities had created a large, triangular maritime zone in the open Atlantic where sailors from Europe's south Atlantic ports operated with confidence.

There is no way to document each discovery, but by the 1350s Europeans had also found Madeira and the Canary Islands, while the Cape Verde Islands were found in the 1400s. By the 1380s European maps show fairly accurate locations for most of these islands, suggesting that several small, undocumented ventures had brought back information to be collated by the map makers. Of the four island groups, the Azores, Madeira, and the Cape Verdes were uninhabited, but the Canary Islands were heavily populated.

Scattered several hundred miles into the Atlantic westward from Africa, the Canary Islands were inhabited by the warlike Guanche people. We know little about these people, since their culture was wiped out before anyone thought to describe it. None of the early invaders or missionaries had the kind of curiosity that led their counterparts in America to describe the Amerindian societies they found. The Guanches were a light-skinned people, probably related to the Berbers of North Africa. They reached the islands well before the time of Christ, and Greek and Roman sources indicate that the islands were known in the classical period. By the 1300s, however, they had been cut off from Africa for centuries. They possessed a stone-age technology, and lived largely by hunting and food gathering. As of 1400 the Canary Islands had 80,000 to 100,000 Guanche inhabitants, organized into small tribal kingdoms. Early invaders found that, despite their stone-age weapons, the Guanches were fierce fighters. Although they lacked European immunities and died rapidly from European diseases, the Guanches put up a prolonged resistance. The final campaign in the European conquest of the Canary Islands did not take place until 1496, a century and a half after the first Europeans settled there.

The Canary Islands appear in modern European documents about 1330. The fact that they were populated and conveniently located off the African coast meant that the Canaries quickly attracted attention, and we have evidence for at least a dozen small Catalan and Mallorcan expeditions before 1390. One expedition, in 1351, carried a papal bull authorizing mission activity, and Pope Clement VI actually created a bishopric for the Canaries that lasted from 1351 to 1393. Early ventures in the Canaries suggest a pattern similar to the conquest of the smaller Mediterranean islands. Groups of militarized nobles organized ventures, which sought financial backing from investors and political legitimacy from an interested ruler. At one time or another Canary Island ventures were chartered by the pope and by the kings of Mallorca, Aragon, Castile, Portugal, and France. These charters gave a veneer of legality to the invaders and created negotiable claims in the future. They also provided a legal basis for royal jurisdiction over conquered lands once a crown had reason to use it.

These enterprises were based on the king–noble vassals model of medieval monarchies in Europe. The conquered lands were defined as fiefs, within which the new lord had wide jurisdictional powers and was authorized to collect rent and taxes on behalf of himself and the king. The crown retained jurisdiction over little except criminal justice and the right of judicial appeal, laying the legal foundation for a decentralized political system. This loosely structured government emerged wherever Europeans established themselves around the world. It was especially common in the first phases of any episode of European expansion. Given the adventurers involved and their distance from royal authority, it was a practical necessity. One irony of this development was that many of the speculators who obtained such "feudal" grants were actually capitalist investors—the type of individual often presented as the antithesis of European feudalism.

The Portuguese were early contenders for control of the Canaries because the islands offered a convenient base for trade with Africa, but the King of Castile also claimed jurisdiction. Until the 1390s the European establishment in the Canaries consisted of no more than a few impoverished outposts. The conflicting claims and grants gradually came under the control of a group of wealthy families in Seville. This group was then approached by two French nobles, Jean de Bethancourt and Gadifer de la Salle, instigators of the first systematic attempt to conquer the Islands.

Both men exemplify the kinds of Europeans prominent in European expansion. For Bethancourt the project combined a search for chivalric status among the European nobility with an escape from debts in France and England. De la Salle was typical in that he was a landless adventurer with a noble name but no patrimony. Such socially marginal mercenaries were common in Europe and were the by-product of the European rebellions and civil wars that followed the bubonic plague.

The original charter for Bethancourt's expedition was granted by the king of France. With support from Seville, however, Bethancourt quickly switched his fealty to Ferdinand III of Castile, who was eager to assert jurisdiction over the project. The invasion force left France in 1402 with 280 men, sixty-three of whom made it to the Canaries. Despite Castilian reinforcements, by 1405 the expedition had captured only a few infertile islands. The whole project was less an attempt to conquer and colonize than it was a search for a base from which Castilians might reach the African gold trade. The colony survived largely because the nearby Guanches died of European disease or were sold into slavery.

The invasion of the Canary Islands was soon overshadowed as Portugal began a more systematic attempt to reach Mali and the gold trade after 1420. This was linked with the ambiguous person known in Western Civilization textbooks as Prince Henry "the Navigator." Prince Henry was a complex person, but has been overrated by historians. The younger brother of the king of Portugal, Henry had few resources of his own and little prospect of becoming king. Beginning in the 1420s he was involved in a series of unaristocratic commercial activities, including the manufacture and sale of soap. At the same time, he promoted a series of small ventures that historians have presented as a grand plan for Atlantic empire. It is equally possible that this "grand plan" was little more than a sequence of ad hoc schemes designed to shore up Henry's fragile finances and enhance his reputation.

Until 1440, despite contacts and raids, only a trickle of African gold had actually reached Portugal. The flow increased notably in the 1440s, and in the mid-1450s one of Henry's commercial agents, a Genoese, sailed up the Gambia and Senegal Rivers and made direct contact with the Mali Empire. From that moment, many African caravans heading north to Morocco were attracted to the more accessible African coast, and serious direct trade with Africa got under way.

As this connection was developing, Prince Henry also encouraged colonization of the Madeira and Azores Islands. Madeira appears on maps before 1400, but only in the mid-1400s, with incentives from Henry, was it actually colonized, possibly as part of his "project" for expanding Portuguese influence. Expeditions visited both Madeira and the Azores, where they scattered seed, left sheep, and possibly dropped off a few settlers. Madeira was subdivided into baronies, with the fief-holders being, in effect, contractors obligated to organize settlement. Portuguese settlers, with the help of Guanche slaves, cut down the ancient forests and sent the lumber to the growing Iberian towns and shipyards. Settlers were also established on the Azores. With fertile virgin soil, both island colonies were soon exporting wheat.

As early as the 1450s, however, a more significant trend appeared: landlords on Madeira began to export sugar. Here again the complex dynamic behind European expansion is apparent. Many of the settler barons were poor, land-hungry nobles who thought in terms of royal legitimation and wealth based on land rents. (See Illustration 3.2.) As a result, development of the Madeira sugar industry depended on capital from investors on the mainland, many of them Genoese. Sugar production differs from many kinds of agriculture in that it requires both large investments in equipment and specialized hard labor. The Genoese had set up sugar plantations in southern Portugal soon after 1400, creating a demand for slaves from the Canary Islands. By the 1450s the growing demand for sugar provided an incentive to expand the industry. The result was a Madeira sugar industry controlled by absentee investors, and by 1480 sixty shiploads of sugar left Madeira every year. In Madeira, and also in the Canary Islands, sugar was produced primarily using the labor of European immigrants with the addition of some slaves.

As an example of expansion, this Portuguese-Atlantic sphere of influence began as a chaotic mixture of weak royal jurisdiction, lesser nobles seeking to improve their status, and merchants and investors looking for new sources of profit. Initially they sought access to Mali and the African gold trade. By 1475 this sphere of influence had evolved into a collection of precarious colonies with impoverished local populations and meager profits. The profits were shared by unruly landlords and mainland investors looking for products which, like sugar, had ready markets in Europe. By this time it was possible to identify Madeira and the Azores as "Portuguese" and the Canaries as "Castilian," but scattered across a vast expanse of ocean, their total population was puny and their commerce represented a tiny fraction of Europe's maritime economy.

Three things stand out about this emerging European sphere of influence in the Atlantic. First, although an example of expansion in the broad sense outlined in Chapter 1, it was dramatically different from the centrally directed, politically organized expansion of the Ottoman Empire, with its hundreds of warships and hundreds of thousands of soldiers. Second, it provided experience and prototypes for two distinctive societies that were to emerge in the Atlantic world: the plantation societies of the tropical part of the Atlantic, and the Ibero-Amerindian civilization of the American mainland that arose from the ruins of the Aztec and Inca empires. Those two new societies in turn played major roles in reshaping the more established civilizations of Africa south of the Sahara and Europe. Third, it provided the Europeans with experience in dealing with unfamiliar societies. This experience, and an understanding of Atlantic navigation, set the stage for Portuguese entry into the Indian Ocean.

**ILLUSTRATION 3.2**
*A SPANISH "HIDALGO" OF THE SIXTEENTH CENTURY.*
*Many of these untitled hidalgos lived at the edge of noble respectability and*
*fought in the various European and Mediterranean wars. They were the targets of*
*both suspicion and derision. The speculative and desperately aggressive adventures*
*of men like these were central to the early behavior of Europeans on the Atlantic*
*islands, on the African coast, and in America.*

Source: James C. Davis (ed. and trans.), *Pursuit of Power: Venetian Ambassadors' Reports
on Spain, Turkey, and France in the Age of Philip II, 1560–1600* (New York: Harper &
Row, 1970), illustration 23, p. 79. Taken from Deserps, *Recueil de la diversite des habits,*
1562. Prints Division, Spencer Collection, New York Public Library. Astor, Lenox, and
Tilden Foundations.

# FROM MALI AND ISLAND "EMPIRES" TO TRANS-ATLANTIC EXPANSION

Initial African contacts, combined with bases in Madeira, the Canaries, and the Azores, made possible a more assertive approach by the Portuguese and Castilians in the late 1400s. The Portuguese became more energetic after Henry the Navigator died in 1460, and by 1475 they had added 2,000 miles of African coast to the trade network, reaching the African kingdoms of Benin and Congo. Their expansion was motivated in part by an awakening interest in reaching Asia, and in part by the prospect of finding Christian allies who would support the crusading commitment of some Portuguese leaders. In 1475, after a century of erratic interest, the Portuguese crown assumed a direct role in African trade, giving Euro-Atlantic expansion a political dimension that it had lacked in the past. Dom João (Don John), king of Portugal after 1481, forced the Castilians out of the African trade. In 1482 he sent a small fleet and construction crew to build a permanent stone fort at São João da Mina near the Volta and Niger deltas. The new fort drew more African trade toward the coast and also protected Portuguese trade from European interlopers.

Initial encounters had taught the Europeans that, although African kingdoms sometimes were small, they generally had effective armies and dangerous coast guards composed of large, fast, and heavily manned war

ILLUSTRATION 3.3

*COLUMBUS' SHIPS.*
*This depiction of Columbus' three ships, with the* Santa Maria *in the foreground, illustrates the small, sturdy vessels which were used in the European expansion in the Atlantic islands and along the African Coast. Note that the* Nina *and the* Pinta *are both shown with the Arab-style fore and aft lateen sails commonly used in the Mediterranean for maneuverability in close quarters and variable winds. They could be (and were) rerigged as square riggers like the* Santa Maria *for the Atlantic crossing.*

Source: Culver Pictures, New York.

canoes. Because those same kingdoms were generally interested in trade, Dom João abandoned the hit-and-run encounters of previous ventures and sent ambassadors to negotiate government-to-government commercial treaties with African countries like Benin, Oyo, and Congo. Portuguese activity on the African coast was adapted from that of the Italian city-states in the Mediterranean and resembled that of trade diaspora societies everywhere. Thus the nature of contact on the African coast was very different from that seen in the Atlantic islands, which became colonies populated by European immigrants. Small groups of Portuguese merchants and political agents established themselves in African ports. They often married locally and became middlemen with the commercial expertise and language skills needed to connect Portuguese trade with preexisting commerce in Africa, including the slave trade.

Dom João also established Christian missions, which met with considerable success and produced the first black African Catholic bishop. They also converted the king of the Congo. Africans, like Europeans, believed in a spiritual or heavenly world separate from the material world. For both, affairs in this world responded to the dictates of a divine power residing in the heavenly world. Both religious systems believed in forms of divine revelation in which priests, holy men, and holy women revealed aspects of that unknowable heavenly world. African religion differed from Christianity in that it did not have an organized, hierarchical priesthood or a formalized theology. It was easy for Africans to accept aspects of Christianity because they coincided with familiar religious assumptions. As a result, a surprising number of slaves who reached America knew something about Christianity before they arrived, and many were actually baptized Christians.

The development of a Portuguese trade diaspora in Africa and of government-to-government negotiations reflected earlier Italian practice, but were also imposed by biology. Just as Canary Islanders had no resistance to European disease, Europeans were vulnerable to the diseases of tropical Africa and died faster there than anywhere else in the experience of European expansion. Few Europeans lasted more than a year, and most of those who did returned home. It was impossible to maintain a large European presence in tropical Africa until the era of modern medicine, a reality that reinforced the autonomy of African states and made it necessary for Europeans to trade with Africans as equal participants in an ongoing exchange. Confronted by unhealthy conditions, effective African governments, and preexisting African trade, the most effective European approach was to insert small groups of European merchants into the existing economy.

The result was a growing African market for European textiles, hardware, luxuries, and weapons, which were traded for African gold, cotton cloth, ivory, pepper, luxury objects, and slaves. Slaves were a small part of African trade in the 1400s compared with their later numbers. In the 1400s small numbers of slaves were bought in Africa and sold in Europe, along with enslaved Guanches from the Canary Islands. Many became household slaves for wealthy European families, but large numbers also ended up on Portuguese sugar plantations or in the shipyards and workshops of Seville. By the early 1500s some 15 percent of the seaport of Seville was African in origin. Initially, however, European participation in the slave trade was internal to Africa. The Portuguese quickly became the middlemen who shipped slaves from the Volta-Niger coast northward to Senegambia, where they were bought by other Africans who used them as labor in the Mali gold mines. Although this chapter talks about the slaving based in west Africa, it is important to remember that as the trade expanded, African slaves were exported from the entire coast of Atlantic black Africa as well as from slave-trading ports on the Indian Ocean side of Africa.

The generally chaotic and small-scale process of European expansion into the Atlantic in the 1400s was the prelude to what became three distinct stories. (1) It facilitated the entry of Europe into the sophisticated world of the Indian Ocean (Chapter 5). (2) It prefigured the creation of a novel Iberian-Amerindian world in mainland America (Chapter 4). (3) It was the first step in the creation of a new Afro–European society in the tropical Atlantic. Each narrative was heralded by specific developments between 1460 and 1499.

In 1488, after the Portuguese had pushed down the African coast as far as Congo and Angola, Bartolmeu Diaz reached the southern tip of Africa and explored enough of the Indian Ocean coast to confirm that he had found the way to Asia. It was ten years before the Portuguese crown sent Vasco da Gama on the first European voyage to India. Diaz's discovery, however, shifted attention in Portugal away from Africa and toward the dual possibility of more profitable commerce in Asia and of connecting with Christian Ethiopia (the legendary kingdom of Prester John) as a way of outflanking the hated Muslims. (This story appears in Chapter 5.)

The second development at the end of the 1400s was the final conquest of the Canary Islands, which provided a blueprint for Spanish conquests in America. While Dom João in Portugal was imposing royal direction on Portuguese–African trade, Ferdinand and Isabella strengthened Castilian authority in the Canary Islands. They launched a new invasion of the Canaries in 1477, aimed at conquering the more fertile and better populated western islands. The final battle in this unedifying conquest did not take place until 1496, twenty years later. The length of the campaign testifies both to the limited resources that Castile could divert from her wars in Granada and Italy, and to the tenacity and ingenuity of the native Guanches. Small groups of invaders faced much larger forces in a complex interplay of differing military technologies and tactics. The territory being invaded was politically divided, and the Castilians learned to play neighboring tribal kingdoms against one another. The Castilians Christianized some of the natives and co-opted some of their local elites. This created a pro-Castilian faction within the islanders' political world. In some cases, as on the island of Gomera, natives were confirmed in the ownership of their land in return for payment of tribute to those who had organized the conquest.

Anticipating a pattern that became common in America, this arrangement broke down when Europeans realized that the land granted to the natives could be used to grow sugar cane. Violations of native rights provoked rebellions between 1478 and 1489, during which the native population was slaughtered or enslaved. The Castilians also resorted to outright treachery, as when local rulers were invited to negotiate and then were slaughtered by the Spaniards. The Canaries thus offered a rich assortment of experiences that were still fresh as the Spaniards forced their way into superficially similar situations in the Americas. (See Chapter 4.)

## SUGAR, SLAVES, AND THE AFRO–EUROPEAN ATLANTIC

The third long-term scenario that emerged from the fifteenth-century expansion of Europe into the Atlantic, and the one that occupies the rest of this chapter, was the construction of a dramatically new society in the tropical Atlantic. This new society, although it incorporated colonial and commercial elements from the Mediterranean past, was unique in the history of the pre-1700 world. It was not planned, nor was it the project of any single European country. The new society, which we can call the "plantation system," was not so much a geographical location as it was a network of scattered but interdependent communities.

Geographically, the plantation system included not only the Atlantic islands already mentioned, but also the coasts of tropical Africa, Brazil, the coastal areas and islands of the Caribbean, parts of the American South, and Atlantic Europe (Spain, Portugal, France, England, and the Netherlands). Socially, this new world depended upon plantation communities composed entirely of immigrants—some voluntary, some coerced. In many cases local society came to include small, free, and white European elites and much larger populations of enslaved Africans. This dichotomy should not be taken too literally, since all of these societies developed marginal groups of poor but free Africans, poor free whites, and growing mulatto communities analogous to the *mestizos* (mixed bloods) who appeared in Spain's mainland empire (Chapter 4).

Slave-based societies were hardly new in the 1500s, but those of the tropical Atlantic were unique in two ways. For one, the ratio of slaves to free persons was often much higher than in earlier plantation communities. While as much as half of the work force on some Brazilian sugar plantations was free, on the Caribbean islands Africans often outnumbered Europeans several times over. For another, Atlantic slave-based societies developed a sharply defined pattern in which whiteness implied free status and blackness implied either slavery or an inferior political and legal status. In previous societies that had included slaves, the perception that slavery had a racial component was much weaker: blacks and whites were found among both free and slave elements. The assumption that blackness meant slavery and inferiority was a heritage of the emerging plantation world.

Economically, this plantation-oriented culture was based on a degree of regional specialization and dedication to mass production never seen before. Europe provided capital, the white elite, manufactures, and food for African and Caribbean consumers. Africa imported European manufactures and weapons, and exported labor in the form of slaves. The plantation colonies specialized in mass production of a few tropical products and imported the capital, labor, and supplies that they needed. During the period that concerns us, the main product was sugar, although by 1700 the plantation system had begun to produce large amounts of tobacco, coffee, cacao, and indigo, a blue dye used by the European textile industry. By the later 1700s slave plantations were also being used to grow cotton.

Sugar cultivation reached the Mediterranean in the Middle Ages and was established in Cyprus, Crete, Sicily, and Muslim Spain. In the early 1400s it appeared in southern Portugal and, as we have seen, it was established in the Madeira and Canary Islands by 1480. While these early examples of sugar plantations included slaves, much of their labor was provided by free farmers. The slaves themselves were more likely to be Europeans, Muslim North Africans, or Canary Islanders than they were to be black Africans.

This changed rapidly after the Cape Verde Islands were discovered around 1450 and the islands of Sao Tomé, Principe, and Fernando Poo were found a few years later. The latter three islands lie off the coast of tropical Africa near the mouths of the Niger and Congo Rivers. These islands were uninhabited, had rich volcanic soil, and, except for the Cape Verdes, were well watered. Their development was a major step in the spread of slave-based sugar plantations around the Atlantic. If Madeira was central to the European sugar trade in 1480, by 1500 that role had been taken by these African islands.

Italian and Portuguese investors, excited by the strong European market for sugar, obtained charters from the Portuguese crown. Once they controlled the land, they made heavy investments in the necessary labor and machinery. They bought the latest sugar processing equipment developed on Madeira and the Canary Islands, but were unable to attract Europeans for their work force. Unlike the first island colonies, these newer places were hot, uninviting, and unhealthy for Europeans, however ideal they were for growing sugar. The solution was at hand in the form of Portuguese connections with African commerce, where slave trading was a normal practice and where the Portuguese were already marketing slaves from the Niger–Congo area to both west Africa and Europe. Not surprisingly, the men developing the new sugar islands turned to this African slave trade for their labor, thus starting the first true plantation societies in the Atlantic.

The plantation system spread steadily. In 1500 Pedro Alvares Cabral discovered Brazil while taking a Portuguese fleet to India. Initial development of Brazil was slow. By the 1540s the success of earlier sugar colonies on the African islands and comparable growing conditions in Brazil were attracting investors to the new colony. The Low Countries (or Netherlands) had become Europe's distribution center for sugar and other luxuries, and by the mid–1500s Dutch, Flemish, and German capitalists had entered the Brazilian sugar boom. Once again investors bought the latest equipment and African labor, with the result that Brazil soon overshadowed the African islands as Europe's largest source of sugar.

By the early 1600s sugar plantations were appearing elsewhere. The English and the Dutch (now independent of Spain) were challenging Spanish and Portuguese authority in the Atlantic. The Dutch seized part of Brazil (modern Surinam) and modernized the sugar plantations they found there. They also captured the Caribbean island of Curaçao, near Venezuela, and became middlemen for sugar, plantation supplies, and slaves throughout the southern Caribbean. The English, meanwhile, seized the islands of Tobago and Barbados and captured Jamaica from Spain in 1654. Their first commercial objective was tobacco, which can be grown economically on small farms, and English entrepreneurs began by recruiting English settlers. Hundreds of European colonists and indentured servants were brought to the islands and, for a few decades, the new colonies successfully exported tobacco. As the demand for sugar grew, however, and the Dutch and Portuguese improved the supply of slaves, English investors shifted to sugar. Bigger processing plants required larger estates in order to supply enough sugar cane to keep expensive refining equipment busy. This increased the demand for grueling labor to cultivate and transport the sugar cane. Capital intensive and labor intensive compared to tobacco farming, the sugar plantations drove out the English settlers. Because this process coincided with the colonization of North Carolina, many Caribbean colonists reestablished themselves as tobacco farmers in that colony. By the 1660s, British sugar production was booming throughout the Caribbean islands.

The plantation system continued to expand as the Portuguese, Dutch, and English were joined by the French and Spanish. As the slave plantation system spread geographically, it was adapted to other mass consumption commodities. The French entered the Caribbean under Louis XIV (1643–1715) and captured Guadalupe, Martinique, and Saint-Domingue (Haiti). By 1700 these French sugar-producing islands had adopted the social and economic structure of the plantation system.

By the mid–1700s the plantation world had begun to diversify. Increasingly, tobacco was produced on slave-worked farms, while Europe's demand for coffee, cacao, and indigo expanded along with its appetite for sugar. The Spaniards had long had slave plantations as part of the internal economy of their American empire, but now they developed full-scale, export-oriented slave plantations in Cuba, Puerto Rico, Venezuela, Peru,

## READING 3.2

*Sugar production was hard, year-round work and sometimes around-the-clock work. While it was capital intensive in terms of mechanical and human machines, it required large amounts of carefully coordinated work under miserable conditions. Here we have a description of slave work on a Brazilian sugar plantation in about 1700, as described by Andre João Antonil, a.k.a. Guiseppe Andreoni.*

The first cane that must be cut is the old cane, that cannot wait . . . and this is cut in time . . . according to whether the climate is more or less cold and the days more or less hot and are without rain. . . . So the male and female slaves work in cutting the cane: commonly the male slaves cut cane and the female slaves tie cane in bundles. One bundle has twelve canes, and each male slave has the obligation to cut seven hands of ten bundles in each finger, that is three hundred and fifty bundles, and the female must tie as many canes into bundles. And if they have time left over, they may spend it freely as they choose, and what is not given to cutting cane, as the work starts at sunrise and ends in sunset. . . . And in counting the task of cutting as stated, in hands and fingers, is accommodated to the rudeness of lately arrived slaves who do not understand how to count in any other manner.

The manner of cutting is as follows: the slave takes as many canes in his left hand as he can, and with the scythe in the right hand he peels off the straw, which afterward is burned . . . and it serves to make the soil more fertile. Then, raising his left hand higher, he puts out the eyes of the cane, and gives them for the cattle to eat. And finally, turning the left hand lower, he cuts the stalk, the closer to the ground the better. Who follows the cutter (usually a female slave) gathers the clean cane stalks as stated, in bundles. . . . The cane is transported in carts; . . . [t]aking the cane by land during rains and muddy weather kills many oxen, especially those who become skinny and weak. . . .

Cane is milled by putting several canes clean of straw and mud (washed, if necessary) between two axles where . . . they are pressed, putting them . . . to be pressed and crushed . . . between the axles that meet during rotations. And after they have passed, the other part is passed to extract more, and yields the liquid which is conserved. And this liquid . . . falls from the press into a broad basket placed below it, and from there runs via a spout to a canal placed in the earth, where it passes to the house of the cauldrons to be purified.

The most dangerous place on the plantation is the sugar mill, because if by misfortune, sleep or fatigue, or some other carelessness, the female slave that feeds cane between the axles places her hand further than she should, she risks having it pressed between the axles and . . . the hand or arm is . . . cut off at once, using a large knife kept near the mill for this purpose, or the mill is . . . stopped to solve the danger. And this danger is greater still at night, during which the mill is as busy as during the day . . . especially if those who work at this occupation are newly arrived Africans or prone to drunkenness.

The slaves needed at the mill are at least seven or eight, three of them to bring cane, one to place the cane, the second to pass the pressed cane, and the third to repair and light the lamps, of which there are five in the mill, and to clean the basin for the juice . . . and the pivots of the mill, and to pour water on them so that they do not burn . . . and another finally to throw out the pressed cane . . . into the river or in the trash bin to burn when there is time. . . .

. . . All of the above slaves need more slaves to relieve them after they have done their time, who come to replace them halfway through the day and halfway through the night. And all together wash the entire mill every twenty four hours. . . . And for the good management of the mill, besides the overseer who sees to everything . . . part of the day and part of the night, there is a guard or watchman of the mill, whose office is to watch in place of the overseer that the cane is well-pressed, the pressed cane is taken away, and that the gears are rinsed and cleaned . . . and in case of some disaster in the mill he must order the mill stopped. . . .

Together with the milling house, called the sugar mill, is the furnace house, these which literally devour the forests, in perpetual fire and smoke and are the living image of the Vesuvius and Etna volcanoes, and almost those of purgatory or hell. These furnaces too have their condemned inmates, who are diseased slaves. . . . Here may also be seen other misbehaved slaves who are held in long coarse chains of iron, working in this laborious process due to the repeated excesses of the extraordinary wickedness, with little or no hope of redemption. . . .

---

From Andreoni's *Cultura e opulencia do Brasil, por suas drogas e minas*, Andree Mansuy (ed.), trans. Linda Wimmer (Paris: Institut des Hautes Etudes, 1968), pp. 165–167, 183–187, excerpted from Stuart Schwartz, Linda Wimmer, and Robert Wolff, *The Global Experience*, Vol. II (New York: A-W-Longman, 1998), pp. 90–92.

Ecuador, Guatemala, and the Gulf Coast of Mexico. Meanwhile, the British were founding the semi-tropical colonies of South Carolina and Georgia. Although these mainland colonies never had the enormous disparities between small white populations and large black ones of the tropical islands, they depended on plantations with African slaves who worked as gangs. The mainland colonies relied less on sugar as a crop and also profited from tobacco, indigo, and rice. The final stage in this sequence came in the later 1700s, when Europeans learned to mass produce cloth from cotton. Cotton plantations, worked with African slaves, quickly spread through the British colonies from Virginia to Georgia. The growing cotton textile industry of eighteenth-century Barcelona prompted similar developments in Spanish Central America.

Various historians have suggested that the Atlantic plantations were the first examples of factory-style, capital-intensive mass production. Like factories, they needed capital for refining machinery, and by pre-industrial standards a sugar plantation required a lot of mechanical equipment and processing facilities. The most chilling aspect of this system was its tendency to look on slaves as machines. Slaves were worked long and hard. Because they were overworked, poorly fed, and vulnerable to Caribbean and European diseases, Africans did not live long as slaves. Their average survival time varied depending on local conditions, but the logic was the same. In parts of Brazil, for example, owners assumed that slaves had a seven-year life span and cold bloodedly depreciated their value over that period, much as a modern industrialist depreciates a piece of machinery. Other owners thought in terms of routinely buying a set number of slaves each year to maintain a particular number of active planation workers. The survival period varied from place to place, but the operators of plantations assumed that the average slave had to be replaced periodically.

In some areas plantation owners allowed slaves to form households, and if the slave population included enough women, the work force eventually began to replace itself. This depended on the willingness of planters and government to recognize slave unions and their family units. Such households evolved a hybrid culture that combined elements from European and African societies. They developed a religion that blended European and African beliefs, sometimes including elements of Christianity that they brought from Africa. Because the Catholic Church defined marriage as a sacrament, whatever a person's status, slave households seem to have been more stable in Spanish, French, and Portuguese colonies. In English North America, however, colonial laws systematically stripped slaves of such civic rights. As the demand for slaves increased in the 1600s and 1700s, this led to the deliberate breeding of children for slave markets without regard for family and household.

This inhuman treatment of Africans was fertile ground for resentment, passive resistance, and rebellion. Thus it is hardly surprising that the slave-based Afro–European plantation colonies of 1400–1700 were far from placid, rigidly controlled agricultural factories. Africans, who came from complex and well-organized societies and economies, did not submit as readily as some stereotypes of slave society would have us believe. They developed techniques that amounted to slow-down strikes and sabotaged plantation operations and equipment. They fled to neighboring plantations and negotiated more favorable conditions for their return. They rebelled frequently against miserable conditions and escaped when they could. Escapees either joined Amerindian communities or set up their own societies in the isolated back country of every large island or country with slave plantations. Organized slave resistance on a large scale was difficult because slaves came from many countries with different languages and customs. Because they were kept illiterate and not allowed to travel, it was hard to formalize grievances and organize large revolts. The depths of African antagonism are hard to comprehend from this distance in time and place, but the violence of events in Haiti during the French Revolution suggests the hidden tensions of the plantation world. In 1792 African Haitians staged a successful revolution, brutally slaughtered the white population, and established the second independent country in America after the United States.

Throughout the slave plantation era individual escape was easier than collective revolt. Thus most Caribbean islands developed refugee communities that were constantly in conflict with the plantation world. Known as Maroons or Buccaneers, these communities lived in the rugged back country of plantation societies. They were populated with a mixture of African and Amerindian peoples, along with a number of outlaw Europeans. In the Caribbean they exploited the rivalry between European countries, traded with privateers and smugglers, and sold provisions for their ships. In Brazil, Jamaica, and Dutch Surinam, these African–American communities organized kingdoms like those they had known in Africa and negotiated as equals with authorities in the plantation colonies.

In Brazil they were subdued only after a brutal, full-scale military invasion. In Jamaica they were never conquered, and their status was eventually recognized by English colonial authorities.

## THE TRANS-ATLANTIC COMPONENTS OF THE PLANTATION SYSTEM

Aside from its social and racial imbalances, the plantation world of the tropical Atlantic was also novel in that it could not survive on its own and was caught up with Africa and Europe in a three-way exchange: Europe exported manufactures and capital to both Africa and the plantations. Africa exported labor to the plantations and imported European manufactures. The plantations specialized in the export of tropical products to Europe and depended on imported food, imported African labor, and imported European capital. It was a system that generated great wealth for a few participants and great misery for many. Europeans used "empty" American and African land on which to build the unique, slave-based societies we have described.[1] Even as they provided the essential components of plantation society, Europe and Africa were themselves changed by their participation in the process. Whether or not we like the consequences, we have to take note of them.

The slave trade not only shaped plantation society, it also played an important role in shaping African politics. It is hard to measure this impact, but its significance is suggested by the expansion of the slave trade itself. In the middle 1400s the European slave trade involved only a few dozen slaves each year, many of whom were destined for slave markets within Africa. The main difference from the older slave trade was that Europeans were now among the middlemen who facilitated the trade. Three centuries later, in the 1780s, Europeans were taking 50,000 to 90,000 slaves from Africa every year, drawing them from African societies all along the Atlantic coast and from Mozambique on the Indian Ocean.

The slave trade provided the kingdoms of coastal Africa with foreign exchange that soon far surpassed the earnings from traditional exports like gold, pepper, cotton cloth, and ivory. As the slave trade expanded, it allowed African elites on the Atlantic coast to buy European ironware, luxury goods, and textiles. It also allowed African rulers to buy European weapons, and by the later 1780s African governments were importing thousands of muskets every year. In some cases the trade produced gruesomely brutal native regimes, in others cases African rulers sought to control the trade. The trade did not undermine African independence, but it did change the balance of power between African states.

---

[1]This deliberately neutral way of describing what happened leaves out the long story of the destruction of local populations in the Canary Islands and Americas thanks to European disease, economic and social disruption, open warfare, and European hypocrisy. These traits often overshadowed the more altruistic behavior of many missionaries and settlers.

The great empire of Mali, which had drawn income from the trans-Sahara trade, lost revenue and prestige and began to disintegrate when trade was diverted to the Atlantic kingdoms. This was accelerated by Moroccan nomads, who also bought guns. Mali was replaced for a time by the Songhai Empire, but previously secondary coastal countries like Benin, Oyo, and Congo gradually captured the initiative in international relations inside Africa.

These and other once-secondary kingdoms along the coast, equipped with new military technology, changed the balance of power between interior and coast. Furthermore, as the slave trade intensified, the exporting states and their slave merchants reached farther and farther inland. The slave trade, along with other Afro-European commerce, was mobilized in part through interlocking trade diasporas. Europeans developed regular contacts in the port cities. African and mixed-blood slave traders, sometimes abetted by selfish coastal rulers, then developed clients inside interior states and subverted traditional loyalties. The slave trade also led to ruthless kidnapping and raids on interior towns. The disruption of the communities that were victims of the slave trade inside Africa eroded their loyalty to governments that were unwilling or unable to protect them. This disrupted families and work, and weakened the economies of interior societies. Armed with European weapons, coastal states had a growing advantage over interior kingdoms unable to protect their subjects from enslavement.

Before about 1800, European traders and soldiers operated in Africa primarily by dealing with local African governments and merchants. Policies regarding the slave trade varied a great deal. Some rulers participated, but some local rulers (as in Benin) successfully limited the trade. In the Kingdom of the Congo, the Portuguese crown used diplomatic channels and treaties to support the King's attempt to regulate the slave trade. Other Portuguese, however, including the entrepreneurs developing sugar plantations on the offshore islands, subverted chieftains inside the Congo, persuading them to raid their neighbors and sell slaves in defiance of their own king. The result by 1600 was the breakup of one important African state (See Reading 3.3). In other areas, the small size of many states allowed both European raiders and African rulers and slave traders to foment wars in order to produce war captives who then became slaves.

Thus the slave trade did not destroy African independence, but it did restructure power relationships within Africa. The sub-Saharan empires of the eighth through the fifteenth centuries had been oriented to the Middle East and North Africa. After 1500 the orientation shifted to the Atlantic. The nature of this independence is highly problematic, since the importance of coastal Africa depended upon Atlantic trade. At the same time, however, there is little evidence that Europeans had to coerce African elites to engage in the slave trade. Initially, Africa's Atlantic trade was a reciprocal exchange of commodities, but that exchange was soon overshadowed by slaving. Thus the new balance of power inside Africa was linked to the developing plantation system and its constant demand

READING 3.3

*Once sugar made the slave trade profitable, the Portuguese government was unable to control many of its agents in Africa, even though the King of the Congo converted to Christianity and sought to Christianize his kingdom. The erosion of authority and the lack of Portuguese control comes through in these letters from the King of the Congo to the King of Portugal:*

(1515) [To the] Very High and Powerful Lord [King of Portugal], We the King [of Kongo] Dom Alfonso . . . our faith is still like glass in this kingdom, due to the bad examples of the men who come here to teach it, because through worldly greed for a few riches truth is destroyed. . . . [B]y entering into a life of sin [these priests] take the key to Hell . . . [and] guide those most blind with them through their bad examples. I ask of you Brother, to aid me in establishing our Holy Catholic Faith, because, Lord my Brother, for us it were better . . . that the souls of our relatives and brothers and cousins and nephews and grandchildren who are innocent . . . see . . . good examples.

(1517) To the King of Portugal from the King of Kongo . . . I have several times written you of the necessity or having a ship, telling you to make me one to buy, and I don't know why Your Highness does not want to consent, because I want nothing more than . . . to use it in God's service . . .

(1526) To the King of Portugal from the King of Kongo [Y]our factors and officials give [so much] to the men and merchants that come to this Kingdom . . . and spread [through it] . . . that many vassals owing us obedience . . . rebel because they have more goods [through trade with the Portuguese] than us, . . . And each day these merchants take our citizens, native to the land and children of our nobles and vassals, and our relations, because they are thieves and men of bad conscience . . . [They] take them to sell . . . [Because of] this we have no more necessity for other than priests and educators, but [send] no more merchandise . . . nor merchants. . . .

(1526) To the King of Portugal from the King of Kongo [M]any of our subjects, through the desire for merchandise and things of this Kingdom which you bring . . . to satisfy their appetite, steal many of our free and exempt subjects. And nobles and their children and our relatives are often stolen to be sold to white men . . . hidden by night . . . And the said white men are so powerful . . . they embark and . . . buy them, for which we want justice, restoring them to liberty. . . .

Taken from *Monumenta Missionaria Africana*, Antonio Brasio (ed.) (Lisboa: Agencia Geral do Ultramar, 1952, Vol. 10, pp. 294–295, 335, 404, 470, 488. As found in Schwartz, Wimmer, Wolff, *The Global Experience*, Vol. II, pp. 5–6.

for African labor. By 1700 Africa was not a distant, exotic place far from Europe—it was a participant in an Atlantic plantation system and the emerging Atlantic "engine of trade" that was destined, for better or for worse, to trigger the Industrial Revolution. (See Illustration 3.6)

If Africa was caught up in the trans-Atlantic plantation system, so too was Europe. To understand that relationship, and some of the unintended consequences, we need to look at this Atlantic engine of trade. It was a European creation, but it could not have existed without America and Africa. One feature of the great engine of trade mentioned earlier was

## READING 3.4

*Olaudah Equiano was an African who became a slave, became literate in English, and published a remarkable autobiography at about the time of the American War of Independence. The following excerpt tells better than any historian can the process whereby the slave trade disrupted African society:*

... I was born, in the year 1745 ... in a charming and fruitful vale named Es-saka. The distance of this province from the capital of Benin and the sea coast must be very considerable for I had never heard of white men ... [Our] markets ... are sometimes visited by stout, mahogany-coloured men from the southwest of us. ... They sometimes carry slaves through our land but the strictest account is exacted of their manner of procuring them before they are suffered to pass. Sometimes indeed we sold slaves to them, but they were only prisoners of war, or ... convicted of kidnapping, or adultery, and some other crimes which we esteemed heinous. ...

When the grown people ... were gone far in the fields to labor, the children assembled together ... to play. ... One day, when all our people were gone out to their works as usual, and only I and my dear sister were left to mind the house, two men and a woman got over our walls and in a moment seized us both ... they stopped our mouths, tied our hands, and ran off with us ... till night came on ... [My sister] was torn from me and immediately carried away while I was left in a state of distraction not to be described. ...

[At] the end of six or seven months after I had been kidnapped, I arrived at the sea coast. ... The first object which saluted my eyes when I arrived on the coast was the sea, and a slave ship [see Illustration 3.4] which was then riding at anchor and waiting for its cargo. These filled me with astonishment, which was soon converted into terror when I was carried on board. I was immediately handled and tossed up to see if I were sound by some of the crew, and I was now persuaded that I had gotten into a world of bad spirits and that they were going to kill me. Their complexions too differing so much from ours, their hair and the language they spoke (which was very different from any I had ever heard) united to confirm me in this belief. Indeed, such were the horrors of my views and fears at the moment that, if ten thousand worlds had been my own, I would have freely parted with them all to have exchanged my condition with that of the meanest slave in my own country. When I looked around the ship too and saw a large furnace of copper boiling, and a multitude of black people of every description chained together, every one of their countenances expressing dejection and sorrow, I no longer doubted of my fate, and quite overpowered with horror and anguish, I fell motionless on the deck and fainted. ... I was not long suffered to indulge my grief; I was soon put down under the decks and there I received such a salutation in my nostrils as I had never experienced in my life, so that with the loathesomeness of the stench, and crying together, I became so sick and low that I was not able to eat ... on my refusing to eat, one of them held me fast by the hands and laid me across, I think the windlass, and tied my feet, while the other flogged me severely.

From Olaudah Equiano, *Interesting Narrative of the Life of Olaudah Equiano, or Gustavus Vassa, the African, written by himself,* published in 1789, excerpted from Oliver A. Johnson (ed.), *Sources of World Civilization,* Vol. II, *Since 1500* (Englewood Cliffs: Prentice Hall, 1994), pp. 141–149.

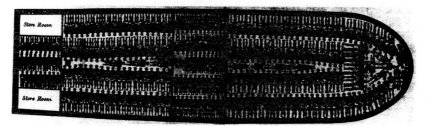

**ILLUSTRATION 3.4**
*DIAGRAM OF HOW SLAVES WERE LOADED ON A SLAVE-TRADING SHIP.*
*This chilling early diagram shows how space was allocated to slaves on ships in the slave trade. Aside from the obvious horizontal crowding, most slaves were chained to bunks that had no more than two or three feet of vertical headroom. There were no bathroom facilities and on days when the weather permitted, slaves were released a few at a time for exercise and hosing down on the deck.*
Source: Stanley Chodorow, Hans W. Gatzke, and Conrad Schirokauer, *A History of the World, Vol. I* (San Diego: Harcourt Brace Jovanovich, 1986), p. 464. Attribution: The Library of Congress.

the complex and reciprocal nature of both the trade and the transfers of credit and profits that emerged. In large measure this trading world was assembled from established ways of doing business. Its unique aspect, however, was the emergence of a European-organized, self-reinforcing expansion that truly was something new under the sun.

The mechanism is best seen through a hypothetical example. By 1700 a Boston merchant could make money selling New England flour and lumber to the tropical plantation colonies, which grew little of their own food and had few forests. The money from those sales was used to

---

READING 3.5

*As the slave trade became larger and more specialized, Africans came to be dealt with as objects, like cattle or pieces of property. This is illustrated by the short descriptions in Readings 3.5 and 3.6, which show how they were processed before being shipped as slaves across the Atlantic. Both are eyewitness accounts of European participants in the slave trade.*

A careful manipulation of the chief muscles, joints, armpits and groins was made, to assure soundness. The mouth, too was inspected, and if a tooth was missing, it was noted as a defect liable to deduction. Eyes, voice, lungs, fingers, and toes were not forgotten; so that when the negro passed from the Mongo's hands without censure, he might have been readily adopted as a good "life" by an insurance company. [See Illustration 3.5.]

From Edward Reynolds, *Stand the Storm: A History of the Atlantic Slave Trade* (London: Allison and Busby, 1989), p. 45, citing Theodore Canot, *Captain Canot, or Twenty Years of an African Slaver* (London: Richard Bentley, 1854), p. 64.

**ILLUSTRATION 3.5**
*EXERCISE PERIOD ON A SLAVE SHIP.*
*This painting of slaves aboard a slave ship shows a small part of the cargo on deck for a period of fresh air and "exercise." Slave ships carried as many as 800 people, and 15 percent to 20 percent of them would die in the Atlantic crossing.*

Philip J. Adler, *World Civilizations, Vol. II* (Minneapolis: West Publishing, 1996), p. 344.
Acknowledged copyright, The Granger Collection.

buy sugar and molasses from the plantations. The molasses was shipped back to New England, where it was processed into rum. The rum was then sold in England, Spain, or the Mediterranean. The profits from those sales were used to buy European manufactures for markets in New England or in the plantation colonies. The sugar bought in the Caribbean was shipped to England or to markets in other places, such as Málaga, Jerez, or Portugal. Those places produced heavy, sweet wines that were popular in England and were exchanged there for English goods. Similar cycles of trade operated between Europe, Africa, and the plantation colonies, in which case they included cargoes of slaves being shipped from Africa to the Americas.

Buried in this complex commerce is a subtle but important development that has escaped many historians. As suggested before, the planta-

READING 3.6

When the slaves which are brought from the inland countries come to Whidah, they are put in prison together. [W]hen we treat concerning buying them, they are all brought out together in a large plain, where, by our surgeons, they are thoroughly examined, and that naked both men and women, without the least distinction of modesty. Those which are approved as good are set on one side; in the meanwhile a burning iron, with the arm or name of the company, lies in the fire, with which ours are marked on the breast. [W]hen we have agreed with the owners of the slaves they are returned to their prisons, where, from that time forward they are kept at our charge, and cost us two pence a day each slave, which serves to subsist them like criminals on bread and water.

From Edward Reynolds, *Stand the Storm*, p. 45, citing Willem Bosman, ed., *New and Accurate Description of the Coast of Guinea* (London: J. Knapton, 1705; 2nd ed, 1721), p. 240.

tions of the tropical Atlantic were the first modern-style mass production factories. They not only used a good deal of machinery in the conventional sense, but they accustomed investors to making large investments in slaves, who were thought of more as machines than as workers. The discovery of how to organize such capital-intensive mass production was an important step toward the Industrial Revolution.

It is, however, only a part of the significance of plantations for economic history. Creation of the modern, capital-intensive factory with fixed equipment and a large scale of output is only one side of the equation. Producers had to be able to sell what they produced, and that also required a new perspective. It required novel market conditions and a new way of visualizing profit on the part of producers and distributors of mass production commodities.

Traditional craft manufacturing was often sophisticated and could produce technically advanced goods. But all pre-industrial societies were basically poor, and poor societies have only a few customers rich enough to buy more than the most basic necessities. Under those conditions the manufacturer made his best profits by getting the highest price he could for each item he sold. Therefore he approached production and sale in a particular way. He invested time in customizing each item so that it could be presented as rare and unique. He spent a great deal of time negotiating with the few buyers available to him. He could not think in terms of mass producing hundreds of identical copies of something, cutting the price, and making his profit by selling them all, since in a poor society he would quickly run out of customers. His marketing psychology instead concentrated on coaxing the highest possible price from each purchaser, emphasizing the uniqueness of each item, and playing on the vanity of the buyer. Until the 1600s most trade and most manufacturing, at least in terms of value, consisted of making and marketing goods within that kind of

**ILLUSTRATION 3.6**
*THE AFRICAN CITY OF LOANGO, A ROYAL CAPITAL ON THE*
*KONGO COAST IN THE 1600s.*
Loango was the capital of one of the African coastal kingdoms that gained impor-
tance because of the slave trade. It was one of several African cities that impressed
Europeans with their size and commercial activity.
Source: Peter Stearns, Michael Adas, and Stuart Schwartz, *World Civilizations: The Global
Experience* (New York: HarperCollins, 1992), p. 624; also Graham Connah, *African civi-
lizations; Precolonial cities and states in tropical Africa: An archaeological perspective* (Cam-
bridge: Cambridge University Press, 1987), cover illustration. Attributed to O. Dapper,
*Description de l'Afrique . . . traduit du Flamand* (Amsterdam: Chez Walfgang, Wesberge,
Boom, and van Somerein, 1686).

market psychology—small volume, individually unique items, and individually negotiated prices.

Sugar changed that. We joke about sugar being addictive, and people everywhere seem to like sweetness. It may not be literally addictive,
but people have always been eager to add it to their diet, especially if most
of their food is sour or bland. In 1400 sugar was an exotic and expensive
rarity for Europeans. Thanks to the plantation system, by 1700 every
English man, woman, and child ate about four pounds a year; in 1800 this
had reached eighteen pounds a year. Sugar was cheap enough for ordinary
workers and farmers to think of it as a basic necessity. In 1901 sugar consumption in England reached ninety pounds per person and had become
an important part of the caloric intake of the working poor. In economic
terms, this means that demand for sugar was very price elastic—a small
decline in its price brought a big increase in demand.

This simple sounding situation is hard to achieve in a poor society
with an unequal distribution of income, but it is essential for the development of modern, capital-intensive factories. Such factories have large
fixed costs in the form of buildings and machinery, compared to the cost

of the raw materials and labor that they use. Technology, machinery, and slaves represented fixed investments to the plantation owner. The logic of sugar production meant that cheap land, combined with machinery and slaves, made it possible for a single plantation to produce a very large volume of sugar. This allowed the investor and producer to spread the high cost of setting up the facility across the entire output. In abstract language, the initial fixed investment, even though it was large, added only a small amount of fixed costs to the day-to-day variable costs—transportation, food for slaves, and maintenance—of producing a unit of goods. At the same time, the fixed capital of the enterprise did much of the work that paid labor otherwise would have had to contribute. This made the cost of producing each unit of the final product much smaller than in traditional handicraft industries. There the fixed capital was small, but so was the volume of output. This means that there were no savings because of the small scale of fixed investment, while the labor costs of each unit of product could be very high. The plantation network and the logic of sugar production created "plantation factories" that took advantage of the returns to large scale possible with capital intensive production.

This logic only made sense if the right market conditions existed in Europe. Sugar, and later tobacco, helped generate market conditions that made returns to scale profitable, possibly for the first time. Most Europeans in the 1500s and 1600s lived like rural populations in third world countries today. They had little disposable income once they obtained food, shelter, and clothing. With diets that were boring, sour, and often mouldy or poorly preserved, sugar was hard to resist and could be marketed in very small quantities. Initially a luxury food, once the price of sugar fell to a certain point, poorer people tried using it. Once people were used to sugar, it began to seem like a necessity and the market expanded quickly. Any small drop in its price greatly increased the number of poor able to try it out. Once it was tried, small farmers and workers reorganized their family economies so as to be able to buy more. Each time sugar got a little cheaper because of bigger plantations or better transportation, the demand grew fast enough to offset the apparent loss of revenue per unit and actually created larger total profits.

This translates into an elastic European market in which any small cut in the price of sugar produced a very large increase in sales. In contrast to traditional assumptions about marketing and profit-making, a reduction in profit *per unit* now produced a significant increase in total profit, encouraging additional increases in the scale of production. Thus the logic of high fixed costs spread over a large, standardized output connected with a market that was expansive enough to be profitable even when the profit per unit declined. This is elementary to anyone in first-year economics, but was a new situation in the pre-industrial world, and required both preconditions and a major reorientation in the minds of merchants and producers. Sugar, slave-powered plantations, and the interconnections we call the plantation system provided Atlantic entrepreneurs with their first large-scale exposure to the logic of capital-intensive mass production and mass consumption, both of which are basic to the twentieth century.

Finally, this intersection of mass production and mass consumption was not a one-time event. Within the Atlantic world of the plantation system, the great engine of trade converted what could have been a brief episode into a self-reinforcing cycle of expanding output, expanding consumption, and increased total profits. As we saw earlier, European expansion began as a chaotic, unplanned process carried out by profit-seeking merchants, land-hungry and unemployed soldiers, and crusading missionary interests frustrated by Ottoman power in the Mediterranean. As time went on, and Atlantic expansion produced profit and tax revenue, the competing governments of Europe took interest and enforced jurisdiction. They created "empires" that diverted part of Atlantic trade to official channels, to the benefit of tax collectors and special interests in Europe. (See Map 3.2.) At the same time, the disorganized, unplanned quality of the process continued and contraband was rampant. Overall it is likely that there was more trade *between* competing "empires" as contraband than passed through official channels.

In spite of that, however, as the 1500s moved into the 1600s European governments built regular navies, hired coast guard vessels, and built better seaports. This put some teeth in government regulation and taxation, but it also cut piracy and reduced the risks that made transatlantic trade costly. Shippers could reduce the size of crews because ships did not have to defend themselves. They could use slower ships, which needed smaller crews and had more capacity. The specialized merchant ship no longer had to outrun pirates and could count on port facilities and resupply bases. All of these things reduced the cost of transporting sugar, slaves, and merchandise around the Atlantic. This in turn reduced the price that the consumer had to pay for his sugar and further increased the demand for sugar. As a result, planters and investors were prompted to expand output and increase the scale of their operations, producing more efficiencies of scale and even lower prices.

The same commercial system reduced costs in another way. Trade (and plantations) operated on credit. Goods were bought on credit and paid for once delivered and sold. Profits from a sale in one place were often used to buy more trade goods in different locations. The Atlantic engine of trade that grew up around the plantation system of the 1500s and 1600s created an efficient mechanism for transferring such credit and profit. The New England merchant grew to trust his French business agent in Martinique, the Dutch slave factor in Curaçao, the English plantation owner in Jamaica, the Portuguese merchant in Madeira, and the English banker in London. He could safely move profits and credits between these people with simple letters of credit and orders for payment. The growing flexibility of this transfer system, which by and large ignored Europe's political "empires" and functioned even when the countries of Europe were at war, reduced interest and insurance rates and al-

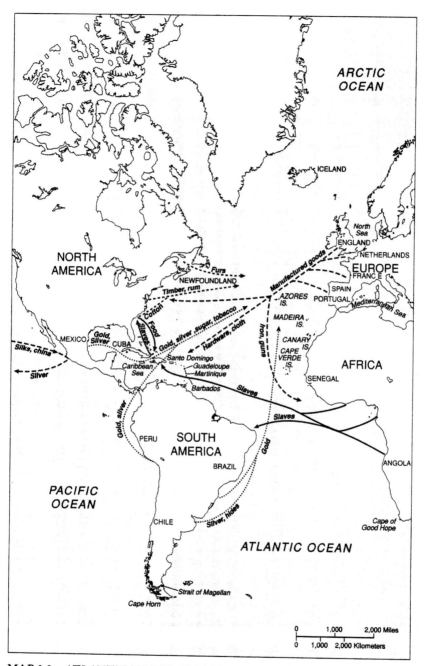

**MAP 3.2**  *ATLANTIC TRADE ABOUT 1700.*
*By 1700 the various European and colonial economies around the Atlantic had
created a self-propelling "engine of trade." This prolonged period of expansion
would culminate in the Industrial Revolution. Because of slavery, many of the
commodities involved could be produced cheaply enough to be bought by Europe's poor, opening up new market possibilities for the economy.*

lowed further reductions in the price that consumers paid for mass produced products like sugar and tobacco.

By 1700, therefore, the European penetration of the Atlantic had created a unique set of plantation societies. It had also laid the basis for a complex, many-sided Atlantic society in which specialized regional economies, at great distances from each other, all depended on the continued operation of the system. That system shaped the Afro–European societies of the tropical Atlantic, it restructured political life in Africa, and it exposed European businessmen to a dramatically new commercial and industrial psychology based on elastic mass markets and efficiencies of scale in capital-intensive production. Many textbooks will tell you that this was first achieved with the early textile mills of England after 1760. Nevertheless, a case can be made that essential elements of that industrial achievement were learned within the tropical plantation system. That system was the unanticipated result of Europe's first haphazard probings into the Atlantic, the availability of easily captured tropical land, the eagerness of African governments and merchants to trade with Europe, and the willingness of many African rulers to participate in the slave trade.

The awkward question about this scenario concerns the profitability of the slave trade. This question cannot really be answered in economic terms, although that is part of the story. Current scholarship suggests that most of the time, slave trading was not spectacularly profitable. Too many countries and traders were competing for prices to stay much above the actual cost of delivering slaves to American markets. At the same time, investors continued to invest and expand the trade, indicating that profits had to be at least as good as in the rest of the commercial system.

On a level that combines economic and moral considerations, the slave trade was vital to the rest of the plantation system. Without it, Europe's profitable export trade to Africa would have been much smaller, plantation owners could never have made the profits that they did, and the colonies of the future United States would not have had markets in the tropical Atlantic. What the slave trade subsidized was not spectacular profits for actual traders, but a whole range of routinely profitable businesses that the Atlantic world could not have sustained without plantations. It may be too much to say that this expanded range of profitable business triggered the European Industrial Revolution. Indeed, many economic historians maintain that internal European demand was adequate to do so. If that is so, it would have been a much slower and later process than it was.

Either way, the outcome in Europe owed a tremendous debt to the millions of Africans who were forced into slavery and lived short, miserable lives uprooted from their own culture. At the same time, the slave trade created the political framework in Africa that was in place when Europeans took direct control in the nineteenth century. The result for the twenty-first century is a chaotic situation in which European concepts of nationhood have been injected into colonial structures that were themselves shaped by a relatively new African political world.

The long-term social and political legacies of this bizarre form of expansion are all around us today. Millions of Africans were forcibly transported to America. In mainland America, from the southern colonies of British North America to Brazil, African slaves and their descendants became a large and permanent part of the population. As they did so, they were forced to live with attitudes and assumptions about their inferior status that are linked to the plantation world's distinction between white = free and black = slave, and to the slave trade that was essential to the "plantation system." In some countries those racial distinctions are modulated by a complex correlation between degrees of color and access to more affluent and influential circles. These social and color gradations give a degree of flexibility to status in places like Brazil, Ecuador, and the Caribbean that is missing elsewhere. In other places, notably the United States, the definitions have become highly polarized, so that any hint of African heritage seems to define one as African–American.

Equally important, if less noticed, the plantation complex gave the modern world a large number of Atlantic countries populated and controlled by the descendants of the Africans who were forced into involuntary migration. They include Liberia and Sierra Leone in Africa, the Cape Verde Islands, and the African island countries of São Tomé and Fernando Poo, which came to have African plantation owners using African slaves. They also include several countries in the Caribbean, from Trinidad and Tobago to Santo Domingo, Haiti, Jamaica, and Cuba. These countries now speak English, French, Dutch, or Spanish, and most of their inhabitants practice a form of Christianity, but their existence and social organization can only be understood as the heritage of the sugar and slave plantation complex created during the age of global expansion.

# 4

# THREE AMERICAN EMPIRES, 1400–1600

# Expansion, Political Power, and Religion

## COMPARING THREE EMPIRES

Between 1400 and 1600, while the Ottoman Turks were building a huge empire in the Mediterranean and the Middle East, and Europeans were haphazardly creating a sphere of commercial and political influence in the tropical Atlantic, three other empires took shape on the mainland of the Americas. All three empires began in the 1400s as regional kingdoms and all three were built by conquest. The Aztec Empire grew out of a small tribal state that appeared in the area around modern Mexico City, probably in the 1300s. The Inca Empire had a similar beginning in the highland valley around Cuzco in southern Peru. (See Map 4.1.) The Spanish empire in America grew out of the medieval kingdom of Castile on the Iberian peninsula, and had its earliest American beginnings in the gradual Spanish penetration of the Caribbean between 1492 and 1519. The Spanish–American Empire on the American mainland then took shape with the Spanish conquest of the Aztecs in 1519–1521 and the conquest of the Incas in the 1530s. The Aztec, Inca, and Spanish empires differed in important ways, but they also had several things in common.

They differed in that markets and trade, which were important in the Spanish case, were less central in the formation of the Aztec empire and were of slight importance to the Incas. These empires also differed in the ways that their ruling elites dealt with conquered societies. The

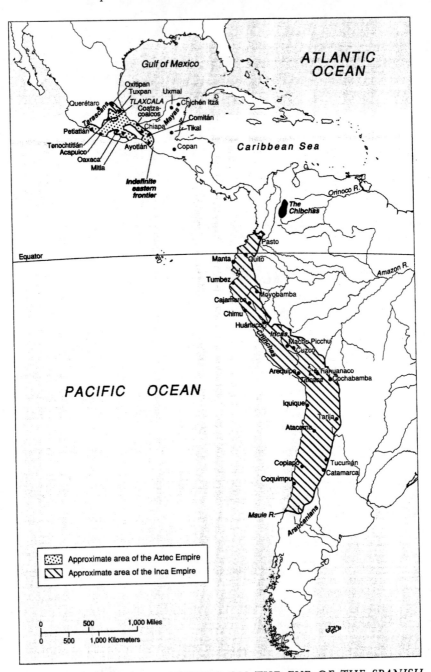

**MAP 4.1**  *AMERINDIAN EMPIRES ON THE EVE OF THE SPANISH CONQUEST.*

Aztecs built a system that depended on military force to ensure submission and extort payment of tribute. Unlike many contemporaneous empires, they made little effort to recruit conquered local elites into an imperial ruling class as a way of widening the social basis of their political system. The Incas, in contrast, created a system that sent royal agents to represent imperial interests in conquered kingdoms and recruited members of local royal families into the ruling elite in the capital city, Cuzco. They also embedded imperial taxes within a system that returned food collected by the government back to local communities when local supplies ran short. The Spaniards took a third approach. They imported a European ruling class large enough to provide local authorities, merchants, landlords, and clergy in the larger communities of their empire. Instead of co-opting local elites into an imperial governing class, they built a dual system of authority that sought to separate Spanish affairs from Amerindian ones. The two systems were theoretically parallel, but there was no question that the Spaniards made the decisions and provided little opportunity for Amerindians to join the European ruling class.

Despite such differences, these American empires were similar in three major ways. Thinking back to the four components of "expansion" (politics, commerce, religion, and culture) we defined earlier, all three involved a conscious drive to assert political control over as many different regional kingdoms as possible, using force where necessary. This military–political element brings to mind parallels with empire building in the Middle East after the nomadic invasions from Central Asia. All three American empires were created by cohesive groups of mobile, militarized warriors who moved quickly, exploited conflicts between neighboring kingdoms, and seized control of kingdoms by capturing their political centers and transferring existing jurisdiction to their own leaders.

Compared with the Middle East, however, religion played a much more central role in the American cases of expansion. Before the eighteenth century, religion and political power were always linked, but in the examples of expansion outlined in Chapters 2 and 3, religion appeared as a secondary factor. Admittedly, the Crusades made religion central to the Christian European invasion of the Middle East in the twelfth and thirteenth centuries, but in later centuries religion was overshadowed by geopolitical concerns in the Mediterranean and by social and economic motives in the Atlantic. In the Ottoman world, Islam provided a rationale for conquest and helped legitimize Ottoman expansion within the Muslim world, but it merely supplemented the ethos of expansion built into the culture of nomadic warriors from Central Asia. By contrast, in all three American empires religion was used systematically to reinforce the political authority of the new ruling elite. This aspect of expansion has to be examined carefully, since it involved both political management of religious matters and sincere and well-meant missionary movements.

As we look at these aspects of the Aztec, Inca, and Spanish empires, we can also review how the densely populated and internally coherent

Amerindian empires became sparsely populated, export-oriented adjuncts to Europe, while at the same time setting out on the path toward a hybrid Euro–American civilization.

## THE AZTEC EMPIRE

The long-term evolution of central and southern Mexico offers interesting, if speculative, parallels to that of Eurasia. By 1200 B.C.E. Caribbean Mexico was the site of the urbanized Olmec culture, which may have involved a political empire. The Olmec were superseded around 200 B.C.E. by the rise of Teotihuacán in central Mexico, a development that coincided with the emergence of the Roman and Han empires in the Mediterranean and China. This culture dominated central Mexico between about 200 B.C.E. and 600 C.E. The remains of the city of Teotihuacán include temple pyramids and a ceremonial complex that dwarf Egyptian and Middle Eastern counterparts and suggest a capital city of 200,000 inhabitants. The society that built Teotihuacán had extensive contacts with the Mayan city kingdoms that flourished in the Yucatan between 200 C.E. and about 850 C.E.

In an intriguing chronological parallel, both Teotihuacán and the Mayan kingdoms fade away by the end of the era of global cooling between 300 and 800 C.E., while the subsequent warming trend (between 800 and 1200 C.E.) saw the emergence of the Toltec empire in central Mexico. Prior to 800, the reduced energy in the hemispheric weather system may have increased rainfall in the Mayan region, while making it less reliable in central and northern Mexico. The connection is speculative, but both changes would have undermined the agricultural systems of the two societies.

As in the Middle East, China, and Africa, changing climate activated tension along the frontier between agricultural and nomadic societies. In Mexico this frontier was about 150 miles north of modern Mexico City. Beyond that frontier the Amerindian tribes could not rely on agriculture and were less sedentary. Dependent on food-gathering and hunting, they were also more warlike. Without domesticated livestock, they were not as nomadic as their Afro–Eurasian counterparts, but seasonal changes in the availability of food and game imposed nomadic migrations. Sharing the militaristic traits of their Afro–Eurasian counterparts, the Amerindians of the plains were regarded as uncivilized by the settled communities with which they interacted.

The weakening of Teotihuacán around 600 C.E. coincided with the southward migration of some of these warlike tribes into the Valley of Mexico. By about 950 C.E. these new arrivals had consolidated power and had created the Toltec Empire, which dominated central Mexico until about 1200. With hemispheric cooling after 1200, the Toltec empire broke up into component kingdoms. As in central Asia, weaker prevailing winds reduced the amount of rainfall in the interior. Just as the Turks and

Mongols of central Asia were encouraged by deterioration of their environment to move into China and the Middle East, the Amerindians of northern Mexico and the American Southwest were forced out of their traditional homelands. This is when the towns and irrigation systems of the Anazazi in Arizona and New Mexico were abandoned, and the warlike *chichimec* (barbarian) Mexicas moved into central Mexico. These Mexica Amerindians, like the Ottoman Turks, began a process of expansion that created a great empire.

Referred to as the Aztecs in history books, the Mexica entered central Mexico around 1300. After fighting in regional wars with mixed success, around 1350 the Mexica were allowed to settle on a muddy island in the lakes of the central valley of Mexico. In return, they became clients of the Tepanec kingdom, the most aggressive state in the valley, and about 1370 the Tepanec imposed a kinglike military ruler on the tribe. By 1400 the Mexica had become a militarized monarchy, in which a warrior nobility controlled the original kinship groups, and were an important ally of the Tepanec. In the 1420s the Mexica turned on their Tepanec sponsors. They formed an alliance with two small tribes in the valley and in 1428 the Mexica conquered the Tepanecs. This "Triple Alliance," dominated by the Mexica, was the foundation of the Aztec Empire.

The 1420s included a military coup that placed control of the Mexica crown within a single royal family. At the same time, the warrior nobility was strengthened as conquered territory was parcelled out to individual warriors, rather than to the kin groups that were the original basis of Mexica society. The new rulers formalized differences between the priestly, military, and commoner classes. The militarized nobility was allowed distinctive dress and, to expand the supply of noble soldiers, warriors were allowed to have several wives.

Between 1428 and 1520 six rulers led the Aztec Triple Alliance in a series of campaigns that brought dozens of kingdoms under Aztec authority and created an empire 700 miles long and 500 miles wide. These successes raise two questions about the Aztec achievement. What gave the Aztec political system its cohesion? What left it so unstable that an empire with several million inhabitants collapsed in the face of a few hundred Spaniards?

Unlike the Turks and the Mongols, the Mexica nomads did not enter agricultural civilization as conquerors. They achieved that goal only after a long period as subordinate mercenaries. This fostered a chronic sense of anxiety about their legitimacy, and the Mexica sought to gain recognition in several ways. Their warriors married women from the elites of the neighboring kingdoms. They also accepted the son of a highly regarded neighboring royal family as founder of their ruling dynasty.

The Mexica also used the religion of central Mexico to reinforce their legitimacy. This manipulation of religion is not easily summarized, but certain elements stand out. To a western observer, the Amerindian religious system has always been hard to comprehend. It apparently viewed the world as driven by a primal force that energized, usually through sun and rain, the actual environment. Worship focused on a collection of what Europeans regarded as gods, although their form and function was confusingly unstable to outside observers. Individual gods were identified with the sun, moon, rain, thunder, and many other phenomena, but their shape and function varied with location and with the religious and seasonal calendar. Thus, at one time and place, a particular god manifested itself with one appearance and power, but at another time of the year its manifestations could be quite different. The nature of these gods also varied from one tribe to another. As a result, the outward forms and powers of Amerindian deities were varied enough to allow the Mexica to reconfigure them to meet specific situations.

A second facet of the religious system is harder to grasp. The Amerindian sense of time and history was cyclical. The past was not a string of events that ran in a continuous line through time. The Amerindians, who were excellent astronomers, had developed an accurate fifty-two year calendric cycle. This cycle was understood as a moment of greatness followed by progressive decline caused by the cyclical waning of cosmic energy. Their view of history, therefore, assumed that distance through time was less important than the place of a past event in the cycle. Events from a particular phase in one historical cycle were readily combined with events from the same phase in other cycles without concern for our idea of chronological sequence. Such combinations simply added insight into the workings of the cyclical pattern, and it was only through understanding that pattern that "history" offered guidance to current events.

Finally, mesoamerican (Mexican and central American) religion fixed on the perception that once a calendric cycle started, it (and human affairs) gradually ran down as the cosmic system used up its store of energy. To counteract that ominous trend, Amerindian societies developed rituals that involved human sacrifice on a scale that is difficult for modern observers to discuss with any kind of objectivity. The practice was to identify sacrificial victims—virgins, children, young men, vigorous warriors—who were full of the energy represented by particular cults. The victims were linked with the god in question and, in theory, were conditioned to think of themselves as joining the divine force. Because this conditioning often involved coercion and narcotics, the degree to which participants really acquiesced in their own death is obviously debatable. Through their ritual death, the personal vital force of these victims replenished the declining power that energized the world, its crops, and its affairs. While mesoamerican religion included many types of human sacrifice, the warriors who entered central Mexico in the 1300s increasingly linked the energy of the sun with the sacrifice of captured warriors and military control of politics. This led to a gruesome increase in the scale of sacrifice of warrior captives during the Aztec–Mexica rise to power. (See Illustration 4.1.)

The leaders of the Mexica coup of 1428 deliberately manipulated this religious system so as to justify their actions. They started with a minor Mexica deity named Huitzilopochtli, who was linked to a Mexica god-hero. They associated Huitzilopochtli with other mesoamerican sun-

**ILLUSTRATION 4.1**
*THE SPANISH VIEW OF AZTEC RITUAL KILLINGS.*
*Many Aztec cults made extensive use of human sacrifice as a way of restoring en-*
*ergy to the cosmos, aspects of which were presented as cult objects identified as*
*"gods" by the Spaniards. That energy was thought to drive the universe and was*
*believed to decline towards the end of the calendric cycle that mesoamerican as-*
*tronomers had documented by studying the heavens. This sixteenth-century*
*drawing depicts sacrifice that involved ritual removal of the beating heart of vic-*
*tims who were military captives. The ceremonies included cannibalism in which*
*Aztec warriors ingested the flesh, and thus the vital energy, of a sacrificed warrior.*

Source: Inga Clendinnen, *Aztecs: An Interpretation* (Cambridge: Cambridge University
Press, 1993), following p. 240. Citation to Codex Magliabechiano, mid-sixteenth century,
small volume of European paper. 92 pages, 15.5 x 21.5 cm. Ms. Magl. CIXIII (Banco Raro
232), Magl. XIII, 11, 3, Biblioteca Nazionale Centrale of Florence. Reproduced in facsimile
as *The Book of the Life of the Ancient Mexicans, Containing an Account of Their Rites and
Superstitions*, intro., trans., and commentary by Zelia Nuttall (Berkeley: University of California Press, 1903).

god cults, each of which reflected a specific time–place–function manifes-
tation of the sun. During the crisis of the 1420s the Mexica apparently destroyed all documents about these deities and replaced them with their
own. The new version placed Huitzilopochtli at the top of the pantheon,
merging him with other sun-god manifestations. This version of the sun
god identified the Aztec emperor as his agent on earth and was "served"
by the Mexica warrior class. The warrior class thus had the sacred duty of
waging war to provide the sacrifices that replenished the sun's energy.

This arrangement did more than justify war and sacrifice. It reconfigured the entire religious system so that the Aztecs, their warriors, and
their emperor became the link between the ordinary world and the energy

that drove the heavenly and agricultural cycles that kept human affairs working. This justified the special status of the warrior class. It also justified wars of expansion, because warfare provided the captives whose sacrifice helped keep things running. It also shaped the way in which war was fought, because it put a premium on taking captives, rather than on killing the enemy. This is part of the explanation for some of the Spaniards' dramatic battle victories. Finally, it was a grim way of keeping conquered kingdoms in line. As the empire expanded, it used the threat of force to exact tribute, rather than constructing a bureaucracy and co-opting local elites. Rebellion thus not only was a challenge to religious authority, but also carried the risk that the warriors of a rebel kingdom would become human sacrifices.

If the anthropologists, archaeologists, and historians have it right, this reconstruction of mesoamerican religion played a major role in building the Aztec empire. It turned religion into an ideological support for a militarized empire with a privileged warrior elite. It also made it sacrilegious to challenge Aztec authority and enhanced the risk inherent in challenging that authority.

Ironically, this same religious system was undermining Aztec power when the Spaniards arrived. Three things contributed to a sense of impending crisis and to tensions in the society underneath the ruling class. One factor was inherent in the structure of the warrior elite. This noble class was accustomed to increasing its wealth through imperial rewards from new conquests. At the same time, thanks to the practice of polygamy, the number of men in this class grew rapidly. Such trends could be sustained only with new conquests or by extracting higher taxes and tribute from the rest of society.

At the same time, in about 1500, the Aztecs' 52-year cycle of greatness and decline moved into its downward phase. This seemed apparent to religious authorities because of crop failures, revolts, and epidemics, some of which were the initial impact of European disease in a population without immunological resistance. The only solution within the Aztec belief system was to step up the number of warrior sacrifices so as to replenish the energy of the cosmic system. This virtually compelled the later Aztec emperors to launch new wars of conquest.

The third factor that destabilized the empire was its size. By 1515 the Aztec army was stretched to the limit. The many subject kingdoms required constant punitive actions. Meanwhile, the empire had become so big that kingdoms that were candidates for conquest were far from the capital, making military logistics difficult. This reduced the effectiveness of Aztec attacks, meant that victories were not clear-cut, and reduced the numbers of captives just when more were urgently needed. The modest returns from later wars also aggravated internal tensions. Without the rewards of conquest, the oversized military class could not maintain its privileges without raising internal taxes. This alienated subordinate classes and kingdoms and further increased the need for police actions.

By 1519, when Cortez arrived in Mexico, the equilibrium that held the Aztec empire together was very fragile. (See Illustration 4.2.) Left

**ILLUSTRATION 4.2**
*THE CENTRAL PLAZA OF AN AZTEC CITY.*
*This is a modern reconstruction of the central plaza of an Aztec city as it might
have looked to Cortes and his men. The whole scene would have dwarfed anything the Spaniards had seen in Seville, which at that time was no more than a
third the size of the Aztec capital, Tenochtilán.*
Source: Bettman/CORBIS, New York.

alone, the empire's leadership might have managed a transformation like
that of the Ottoman Turks after the invasion by Timurlane. Most observers, however, think it likely that the empire was about to disintegrate
into its constituent kingdoms. Either way, Mexico was an ideal world for
the Spaniards' tactics of local alliances, participation in local conflicts, and
piecemeal conquest, tactics they had learned in Andalusia, Granada, the
Canary Islands, and the Caribbean.

## THE INCA EMPIRE

Chronologically, the rise of the Inca Empire is similar to that of the Aztec
Empire. Religion played a similar role in shaping the imperial elite and in
legitimating imperial authority created by conquest. At the same time,
there were differences in the way that this empire evolved and in the crisis
that confronted it when the Spaniards landed in Peru.

Complex societies existed in the Andean region by the second mil-
lennium B.C.E., and archeological remains document a culture in northern
Peru that was building large stone temples and palaces by 1700 B.C.E. By
200 B.C.E. there were two development zones in the Andean world. In the

highland interior, Nazca culture flourished over a large area from about 200 B.C.E. until around 700 C.E., while a complex urban culture appeared on the northern coast of Peru. This Moche culture included city-states with complex governments, cities, and irrigation systems with main canals seventy miles long. Both the Moche and Nazca cultures faded out near the end of the global cooling trend that lasted from about 300 to 800 C.E.

Meanwhile, the Andean interior came to be dominated by the Tiahuanaco culture. Centered on Tiahuanaco city, near modern La Paz, Bolivia, this culture left distinctive remains over much of the Andean interior between 600 and 1100 C.E. By 900, possibly assisted by global warming and improved rainfall, the Peruvian coast again saw the rise of city-states and their consolidation into what is known as the Chimu empire. The ruins of its capital document palaces, temples, and sophisticated irrigation systems that brought water from the mountains to the coastal plain. The Chimu empire flourished after 900, was absorbed into the Inca Empire in 1465, and faded rapidly after Spanish conquest.

After about 1100, the Andean interior was divided into several regional kingdoms. The Incas themselves constituted a small tribal state near the city of Cuzco. In the 1200s and 1300s several kingdoms contended for power in the Andean valleys and around Lake Titicaca. As a secondary tribe, the Inca participated in the struggle with mixed results. The situation altered in the early 1400s under the first historically credible Inca ruler, Viracocha Inca (died 1438). After participating in complex diplomatic and military maneuvering around Lake Titicaca, Viracocha Inca and his warriors were nearly defeated by their neighbors in 1438.

After a heroic defense of Cuzco, Viracocha's successor, Pachakuti (ruled 1438–1471), began a remarkable career of internal revitalization and imperial conquest. By 1463 he controlled the Andean valleys from Lake Titicaca to Lake Junin, a strip of territory 600 miles long. Inca armies then moved into the populous and sophisticated Chimu empire, which acknowledged Inca authority by 1465. When Pachakuti died in 1471, the Inca had conquered all of northern Peru and much of highland Ecuador. The next emperor, Topa Inca, turned his attention south. By 1493, when Columbus stumbled upon the Caribbean Islands, Topa Inca had added southern Peru, Bolivia, western Argentina, and Chile as far south as Santiago to the Inca Empire. The last great Inca leader, Huayna Capac (ruled 1493–1525), added the inland valleys of central Peru to the empire and pushed north to the border of modern Colombia. In eighty years these three remarkable rulers created a political empire 3,000 miles (4,300 km) long—the distance from Boston to San Diego.

As in the Aztec Empire, this story poses some questions. How did the leaders of an empire of conquest legitimize themselves so as to minimize resistance, and what made their empire collapse when confronted by a few dozen Spaniards? Just as Aztec leaders reconfigured mesoamerican religion to reinforce a military empire, Inca leaders modified Andean religion so as to fit themselves into religious beliefs about the power that controlled the cycles of weather, seasons, and daily life and death. The beginnings of successful expansion in 1438 forced the Inca elite to organize itself into a coherent ruling class and to consolidate royal leadership. Moreover, just as Aztec leadership saw itself confronted by crisis after 1500, the Inca empire confronted an internal crisis in the 1520s. The similarity is deceptive, however, because the policies that integrated the Inca Empire were different from those of the Aztecs, and the crisis that the Spaniards were able to exploit was also different.

Andean religion resembled that of Mexico in basic ways, but had some distinctive traits. Andean culture was conscious of the cyclicality of heavenly events, but was less obsessed by cyclical rise and decline. The conceptual framework was similar in that, while Andean religion had religious figures that Europeans identified as gods, such figures had different features and functions depending on time and location. Leadership in a kin group or kingdom was generally associated with one of these godlike cults, connecting political authority with higher forces through a deity that shared its power with the local leader. Among the manifestations of the power that drove the universe were the sun, the moon, Venus (seen as two entities because it appeared in different places and in different seasons), thunder, and rain. Andean religion included human sacrifice; compared with Mexico, however, it was on a small scale. What emerges is a religion as adaptable as mesoamerican religion, but less pessimistic and bloodthirsty.

To understand how the Inca elite exploited religion, we must understand two other aspects of that religion. One is the concept of the *huaca*. Andean peoples assumed that, although there was a barrier between human affairs and the forces that moved the universe and caused crops and animals to grow, that barrier could be penetrated. The places or objects through which contact between the two spheres took place were called *huacas*. The word could be applied to a magical spring or grotto, to a good-luck amulet, to a tribal god-figure, or to the mummy of a dead ancestor. Priests or rulers who were able to penetrate the barrier and draw upon supernatural forces were respected and powerful people.

The most politically significant practice associated with huaca (pl. huacas) was a form of ancestor worship. When an individual died (to use a European word), he did not cease to exist or to participate in affairs. Instead, he was thought of as having crossed the barrier between realms. His body was mummified and became a huaca, a point at which the barrier between worlds was permeable because the dead individual was assumed able to communicate with the living. Mummified persons were treated with respect and allowed to advise on everyday affairs. They were given lodging, food, and water, and brought out to participate in village festivals and meetings. While they obviously didn't say much, they were treated as members of the spiritual world who sometimes took notice of the material world and signaled good or bad fortune.

Inca leaders reconfigured the Andean religious system after 1438 so as to reinforce their authority. The god-figures associated with the sun and the moon were the most powerful in the Andean pantheon, and the Inca linked together the emperor and the sun god. At the same time, they formalized a hierarchy of god-figures through which cosmic energy descended from the sun and moon to the primal elements of the real world. The sun and moon were identified with emperor and empress, the two Venuses with local kings and queens, and earth and water with man and woman. This placed the sun, and therefore the emperor, above local cults and rulers, and implied that the emperor was the symbolic father of local rulers.

This hierarchy was reinforced in other ways. The paternal aspect of rule over subordinate kingdoms was reinforced by "inviting" the children of conquered rulers to the palace in Cuzco. Politically important women became secondary wives of the emperor and the rest entered a form of royal service that prepared food and clothing for ritual use. The men were trained as soldiers and administrators who identified with the imperial government and became officials and army officers. In this way the Inca government recruited a bureaucracy and co-opted regional elites into the imperial ruling class. Simultaneously, Inca rulers transferred the cult images associated with local rulers to Cuzco. This reinforced their subordination to the sun and moon, and toward the imperial government. The recruitment of royal offspring to the court and the transfer of local cults to Cuzco sound suspiciously like hostage taking by Inca conquerors, but, together with the reconfiguring of religious ideology, they suggest a shrewd approach to legitimating imperial rule. (See Reading 4.1.)

The Incas combined military logistics with a form of paternalist redistribution to strengthen their authority. Conquered peoples were forced to contribute part of their land and labor to construct terraces and irrigation systems. (See Illustration 4.3.) They then had to provide labor to cultivate the terraces in order to produce supplies which were stockpiled in imperial warehouses. These supply depots allowed Inca armies to travel rapidly because they did not have to carry supplies as they marched through the empire. As a result, Inca armies could reach a war zone or a rebel kingdom with remarkable speed. The coercive potential of this arrangement was masked by the fact that emperors released supplies from the royal storehouses when communities were caught short by bad weather and crop failure. In this way the imperial system allowed the emperor to counteract the forces of nature and verify his nearness to the power that drove the universe.

Inca rulers also exploited ancestor worship as a way of enhancing imperial prestige. (See Illustration 4.4.) When an emperor died, his body was mummified. Because he did not die in the European sense, his private property did not pass to his heir. In a form of divided inheritance, the dead emperor was treated as though he had retired from office. The prerogatives of rule passed to his heir, but because he was not really "dead," the late emperor's palaces and property remained "his." The "retired" emperor continued to "live" in his palace and was served by noble families who administered his estates for him, and, of course, supported themselves in the process.

This opulent world of ritual and ceremony enhanced the status of imperial office, but it created a long-term problem for the empire. Each

READING 4.1

*The Inca left no written history of their own and all that we have about their empire comes from oral tradition and observation by the first Spaniards to arrive in Peru. The following account of how the Inca incorporated new territory into their empire was written by the Spanish historian Bernabé Cobo in 1653 and was based on a careful compilation of available material.*

Although it was very extensive and composed of many and very different nations, the entire empire of the Incas was a single republic, governed by the same laws, privileges, and customs, and it was observant of the same religion, rites, and ceremonies; however, before being brought under Inca rule, the several nations had their own common law and a different way of living and governing themselves. . . . The first thing that these kings did when they won a province was to take out of it six or seven thousand families . . . and send them to other parts of the quiet and peaceful provinces; . . . and in exchange for them they put the same number of other people, who were made to leave the places where they first were settled, or from wherever the Incas wished, and among them were many *orejones* of noble blood. . . . Care was taken in this transmigration that those who were transferred, the recently conquered as well as the others, did not move to just any land, in a haphazard way, but to the places that were of the same climate and qualities or very similar to those they were leaving and in which they were raised. . . . And, as would be the case with warriors they [the new settlers] were given some privileges so that they would appear to be more noble. . . . With this skillful plan, as long as these *mitimaes* [new settlers] were loyal to the governors, if the natives rebelled soon they would be reduced to obeying the Inca, and if the *mitimaes* made a disturbance and started an uprising, they would be repressed and punished by the natives; and thus, . . . the king kept his states secure from rebellion. . . . [T]he Incas obliged everyone to accept their language, laws, and religion, along with all of the opinions related to these matters that were established in Cuzco. . . . [U]pon conquering a province, the Incas had the people's main idol taken away and placed in Cuzco with the same services and cult that it used to have in the province of its origin, and the natives were obliged to take care of all this, exactly as had been done when the aforementioned idol was in their province. For that reason Indians from all the provinces of the kingdom resided in Cuzco. These Indians . . . after returning to their own province . . . maintained the practices they had seen and learned in the court, and they taught all this to their people.

Bernabé Cobo, *History of the Inca Empire* (1653), excerpted from Mark Kishlansky, *Sources of World History*, Vol. I (New York: HarperCollins, 1995), pp. 280–285.

new emperor had to accumulate new wealth and new lands to be personally wealthy. This was one factor that drove successive emperors to make new conquests. As in Mexico, when the empire grew large, conquests became more difficult and the returns were increasingly meager. At the same time, the noble cliques that lived off the estates of the dead emperors constituted a growing aristocracy that was independent of royal favor and thus capable of undermining royal authority.

The potential for internal strife came to a head in the 1520s, just as the Spaniards were preparing to invade. Emperor Huayna Capac died in 1525 of a plague, possibly one that came to America with the Spaniards.

**ILLUSTRATION 4.3**
*INCA AGRICULTURE.*
*This picture shows Inca farming, often done with carefully laid out raised beds near the lake shore. In this picture the growing corn is being irrigated during the dry summer season. The careful layout and the stone-built reservoir show how labor intensive Inca farming was. As suggested in the text, the religious system constructed around the imperial cult integrated royal fields and accompanying storehouses into the symbolic array that asserted the legitimacy of Inca rule.*

Source: *El primer nueva cronica y buen gobierno,* by Felipe Guaman Poma de Ayala, Granger Collection, New York.

**ILLUSTRATION 4.4**

*An Inca nobleman receives a report from one of his officials, who holds a quipu for counting and recording important facts. It shows how, even without formal writing, the Inca maintained an effective bureaucracy.*

Source: Sixteenth-century Spanish manuscript, The Granger Collection.

This precipitated a succession crisis. Legally, the succession could pass only to a son of the emperor and the empress, who was also the emperor's sister. Brother–sister marriage guaranteed that each new emperor would inherit fully the cosmic power inherent in the identification of the sun with the emperor and the moon with the empress. The emperor also had "secondary" wives from royal families of subordinate kingdoms. The sons of these marriages, being only half divine, were not eligible to rule. At the same time, because they *were* half divine, they became key figures in the army and administration.

When Huayna Capac died, the authorities in Cuzco crowned his legal heir, Huascar, as emperor. Huascar, however, seems to have been an unpleasant, paranoid intriguer who alienated many of his supporters. In his last years, Huayna Capac had favored a half-royal son named Atahualpa, who proved to be a superb general and leader. When the Spaniards arrived in 1532, Atahualpa had just won a series of battles, had captured Huascar, and was on his way to take control of Cuzco, the imperial capital. Thus Pizarro arrived at a moment when the institutions of empire were challenged both militarily and ideologically. One wonders, however, if things would have been different had the Spaniards arrived a year or two later. Atahualpa might well have used his victory to change the succession and reform the institutions that had created internal dissension. The tenacity with which the Inca sought to recapture Cuzco from the Spaniards in 1536, and the fact that the last Inca government in exile survived until 1572, indicate that the Inca state was not as inherently fragile as the Aztec empire.

## THE SPANISH–AMERICAN EMPIRE

The third great American empire, that of the Spaniards, was built upon the ruins of the two that we have just described. It also evolved through two distinct phases. It began as a semi-feudal society of conquest created by a fast moving military elite and evolved into a complex, centrally administered empire. The invading Spaniards first tried to take control of existing societies, partly by supporting puppet successors to the Aztec and Inca thrones, partly by personally replacing local kings and chieftains. Initially the invading European adventurers and entrepreneurs thought in terms of reshaping a densely populated agricultural society into a pattern reminiscent of late medieval Castile. Once they had seized and shipped home the precious metals and valuable goods accumulated by the defeated Amerindian rulers, the costly shipping route to Europe forced the early Spanish conquerors to look for wealth and status as landlords in a populous but self-contained American world. This agenda was subverted by European disease and by the discovery of silver in Mexico and Peru.

The first European presence in America was an extension of the Iberian experience in the Atlantic islands. It was spearheaded by a search for wealth and status by people who, because they were part of the marginal fringe of European nobility and the speculative fringe of Mediterranean capitalism, were willing to undertake very risky ventures. Admittedly Columbus thought in terms of getting to Asia, and his plan was not entirely implausible, but his reasoning was representative of the rationales of early Atlantic adventurers. Although Europeans could measure latitude and estimate north–south distances, their ability to calculate east–west distances was limited. The world was known to be round, and the Greeks had left calculations of its circumference, some of them accurate. Columbus, however, made the case for his venture using Greek sources that underestimated the distance. Meanwhile, contemporary estimates of the size of Asia placed China and Japan farther east than they are. Combining two sets of data that minimized the size of the world, Columbus argued that Asia was situated about where America is located. It was his peculiar luck that *something* was out there, since Asia was not.

Early Spanish settlements in the Caribbean were much like those in the Canary Islands, although the islands of Santo Domingo and Cuba were larger, and the local societies more complex. Santo Domingo actually had alluvial gold worth mining if you could force the Amerindian population to do the work. Nevertheless, it took the 25 years after 1492 for the Spaniards to establish settlements in Santo Domingo, Cuba, Jamaica, and Panama and to develop a sense of Caribbean geography. They also picked up information about the Aztec empire and stories about the Incas, although the latter, filtered through Amazonian natives, were fanciful and eagerly misinterpreted. Most initial contacts were shaped by mutual curiosity, but given the social background of most of the first European invaders, initial contacts easily moved from friendly curiosity to violence. (See Readings 4.2 and 4.3.)

Until 1520 the Spanish crown was a fairly passive participant in this expansion. Preoccupied with a succession crisis that lasted from the death of Isabella I in 1505 to the end of the Castilian Comunero Revolt in 1521, the rulers of Castile had little time for a distant and unprofitable venture. In this phase of Atlantic expansion the crown did little more than grant charters, acknowledge rights of conquerors, and appoint a few officials. The reliability of such appointees, however, was limited by the danger involved, meager results, and the type of individual willing to accept such risky appointments.

Religion was involved from the beginning, but its role changed a great deal during the 1500s. Sixteenth-century Europeans could no more set out on an expedition without churchmen than they could leave without cooks or blacksmiths, but religion played a secondary role in the first phase of expansion into America. The church did legitimize conquest, however, by maintaining the Christian obligation to bring the word of God to the heathen, even if they had to be forced to listen. Among other things, this led to the *requerimiento*, a product of the European preoccupation with legality. (See Reading 4.4.) The Spaniards concluded that it was legal to conquer Amerindians if they first were told about Christian-

## READING 4.2

*From a Letter by Amerigo Vespucci, written in 1499.*

[We] went to another island. We found that this other island was inhabited by very tall people. We landed to see whether there was any fresh water, and not thinking it was inhabited, as we had not seen anyone, we came upon very large foot-marks in the sand, as we were walking along the beach. We judged that if the other measurements were in proportion to those of their feet, they must be very tall. Going in search, we came into a road which led inland. There were nine of us. Judging that there could not be many inhabitants, as the island was small, we walked over it to see what sort of people they were. When we had gone about a league [four miles] we saw five huts, which appeared to be uninhabited, in a valley, and we went to them. But we found only five women, two old, and three children of such lofty stature that, for the wonder of the thing, we wanted to keep them. When they saw us they were so frightened that they had not the power to run away. The two old women began to invite us with words, and to set before us many things, and took us into the hut. . . . Our intention was to take the young girls by force, and to bring them to Castile as a wonderful thing. While we were forming this design there entered by the door of the hut as many as thirty-six men, much bigger than the women, and so well made that it was rare thing to behold them. . . . They carried very large bows and arrows, and great clubs with knobs. They talked among themselves in a tone as if they wished to destroy us. Seeing ourselves in such danger, we made various suggestion one to another. . . . We at last agreed to go out of the hut, and walk away in the direction of the ships as if nothing had happened, and this we did. Having taken our route to return to the ships, they also came along behind us a distance of about a stone's-throw, talking among themselves. I believe they had not less fear of us than we of them. . . . At last we came to the beach, where the boats were waiting for us. We got in, and, when we were some way from the shore, the natives rushed down and shot many arrows; but we then had little fear of them. We replied with two bombard-shots, more to frighten them than to do them harm. They all fled into the woods, and so we took leave of them, thankful to escape after a dangerous adventure.

Taken from C. R. Markham (ed. and trans.), *The Letters of Amerigo Vespucci* (London: Hakluyt Society, 1894), pp. 27–28, presented in Merry Wiesner, Julius Ruff, and William Wheeler (eds.), *Discovering the Western Past: A Look at the Evidence*, Vol. I, *To 1715* (Boston: Houghton Mifflin, 1989), pp. 273–274.

ity and then refused to convert. This led to the ritual in which Spanish officials faced the natives and solemnly read aloud (in Spanish) a short explanation of Christianity, along with an offer of baptism. Not surprisingly, this made little impression on the Amerindians, although it satisfied the European concern for legality. Paradoxically, such legal niceties also laid the legal basis for a missionizing effort that sought conversion by validating the culture of newly conquered communities.

By 1519, when Hernan Cortez was ready to invade Mexico, the Spaniards still had only a few thousand Europeans in the Caribbean. They had acclimatized horses and European livestock, and had established an island base from which to move onto the mainland. We should

READING 4.3

*This letter, written by one of Columbus' crew members, Michele de Cuneo, on 28 October 1495, needs little comment regarding Spanish attitudes toward Amerindian women.*

While I was in the boat I captured a very beautiful Carib woman, whom the said Lord Admiral gave to me, and with whom, having taken her into my cabin, she being naked according their custom, I conceived a desire to take pleasure. I wanted to put my desire into execution but she did not want it and treated me with her finger nails in such a manner that I wished I had never begun. But seeing that (to tell you the end of it all), I took a rope and thrashed her well, for which she raised such unheard of screams that you would not have believed your ears. Finally we came to an agreement in such a manner that I can tell you that she seemed to have been brought up in a school of harlots. . . .

From *Journals and Other Documents in the Life and Voyages of Christopher Columbus*, S. E. Morrison (ed. and trans.) (New York: Heritage Press, 1963), p. 212, found in Marvin Lunenfeld, *1492: Discover, Invasion, Encounter* (Lexington: D. C. Heath, 1991), p. 283.

not dramatize this phase of European expansion, however, since it took twenty-seven years to accumulate those modest resources. Moreover, the surviving Europeans were at best a third of those who set out for America. The remainder had died from disease, malnutrition, shipwreck, or (occasionally) in battle. The survivors were as ruthless as any army that Europe ever produced. This ruthlessness went beyond that of conventional military conflict, since these men had taken tremendous risks and, numbering only in the hundreds, were thousands of miles and many months from any possible reinforcements. In addition to their rough understanding of the politics of Amerindian kingdoms, horses and guns gave them an additional psychological edge in combat that lasted long enough for them to knock apart the American empires and pacify their component kingdoms. Tactically, the Spaniards fought with the goal of killing the enemy in battle, rather than capturing him—an approach to field tactics that was different from that of many Amerindians. The Spaniards stuck together, rallied each other, and fought to kill with a ferocity that stunned their opponents. The battle formations used by the Amerindians were often broken by such ruthlessness, leading to Spanish victories against improbably large forces.

Moreover, it was easy to find Amerindian allies ready to challenge Aztec and Inca authority. Because both Amerindian empires were new, their subject kingdoms still remembered defeat. In Mexico, there were important kingdoms, like that of the Tarascans, which had never been brought under Aztec rule and may even have been left independent so as to justify periodic wars and a supply of sacrificial victims. When Cortez arrived in front of the Aztec capital of Tenochtitlán, therefore, he not

## READING 4.4

*For various reasons, including the maintenance of a degree of legal rights to their conquests and the maintenance of royal claims to jurisdiction, Spaniards felt compelled to offer Christianity and the divinely ordained authority of the rulers of Spain to the Amerindians before forcing them to accept it. Therefore they routinely tried to read a version of the following document to the communities and armies that they confronted. Given the linguistic and conceptual distance between Spaniards and Amerindians, the exercise was more important within the culture of the conquerors than to the outcome of the struggles that ensued.*

On the part of the King, Don Fernando, and of Dona Juana, his daughter, Queen of Castile and Leon [N.B.: this version was created after the death of Isabella I and before Charles V was old enough to rule], subduers of the barbarous nations, we their servants notify and make known to you, as best we can, that the Lord our God, Living and Eternal, created the Heaven and the Earth, and one man and one woman, of whom you and I, and all the men of the world, were and are descendants. . . . Of all these nations God our Lord gave charge to one man, called St. Peter, that he should be Lord and Superior of all the men in the world. . . . And he commanded him to place his seat in Rome as the spot most fitting to rule the world from; but also he permitted him to have his seat in any other part of the world, and to judge and govern all Christians, Moors, Jews, Gentiles, and all other sects. This man was called Pope. . . . The men who lived in that time obeyed that St. Peter; . . . so also have they regarded the others who after him have been elected to the Pontificate. . . .

One of these Pontiffs, who succeeded that St. Peter as Lord of the world, . . . made donation of these isles and *terra firme* [mainland] to the aforesaid King and Queen and to their successors, our lords, with all that there are in these territories, as is contained in certain writings, which passed upon the subject as aforesaid, which you can see if you wish. So their Highnesses are kings and lords of these islands and land of *terra firme* by virtue of this donation; and some islands, and indeed almost all those to whom this has been notified, have received and served their Highnesses, as lords and kings, in the way that subjects ought to do, with good will, without any resistance, immediately, without delay, when they were informed of the aforesaid facts. . . . Wherefore as best we can, we ask and require you that you consider what we have said to you, and that you take the time that shall be necessary to understand and deliberate upon it, and that you acknowledge the Church as the Ruler and Superior of the whole world and the high priest called Pope, and in his name the King Don Fernando and Queen Dona Juana our lords, in his place, as superiors and lords and kings of these islands and this *terra firme*. . . .

If you do so, . . . [we] shall leave you your wives, and your children, and your lands, free without servitude, that you may do with them and with yourselves freely that which you like and think best, and they shall not compel you to turn Christians, unless you yourselves, when informed of the truth should wish to be converted to our Holy Catholic Faith, as almost all the inhabitants of the rest of the islands have done . . .

[I]f you do not do this, and wickedly and intentionally delay to do so, I certify to you that, with the help of God, we shall forcibly enter into your country and shall make war against you in all ways and manners that we can, and shall subject you to the yoke and obedience of the Church and of their Highnesses; we shall take you and your wives and your children, and shall make slaves of them, and as such shall sell and dispose of them as their Highnesses may command; and we shall take away your goods, and shall do all the harm and damage that we can, as to vassals who do not obey. . . . And that we have said this to you and made this Requirement, we request the notary here present to give us his testimony in writing, and we ask the rest who are present that they should be witnesses of this Requirement.

From *The Spanish Conquest in America and Its Relation to the History of Slavery and to the Government of the Colonies* (London: J. W. Parker & Sons, 1855–1861), Vol. I, pp. 264–267, as excerpted from Marvin Lunenfeld, *1492: Discovery, Invasion, Encounter* (Lexington: D. C. Heath, 1991), pp. 189–190.

only had several hundred Spanish soldiers; he also had thousands of Amerindian allies. Even so, the actual Spanish conquest of Tenochtitlán suggests that the outcome could have been different if the Aztecs had not been hit by a devastating European epidemic. (See Reading 4.5.)

This epidemic reminds us that at every step of the way the Europeans in America were aided by a silent ally, European disease. Isolated from Eurasia for at least 10,000 years, the Amerindians had had no exposure to Eurasian diseases like smallpox, mumps, measles, tuberculosis, and bubonic plague. As a result, they had none of the accumulated resistance and antibodies that had built up in the European population. Even measles or mumps, mild childhood afflictions in Europe, were fatal to most Amerindians. Starting with Santo Domingo in 1500 and lasting well into the twentieth century, the exposure of isolated Amerindian communities to such diseases produced epidemics that killed as much as 90 percent of given towns in one epidemic. (See Reading 4.6.) The situation was similar to what happened to Europeans in tropical Africa, where most Europeans died within a year or two of diseases that were not usually fatal to Africans.

This silent ally was helpful to Europeans in some crucial situations. The epidemic that coincided with the capture of Tenochtitlan greatly weakened the Mexica defense. The death of the Inca emperor from what probably was a European disease created a fortunate opening for Pizarro. At the local level, resistance was impossible.

In the longer run, disease was a problem for the victors as well, because an empire and an economy cannot function without a population. By 1600 Peru had lost 70 percent of its preconquest population, while Mexico had lost 90–95 percent of its preconquest population. A once-crowded world had become a vast, empty space that posed complicated problems for the new Spanish Empire.

Religion played a dual role in the Spanish conquests. As we have seen, certain rituals were developed to rationalize conquest and make it legitimate in the European context. At the same time, Christian missionaries were deeply convinced of their obligation to spread Christianity by education and conversion. Finally, the imperial government sought to manage both aspects of religion so as to enhance royal authority. Initially, the aspects of religion that served to legitimize conquest were most evident.

## READING 4.5

*When the Spaniards first arrived at Tenochtitlan (Mexico City), Emperor Moctezuma allowed them to enter. After various events and arbitrary actions by the Spaniards, they were evicted from the city in a bloody battle. The Spaniards reorganized, acquired more Indian allies, and mounted a 75-day siege (according to Cortes himself) in which they conquered the Aztec capital. Cortes' account describes Spanish heroics, but the major reason for the victory is found in indigenous accounts of the fall of Tenochtitlan.*

When the Spaniards left Tenochtitlan, the Aztecs thought they had departed for good and would never return. Therefore they repaired and decorated the temple of their god, sweeping it clean and throwing out all the dirt and wreckage . . .

While the Spaniards were [recovering] in Tlaxcala, a great plague broke out here in Tenochtitlan. It began to spread during the thirteenth month and lasted for seventy days, striking everywhere in the city and killing a vast number of our people. Sores erupted on our faces, our breasts, our bellies; we were covered with agonizing sores from head to foot.

The illness was so dreadful that no one could walk or move. The sick were so utterly helpless that they could only lie on their beds like corpses, unable to move their limbs or even their heads. They could not lie face down or roll from one side to the other. If they did move their bodies, they screamed with pain. A great many died from this plague, and many others died of hunger. They could not get up to search for food, and everyone else was too sick to care for them, so they starved to death in their beds.

Some people came down with a milder form of the disease; they suffered less than the others and made a good recovery. But they could not escape entirely. Their looks were ravaged, for wherever a sore broke out, it gouged an ugly pockmark in the skin. And a few survivors were left completely blind. The first cases were reported in Cuatlan. By the time the danger was recognized, the plague was so well established that nothing could halt it, and eventually it spread all the way to Chalco.

---

Presented in Miguel Leon-Portilla (ed.), *The Broken Spears: The Aztec Account of the Conquest of Mexico* (Boston: Beacon Press, 1962) as found in Stuart Schwartz, Linda Wimmer, and Robert Wolff (eds.) *The Global Experience: Readings in World History*, Vol. II (New York: Addison Wesley Longman, 1998), p. 16.

As the church became serious about bringing Christianity to the Amerindians, however, religion became a complicated issue for the conquerors. Conquest was followed by missionaries, the most prominent being the Franciscans. The Franciscans of the time were committed to celibacy and poverty, convinced of the rightness of their goals, and well educated in religion, law, and language. They took seriously the possibility of turning Aztecs, Incas, and Mayans into Christian *gente de razon* (civilized people). To this end the missionaries got royal permission to create missions that separated the natives from both their own culture *and* from the Europeans. In that context the missionaries earnestly and vigorously tried to educate, convert, and train Amerindians to coexist with a European world while trying to keep them separate from the emerging society of the Spaniards. This ran counter to interests of the early con-

READING 4.6

*European disease also devastated the Mayan regions of Yucatan and Guatemala beginning as early as 1519 and repeatedly thereafter. We see this in* The Annals of the Cakchiquels, *the historical tradition of a Mayan community.*

It happened that during the twenty-fifth year [1519] the plague began, o my sons! First they became ill of a cough, they suffered from nosebleeds and illness of the bladder. It was truly terrible, the number dead there were in that period. . . . Little by little heavy shadows and black night enveloped our fathers and grandfathers and us also, oh, my sons! when the plague raged. . . . During this year [1520] when the epidemic broke out, our father and grandfather died, Diego Juan. [In 1521] when the plague began to spread . . . [i]t was in truth terrible, the number of dead among the people. The people could not in any way control the sickness. . . . Great was the stench of the dead. After our fathers and grandfathers succumbed half of the people fled to the fields. The dogs and the vultures devoured the bodies. The mortality was terrible.

On . . . [February 20, 1524] the Quichés were destroyed by the Spaniards. Their chief, he who was called Tunatiuh Avilantaro [one of Cortes' subordinates, Alvarado], conquered all the people. . . . [During 1530] heavy tribute was imposed. Gold was contributed to Tunatiuh [Alvarado], four hundred men and four hundred women were delivered to him to be sent to wash gold . . . . Four hundred men and four hundred women were contributed to work in Pangan on the construction of the city, by order of Tunatiuh.

. . . [T]here came to our church the Fathers of St. Dominic, Fray Pedro de Angulo and Fray Juan de Torres. They arrived from Mexico on February 10, 1542. The Fathers of St. Dominic began our instruction. The Doctrine appeared in our language. . . . Up to that time we did not know the work of the commandments of God; we had lived in utter darkness. . . .

In the sixth month after the arrival of the Lord President in Pangan, the plague which had lashed the people long ago began here. Little by little it arrived here. In truth a fearful death fell on our heads by the will of our powerful God. Many families [succumbed] to the plague. Now the people were overcome by intense cold and fever, blood came out of their noses, then came a cough growing worse and worse, the neck was twisted, and small and large sores broke out on them. The disease attacked everyone here. . . . Truly it was impossible to count the number of men, women and children who died this year [1560]. My mother, my father, my younger brother, and my sister, all died.

From Adrian Recinos and Delia Goetz (eds. and trans.), *The Annals of the Cakchiquels* (Norman: University of Oklahoma Press, 1953), pp. 115, 119, 129–133, 143–144. Excerpted from Marvin Lunenfeld, *1492: Discovery, Invasion, Encounter* (Lexington: D. C. Heath, 1991), pp. 312–313.

querors, who saw those same natives as the captive labor that they needed for their estates.

In the very first stages of occupation the conquerors on the ground had the upper hand in the control of inhabitants. As America was pacified, the invaders set up provisional governments. They created self-governing, Spanish-style towns in anticipation of royal confirmation, and awarded themselves *encomiendas*. The *encomienda* is best described as a kind of provisional trusteeship held in the name of the king. As *encomenderos*, soldiers administered Amerindian communities in place of native rulers, collected tribute, and provided justice. They also sought to convert *encomiendas* into private estates with manor houses and European crops. Many of them married the daughters of deposed chieftains so as to gain legitimacy in the eyes of the natives. The early conquerors acknowledged royal jurisdiction because it legitimized their control to themselves. At the same time, they tried to limit the development of autonomous communities of Amerindians sponsored by the missionaries. As of 1540 their American conquests did not constitute a centrally controlled empire. It was a loosely organized conquest society evolving toward European forms of land tenure, farming, and grazing. This situation was to change dramatically in the next twenty years.

As it developed, the Spanish empire in America came to resemble its Amerindian predecessors in several ways. Like the Aztecs and Incas, the Spaniards used force to take control and they exploited friction between American kingdoms to gain allies. Engaged in a war of conquest that was morally dubious in European terms, the Spaniards used religion to justify their actions. More significantly, religion was used to normalize Spanish control and strengthen royal authority at the expense of local elites. Ultimately, two things conspired to promote a centralized Spanish empire. One was the discovery of silver in Mexico and Peru; the other was the collapse of the Amerindian population.

The discovery of silver mines in Mexico and Peru quickly brought strong royal authority to the Spanish empire in America for four reasons. Silver was used throughout Europe for coining money and was a universal form of foreign exchange. As we saw, the Europe of the 1500s was confronted by an Ottoman–Turkish invasion and by ongoing struggles between the kings of Spain, France, and England. This situation was complicated by the politically subversive Protestant Reformation after 1517. In that context, every government had to raise taxes, preferably collected in silver, to keep up its international commitments. As we saw in Chapter 2, European kings had difficulty with this because they constantly had to negotiate with local elites who preferred that their kings remain weak. This created a real advantage for a European king who had access to large supplies of silver that would provide him with foreign exchange and a better credit rating with European bankers. When word of American silver reached Spain, it is not surprising that Charles V (1515–1555) and Philip II (1555–1598) moved quickly to develop the American mines and to strengthen imperial authority in the new empire.

This was reinforced by a second aspect of silver. European kings had weak taxing powers, but they had well-established rights to subsoil assets. Thus they were in a good legal position to collect royalties from mining. This meant that the Spanish crown could claim 20 percent of the output of the American mines. By the 1560s these royalties alone were worth more than Charles V's entire average annual budget prior to 1555. It had become worthwhile to assert royal authority in America.

Silver helped the royal treasury in another way. Like oil in the modern economy, silver is a highly commercial commodity. The 80 percent of mining output that went into private hands entered the economy as mine owners paid workers, bought European machinery, purchased supplies, and bought expensive imports so that they could live like rich Europeans. Most of the European economy was agricultural, and agriculture was hard to tax. Trade, however, used seaports and marketplaces and was hard to hide. A king who had a lot of trade within his jurisdiction thus had an easier time collecting taxes. As the American silver industry developed, therefore, the kings of Spain diverted the trans-Atlantic commerce that it created to Spanish seaports. In addition to royalties, therefore, they could tap a second bonanza by taxing the commerce that silver generated.

Finally, silver is small in bulk for its value. Because two or three tons of silver were worth as much as hundreds of tons of trade goods, it was feasible to exploit American mines even though Atlantic shipping in the 1500s was risky and expensive. Until the discovery of silver, America produced little that could be shipped to Europe profitably. This meant that the first Europeans in America could not easily acquire the foreign exchange they needed to buy European products, particularly in view of the high cost of transatlantic shipping.

American silver changed this. To secure the silver trade, the Spanish crown created a militarized version of an Italian-style trade diaspora. It was based on a chain of fortified trade centers that started in Seville and went to Santo Domingo. From there one route went to Veracruz and Mexico City, where it divided. One branch ran north to the silver mining towns, another to Acapulco and across the Pacific to Manila. The second route ran from Santo Domingo to Panama, then down the coast to Lima and inland to Cuzco and the mines at Potosí. The profits from silver mining sustained a system of ship convoys and overland pack trains that protected the silver from pirates. The security of the silver supply required large, sturdy ships that could withstand Atlantic weather and fight off attackers. At the same time, the value of the silver recommended that it be distributed among several ships so as to reduce the risk implied by shipwreck.

The result was a shipping system with excess capacity beyond the space needed by the silver itself. Because silver subsidized the shipping infrastructure, the extra space on the ships could be filled with goods that didn't pay the true cost of shipment. Anything that generated enough revenue to pay for handling and contributed even a small amount to the operating costs of the ship was potentially worth sending.

## FROM CONQUEST TO EMPIRE

These aspects of the silver industry revolutionized the emerging structure of Spain's American empire. The original drift toward an autonomous and largely self-governing agricultural society was overshadowed by a complex commercial economy as the new mining centers demanded timber, fuel, food, and clothing. This development made it possible, even urgent, for the authorities to control resources in America, especially the supply of labor.

This brings us back to the greatest unintended consequence of the European entry into America, the massive decline of the Amerindian population. This topic has become a standard part of colonial Latin American history, but it is helpful to see how it played out. In 1515 Mexico had between 10 million and 25 million inhabitants. The figure is debatable, but even the lower estimate makes the point. By 1600 Mexico had only 1 million Amerindians and mestizos and something like 100,000 people of European stock. The collapse in the Andean region was less spectacular because European diseases were not as easily transmitted in the cooler Andean highlands. Even so, the population fell from 7 or 8 million to around 2 million.

Under these circumstances it is not surprising that the royal government sought to control the Amerindian population. Just as it is important today to keep the oil flowing out of the Middle East, it was crucial for Charles V and Philip II to keep the silver flowing from Mexico and Peru to Seville. In a world where all production was labor intensive, the supply of manpower was strategically vital.

Consequently, Spanish authority in America focused on organizing and reorganizing the Amerindian population, a story that involves attitudes about slavery, conversion, and government. The link between religion and empire here offers parallels to the Aztec and Inca empires. We have seen that from the beginning of the European occupation of America, Christianity played an ambiguous role. It was important to the conquerors that their actions be accepted as legal in Europe, and for that they needed religious sanction. So they had no choice but to accept churchmen dedicated to converting the Amerindians. Yet the missionary project of the Franciscans sought conversion within self-sustaining native communities. Thus, even before the discovery of silver, tension existed between the conquerors, who wanted to turn the Amerindians into a dependent labor force, and the missionaries, who favored freestanding native communities.

Behind this real-world tension was debate in Spain about the humanity of the Amerindians and concern for the legalities of royal vs. local jurisdiction. The debate involved missionaries and theologians such as Bartolomé de las Casas and Juan Jinés de Sepúlveda. It concluded that, while black Africans could legitimately be enslaved, Amerindians had souls and were potentially *gente de razon* (civilized people). Using arguments derived from Aristotle, Africans were defined as less than human and as requiring more development before they could be treated in the same way as Amerindians. This conclusion fitted conveniently with the plantation system discussed in Chapter 3. It also fitted nicely with the crown's concerns about the legal situation in America. Such conclusions sound odd to the modern ear, but they mark an important step in European thinking. The debates in question resulted in the conscious formulation of the possibility that non-European culture had its own validity—a crucial step to the ideal of plural society.

If the Amerindians were not natural slaves, they did not belong to the conquerors who seized their lands. If they had souls, they were by definition subjects of the king, and the jurisdiction once held over them by the Aztec and Inca emperors transferred directly to the Spanish emperor. This may seem legalistic, but in a European world where kings had to defend their prerogatives in complicated legal disputes, it meant that, short of rebellion, royal jurisdiction over the native population could not be challenged.

Even before it confronted population decline and the silver industry, therefore, the crown supported the missionaries in America. It established missions all over the empire, gave them military protection, and granted them autonomy from the town governments set up by the first conquerors. The Franciscans in particular learned local languages and looked for parallels between Amerindian religion and Christian practices. They modified Christian rituals and processions with local religious symbols in an effort to present a visually accessible form of Christianity to nonliterate converts. They developed writing systems for Amerindian languages, making it possible for the language of the Aztecs to become the language of literacy and legal record in much of colonial Mexico. In this way the missionaries brought the Amerindians part way into Christianity within a framework that assured royal jurisdiction over their communities. They also began the process of developing the western ideal of tolerance for different values and beliefs.

As this developed, the crown formalized a system of dual jurisdiction: a *República de los Españoles* and a *República de los Indios*. The Republic of Spaniards included the network of municipalities, seaports, guilds, commerce, and courts created by the European conquerors. Numerically much smaller, this was the institutional world of the European elite of the Spanish–American empire. The Republic of Indians was theoretically parallel to the first. City-based kingdoms and smaller communities with stable governments before the conquest were Christianized and given Spanish-style town governments. These governments were staffed with members of the Amerindian community who supervised local affairs and were subordinate to the Viceroy in Mexico or Lima.

However autonomous these communities may have been, they included churches staffed by Spanish clergy. This religious presence was maintained either by the missionary orders or by the secular clergy of the church. While the missionaries sought parallels between local religion and Christianity, so as to facilitate conversion, the bishops and priests of the church hierarchy were preoccupied with maintaining the integrity of Christian doctrine.

Early missions had mixed results, as in the Yucatan in the 1540s and 1550s. There the Franciscans brought the sons of regional leaders into mission schools, exposed them to Catholic ritual, and taught them to recite Christian prayers and gestures. This approach was based on the assumption that by regulating external actions one could reshape the person inside. Amerindian leaders, not surprisingly, thought differently. They believed that religion involved a cosmic force that reached the human world through a variety of channels, some of which the Europeans identified as gods. They could translate the idea of the Trinity into terms they understood, but the idea of monotheism made no sense to them. Because the European God and his rituals had proven more effective than their own cults, it made excellent sense to add that God's rituals to those they already used. This pragmatic approach to spiritual power was anathema to the Franciscans and the church, and led to brutal investigations and heresy trials in the Yucatan in the 1560s.

Behind this vignette is the reality that the crown invested heavily in making Christianity accessible to Amerindians. This reflected the conviction within Catholicism that the church was required to bring salvation to all souls. This was as obvious to late medieval Europeans as the merits of capitalism, science, and technology are to us. At the same time, this religious urge was managed by the Spanish crown. By allowing the missionaries to separate part of the Amerindian population from the soldiers who conquered America, the crown gained two advantages. It precluded the conquerors from preempting royal jurisdiction over the population. More practically, the missions helped to create a parallel Republic of Indians, a development that proved useful to the crown with the advent of the silver mines and demographic collapse.

The link between religion and politics came to the fore again later in the sixteenth century. As more silver mines were opened, and the native population declined, royal officials were faced with the problem of maintaining the supply of labor. Mines, manufacturing, and commercial agriculture all needed labor, and the Republic of Indians, however much it was violated, was a barrier to rampant exploitation. The official reaction to declining population and increasing demand for labor had three components.

One was resettlement. In a world that went from over 10 million Mexicans to 1 million, and from 8 million to 2 million Andeans, hundreds of Amerindian communities became ghost towns with only a few families. The Spaniards systematically consolidated the remnants of these communities into new towns with Spanish-style governments. While this policy created towns that were economically viable and easier for the church to serve, it *also* made it easier for the crown to regulate the supply of manpower.

The second component of this labor policy was a system of conscripted labor. Called the *repartimiento* in Mexico and the *mita* in Peru, this system required town authorities to maintain lists of adult male residents. These men were drafted to spend several years working in the mines, workshops, and fields that were crucial to the Republic of Spaniards. The workers were supposedly paid a reasonable wage, given decent living accommodations, and were free to return home when their term was up. This was not, strictly speaking, slavery, and was actually a logical extension of routine practices in Spain. From the crown's perspective it was essential, because it was the only way to assure that locally powerful Spaniards would not preempt labor for their estates and disrupt the flow of silver to Spain.

From the Amerindian perspective, the system had serious drawbacks. In a society disintegrating demographically, the labor drafts deprived communities of the labor needed to feed the population. It also deprived communities of the age group of men essential to family formation and reproduction, aggravating the difficulty that Amerindian populations had in offsetting European diseases. This was worsened by the often-dangerous work that draftees were forced to do, especially at the mines. The mine pits themselves were primitive, dangerous, and poorly ventilated. Moreover, the silver refining process used mercury, and thousands of workers were exposed to heavy concentrations of mercury vapor. As a result, many labor draftees never lived to return home.

The third part of the royal solution to population and labor problems takes us back to religion. The mission system originally provided a degree of separation between Amerindian communities and avaricious conqueror–landlords, an arrangement that initially met royal goals. By the later 1500s, however, this had changed. The missions now tried to protect Amerindians from the labor draft, and the crown reacted to this by secularizing the missions. Following an investigation into the Catholicism practiced by the missionaries, the church hierarchy concluded that the missionaries had allowed pagan symbols, practices, and ideas to penetrate the faith. This gave the crown a reason to cancel mission charters and turn their churches over to priests selected by the church hierarchy. This more puritan form of Catholicism reformed ritual, painted over the murals that had provided a visual bridge to Christianity, and exposed everyone to the workings of the Inquisition.

Behind this transition was the fact that the Spanish crown had more control over the Catholic hierarchy than it did over the missionaries. The missionary orders were more directly connected with the papacy. The American bishops and parish clergy were appointed and controlled by the crown through the Patriarch of the Indies and the royal Council of the Indies. By shifting Amerindian communities to clergy appointed in Madrid, the crown removed an obstacle to the labor drafts needed by the silver industry.

## THE LEGACY OF THE AMERICAN EMPIRES

By the 1600s, therefore, the Spaniards had created an American empire built upon the ruins of its Amerindian predecessors but structured around silver and the significance of silver in Europe. The institutional backbone of this new empire included the regulated transatlantic trade called into existence by the discovery of silver, a network of Spanish officials and judges, some 200,000 people who considered themselves Spaniards, and an Amerindian population dramatically reduced in size from its preconquest numbers. This native population had been Christianized, at least superficially, and many of them lived in communities run by Spanish-style institutions but staffed by their own people. The autonomy of those communities was limited by the policy of resettlement, the shift of churches from mission to parish status, and the system of labor drafts.

This image of control imposed from the imperial center is obviously oversimplified. Moreover, a case can be made that the Spanish empire suffered the same abrupt end as its two predecessors. In 1808 the Spanish monarchy was dismantled by France much as the Spaniards had dismantled the governments of the Aztecs and Incas. That story is beyond the scope of this book, but it caused mainland Spanish America to fragment into the regional societies that we know in today's Latin America.

Early in this chapter we suggested that, while a Spanish empire replaced the Aztec and Inca empires, inside that third American empire a distinctive new civilization was taking shape. Several trends already pointed in that direction as early as 1650. The separation between Amerindians and Europeans blurred as the population came to include more and more mixed-blood (*mestizo*) Americans who did not fit either of the Republics of the sixteenth century. At the same time, by 1650 the population of Spanish America was again growing. Acquired immunities had finally reduced the killing power of European disease. Both trends point to the dynamic and complex societies that emerged after 1808.

At the same time, the empire itself was the context for many ad hoc autonomies and local balances of power. A subtle shift took place within the European sector. By the early 1600s both Mexico and Peru had complex, dynamic economies with internal markets, industry, and sources of capital. As a result, more silver remained in America and it was less attractive for Spaniards in America to use the monopolistic trade system designed to deliver silver to Seville. (See Map 4.2.) Spain, however, was more dependent than ever on American silver to maintain its place in European affairs. Thus, although political control seemed to come from Madrid, by the 1640s the collective decisions of miners, merchants, and plantation owners in America determined whether the Madrid government got the resources it needed. This ability of colonial elites to quietly undermine the imperial government is the first hint of eventual Latin American independence.

At the same time, colonial elites accepted working arrangements with Amerindian communities that suggest mutual accommodation. This is not to minimize the exploitation that went on, but suggests that Amerindian culture retained more freedom of action than is apparent to the modern observer. One example involves the silver economy in Peru. The Inca empire had an elaborate system of roads and inns maintained by communities along the royal roads. The Spaniards tried to insert themselves into the Inca chain of command with little understanding of how it worked. Rather than working under duress for the Spaniards, the transporters faded into the mountains. Once the Spaniards had given them Spanish-style institutions, the transporters adapted those institutions to their own purposes, providing transport between Lima and the silver mines. Before long, Amerindian transporters had a monopoly on the transport of mercury and silver to Potosí. Their adaptability gave them the strategic leverage that guaranteed reasonable contracts and autonomy from Spanish authority.

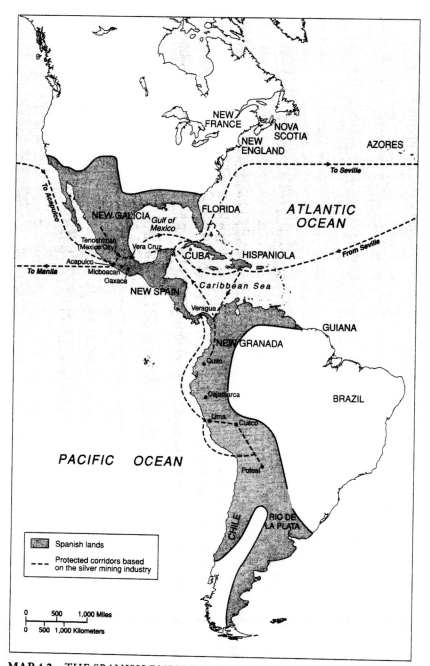

**MAP 4.2**   *THE SPANISH EMPIRE IN AMERICA ABOUT 1600.*
*The backbone of the empire was the silver mining industry and the trade that it supported. Once this system of protected trade was in place, the original Caribbean settlements became marginal to the Spanish. Thus they were more easily captured and exploited by other Europeans interested in contraband and sugar production.*

One could cite many similar anecdotes, but the underlying situation is clear. The empire had become a network of interdependencies and compromises. Madrid had to put up with the autonomy of colonial Europeans who, in turn, needed the legitimacy of imperial authority and therefore acknowledged some imperial demands. The European elite in the empire was heavily exploitative, yet it was outnumbered and had only rudimentary policing mechanisms. This meant that they had to accept working arrangements with Amerindian communities. The Amerindian world preserved more of its preconquest culture than a modern observer might expect. At the same time it accepted (somewhat selectively) Christianity and learned to use Spanish institutions to defend Amerindian interests. While the Spaniards developed a bureaucracy around the Viceroys and royal courts, it was a political system that balanced coercion with compromise. On that basis the Spanish empire in America lasted from 1519 until the early 1800s.

Meanwhile, America exported thousands of tons of silver. Historians have estimated that by 1600 the American mines had tripled the amount of silver in the European money system. Silver subsidized the trading system between Europe and America, and American mines gave Spain the resources to contain the Turkish invasion of Europe and to maintain her power in Europe. Silver also changed Europe's relations with Asia by giving Europeans a commodity that the Asians wanted. Indeed, by 1600 the silver industry in America affected politics in Japan and market conditions in India. That development is a part of the story in Chapters 5 and 6.

# 5

# CROSSROADS OF THE WORLD

# South Asia and the Indian Ocean

## THE INDIAN OCEAN AS CROSSROADS

The lands bordering the Indian Ocean have never been part of a single great empire, and there is no one political narrative that defines the region. At the same time, several economic, cultural, and religious reasons prompt us to view the Indian Ocean basin as a coherent region. At one time or another in the centuries between 1200 and 1700, Chinese, Europeans, Ottomans, Safavids, and Mughals expanded into lands around the Indian Ocean, and the different outcomes of those invasions only make sense when they are placed in their regional context and within the structures that gave the region its coherence. The four kinds of expansion outlined in Chapter 1 all were at work, but the combinations were complex and varied.

In the 1300s this huge region included a handful of large countries and empires along with a great many smaller ones, but by 1450 most of the larger states had lost their coherence. As of 1500 the prevalence of smaller powers was pronounced throughout the Indian Ocean basin. Nominally the most important power in the area was the Mameluk Empire of Egypt (1260–1517), which controlled the Muslim holy places and the entrances to both the Red Sea and the Persian Gulf. Northern India in 1500 was weakly ruled by descendants of Turkic Muslim warriors who had founded the Sultanate of Delhi in 1206. Like the Ottoman Empire, the Sultanate of Delhi had been devastated by Timurlane (1398). Unlike the Ottoman Empire, it never recovered, and had lost much of its internal cohesion by the mid–1400s. In southern India the large Hindu Vijayana-gara Kingdom emerged in 1336, while the Kingdom of Siam, nucleus of modern Thailand, emerged in Southeast Asia at the same time. In 1431 the Thais conquered the remnants of the Cambodian empire and its capital at Angkor Wat. Another important kingdom emerged in Java after the fail-ure of a Mongol–Chinese invasion in the 1290s, but by the 1400s it no longer dominated the region. A bit later, in the 1500s, a strong Kingdom of Burma emerged, as did the country of Viet Nam. In 1500, however, most of the Indian Ocean basin was a mosaic of small and midsized prin-cipalities and city-states.

To the extent that it is safe to generalize about a world that stretches 10,000 miles from Mozambique in East Africa to the Moluccas Islands in Indonesia, these small states shared certain characteristics, some of which resembled those of their Mediterranean counterparts. Their underlying economies were agricultural, but most coastal states were centered on cities that functioned as political capitals, market centers, and seaports. The agricultural sector was at least partly oriented to producing cash crops, some of which were exported. This commercial agriculture was supplemented by manufacturing, which supplied overseas as well as local markets. This industry was labor intensive, depended on skilled artisans, and in several places it produced high-quality textiles and metal products ranging from nails to gold tableware. A few ports, located at key cross-roads (Aden, Hormuz, Calicut, and Malacca), specialized in providing warehouse and financial services for long-distance trade.

The commodities exported around the Indian Ocean varied widely. A short list includes gold and slaves from east Africa, sugar, dates, and coffee from the Red Sea and the Persian Gulf, and rice, cotton, and tex-tiles from India. Cinnamon came from Sri Lanka and other spices from Indonesia. Silks and porcelain entered the system in Chinese ships that stopped in Thailand, Sumatra, and Java. These goods were redistributed throughout the Indian Ocean and exported to China, the Middle East, and the Mediterranean. The specific commodities are not so important as the web of long-distance economic and cultural interaction represented by the trade itself.

Larger coastal countries maintained navies, although they served mostly to protect trade from piracy. Ship technology varied from one part of the Indian Ocean basin to another and included at least four solu-tions to the problems of long-distance overseas transport. In the western Indian Ocean, where the Mameluks of Egypt were responsible for pro-tecting the pilgrim trade to Mecca, the ships guarding the routes were oared galleys similar to those in Mediterranean navies. They were long, narrow, light, and fast, and could maneuver independently of the wind. They were heavily manned and could be fearsome enemies when the tactical goal was to ram and board the enemy, thus creating a miniature land battle. The disadvantage of galleys was that their narrow, light design made them vulnerable to rough weather. They also had little room for supplies and could not operate far from secure bases.

Arab merchant ships, developed in the western Indian Ocean, were sturdy, modest-sized vessels in which the hull planks were fastened together with coconut fiber rope, the hull being reinforced with ribs locked into place after the hull was formed. The technology has been known in east Africa for at least two thousand years. These ships carried a fore-and-aft lateen rig that allowed them to sail into the wind by tacking, but which also worked well when running before a steady wind. Such ships carried as much as a hundred tons of cargo. They could sail thousands of miles across the open ocean and, by the eleventh century, they often travelled the entire eight thousand miles between Arabia and China. For centuries this was the basic type of merchant ship in South Asia.

In the huge collection of islands that we call Indonesia, islanders used a ship design that resembled a large outrigger canoe. (See Illustration 5.1.) Capable of holding 40 to 50 tons, they carried a large sail and had outriggers for stability. Small and relatively fast, they were used for inter-island shipping throughout the two-thousand-mile reach of Indonesia. Similar vessels travelled thousands of miles between the Pacific Islands and made possible the colonization of such distant places as Easter Island

**ILLUSTRATION 5.1**
*INDONESIAN SEAGOING VESSELS.*
*Indonesia was familiar with war galleys similar to those of the Indian Ocean and Mediterranean Sea, and also used large outrigger canoes. When used for freight, they could easily carry forty tons. In this print we see an armed galley from an Indonesian sultanate and the royal canoe or korakora of the Sultan of Ternate. It was big enough to carry rowers in the outriggers and mounted seven cannon. Ternate was one of the Portuguese first targets in the Spice islands.*

Source: Anthony Reid, *Southeast Asia in the Age of Commerce, 1450–1680* (New Haven: Yale University Press, 1993), Vol. 2, p. 231, fig. 31b.

and New Zealand by Pacific Islanders. With a large crew to paddle, this type of vessel was favored by pirates in southeast Asia.

Finally, any large port in southeast Asia routinely saw Chinese junks. With flat bottoms and flat sides, junks were built of sturdy lengthwise planks fastened to solid bulkheads that ran from one side of the hull to the other, dividing it into watertight compartments. This created a strong hull design that could be used for ships of moderate to very large size. Bigger junks carried several masts with large sails and made voyages that lasted several years and crossed thousands of miles of Pacific and Indian Ocean. By 1500, Chinese junks were no longer common in the western Indian Ocean, but no one was surprised if one showed up to trade at Hormuz on the Persian Gulf.

Despite the lack of political unity in the Indian Ocean, certain factors produced a long-term regional equilibrium. One such feature was its system of long-distance trade. Because transport and communications were slow by modern standards, individual transactions in such a huge region took a long time to complete. Not only did it take time to move goods, but most commodities were derived from agriculture or livestock and appeared on the market in annual cycles. Moreover, the seasonal changes in prevailing winds meant that long voyages could take place only during certain seasons.

As a result, buyers and sellers had to do much of their business on credit. They bought goods in anticipation of the sale of other commodities, used letters of credit, and made loans timed to come due when crops were harvested or when winds would allow completion of particular voyages. Exporters contracted to buy agricultural commodities from producers months before crops were harvested, providing credit to the agricultural world. Merchants holding notes that would not be paid off for several months could sell them for less than their full value (that is to say, at a discount) to merchant bankers. The seller of such a note thus surrendered a part of the return he expected in the future in order to have the rest of his money right away. The banker who bought the discounted note eventually collected the loan at full value, earning interest on his earlier advance to the small merchant.

Credit-based trade requires trust and understanding among all participants. In many cases the participants in a transaction did not know each other and depended on middlemen known to have reliable information on the creditworthiness of people in the commercial system. Such a system of personal trust works better if participants can expect courts throughout the trade network to enforce contracts. Interdependence between individuals and consistent legal enforcement were reinforced by the fact that many local economies were so specialized in exports that they depended on reliable imports for essential food and raw materials. That dependence was a powerful incentive for governments and their judges to respect the rights of foreign merchants. As in the medieval Mediterranean, these factors favored governments that were responsive to merchants, protected trade, avoided arbitrary taxation, and did not maintain expensive military establishments. This does not mean that arbitrary rulers and military conflicts were unknown, but it tells us that commercial interests were influential and that most governments thought twice before disrupting trade.

This network of interdependence freed the shippers of the Indian Ocean from the need to travel the entire distance from Arabia to Indonesia or China in order to deal in goods from those places. As a result, we can identify seven or eight autonomous trade circuits within the intercontinental system of the Indian Ocean. (See Map 1.4.) It was more efficient for different ships to make annual voyages between Hormuz and Ceylon, between Ceylon and Malacca, and between Malacca and China than for a given ship to make the entire trip. Seasonal winds forced such long-distance ventures to wait several months at each transfer point, a waste of shipping capacity that added to the cost of the transaction. A trade system in which governments respected both trade and commercial law allowed merchants in each section of the Indian Ocean region to find the goods they needed at key transit points without having to go to the places where they were produced. The result was a system in which a remarkable quantity and variety of goods travelled halfway around the world while few merchants visited the sources of the goods they bought and sold.

Regional interdependence was reinforced by cultural exchanges, the most notable of which was the spread of Islam. The antimodern tendencies of some current Islamic communities distract us from the fact that Islam has long been more open to trade and business than many religions, including Christianity. Mohammed himself started as a merchant and, unlike China or Europe, commercial backgrounds did not exclude businessmen from court life in Muslim governments. As in west Africa (see Chapter 3), Islam spread across the Indian Ocean and Indonesia along trade routes. The degree to which local populations converted to Islam varied, just as in the Balkans and Africa. By 1300, however, most of the commercial and governing elites around the Indian Ocean were Muslim, especially in the zone between east Africa and India. This made Arabic available as a common language and disseminated Muslim law and Arabic commercial techniques throughout the Indian Ocean. In this way common legal precepts were available to reinforce the mutual trust and respect for contract essential to a complex trading system.

This should not be taken as a universal generalization. Hindu religious traditions and social elites moved between India and Burma along with trade in the Bay of Bengal, while Neo-Confucian ideas and Chinese administrative techniques travelled from China to Japan, Siam, and Viet Nam. Across the region as a whole, however, the influence of the code of behavior associated with Islam was a major element in regional interdependence. (See Map 1.3 on the spread of Islam.)

In this way the immense reaches of the Indian Ocean and southern Asia worked as a region despite political fragmentation. Mutual interdependence made it risky for countries to engage in empire building that would upset the equilibrium, because everybody depended upon the regular flow of trade. This was reinforced by the presence of Islam and by its role as a vehicle for common legal precepts and commercial practices. The region lacked an obvious political center, and without a dominant political power its history is hard to present effectively. By 1300, however, the shores of the Indian Ocean had developed a distinctive combination of fragmented political power, economic interdependence, sophisticated commercial and maritime techniques, and acceptance of Islamic religious and legal precepts. This system proved remarkably durable in the face of intervention until after 1750.

An interactive commercial and cultural network that spans ten thousand miles and connects three continents merits the label "world system" or "crossroads of the world" in its own right. Between 1200 and 1700, however, this region became a global crossroads in more emphatic ways. This is because the Indian Ocean region was the target of at least five major surges of expansion from peoples and empires attracted to it.

One of these was the construction of a Chinese presence. As we will see in Chapter 6, China maintained a strong military and diplomatic thrust into South Asia between the mid 1200s and the 1420s. This began with a number of Mongol Chinese invasions of Java and other parts of Indonesia. It culminated in several huge naval expeditions that ranged as far as India, Arabia, and East Africa between 1400 and 1433. The result was an enduring legacy of Chinese commercial links, a legacy particularly strong in Viet Nam and Siam.

The other expansive surges entered the Indian Ocean from the north and northwest. The Ottoman Empire, in addition to its offensive in the Mediterranean and eastern Europe (see Chapter 2), penetrated the Indian Ocean and created an important sphere of influence. Concurrently, the Safavid Empire in Iran extended its influence to the Indian Ocean, seeking a share of Eurasian trade and political influence. In the early 1500s Turkic nomads living in Afghanistan invaded India. In a few short decades they created the Mughal Empire, after China, the largest and wealthiest empire in the Asia of the 1600s. Finally, Europeans appeared in the region, first the Portuguese, later the Dutch and English. Some Europeans sought to build political empires or, in the case of the Portuguese, even to continue the Crusade for control of the Christian Holy Land, but the dominant goal was access to Asian products that could be marketed in Europe.

To a degree these stories must be told independently, since they have different dynamic elements. At the same time, however, they interacted in ways that created a complex matrix, one which verifies the idea that the Indian Ocean was a global crossroads. Thus the European presence did not change Asian history very much until after 1700, and for that reason does not appear at this point in our story. Nevertheless, it is important to keep in mind that Portuguese warships were on the scene from 1500 onward and were accompanied by merchants and missionaries. Even so, as late as 1700 the societies of the Indian Ocean had both resisted and borrowed from various invaders with considerable success. At the same time, however, the Europeans who had entered the scene were setting the stage for a shift in the relationship between the Indian Ocean and the rest of the world. The region remained a global crossroads, but after 1700 the decisions that shaped its commerce and politics increasingly were made in Amsterdam and London.

# THE GUNPOWDER EMPIRES OF THE TURKS, SAFAVIDS, AND MUGHALS

The most prominent feature of the process of expansion within the Indian Ocean region took the form of three examples of militaristic empire building. Together the three cases were a heritage of the centuries-long sequence of conquests by nomadic warrior elites that we associated in Chapter 1 with the Mongol Empire of the 1200s. The outcome in the Indian Ocean was the three so-called "gunpowder empires": the Empire of the Ottoman Turks (centered in Turkey), that of the Safavid Turks (centered in Iran or Persia), and that of the Mughal Turks (centered in northern India). (See Map 5.1.) As large inland empires, their participation in long-distance commerce varied, but all had a major impact on the intercontinental trade that flowed through Asia and across the Indian Ocean. Thus they are important for any understanding of how Europeans were able to fit themselves into the region after 1500.

## THE OTTOMAN DRIVE TOWARD THE EAST

As we saw earlier, before about 1500 the largest empire involved in the Indian Ocean was the Mameluk Empire. The Mameluks based their political control of the Red Sea and the Persian Gulf on a military protectorate that was reinforced by the moral authority of the Caliph of Cairo, the titular head of Islam. This reliance on the authority of the Caliph brought the Mameluk Sultans diplomatic prestige, but it also brought obligations. It made the government in Cairo responsible for the Muslim Holy Places in Mecca and Medina and for protecting Muslim pilgrims travelling there.

Because all good Muslims were obligated to try to visit Mecca once in their lives, this pilgrim trade was substantial even in the era from 1200 to 1700. Much of the population of east Africa and Southern Asia had converted to Islam, and a large part of the trade around the Indian Ocean was dedicated to transporting pilgrims. Some came from as far as the Philippines, although the pilgrimage trade was most intense in the area between western India and eastern Africa. For this reason the Mameluk Sultans maintained a naval base at Suez and a fleet of galleys that patrolled the Red Sea and the coasts of Arabia and Persia.

We saw in Chapter 2 that by the 1490s European interest in Atlantic expansion was in part the result of a tense political situation in the eastern Mediterranean and the Middle East. There Shah Ismail, head of the Safavid dynasty in Iran, was rebuilding the Persian Empire from his base in northwestern Iran. This led to invasions of Iraq, Syria, and the buffer zone between the Mameluk and Ottoman Empires. The Ottomans, meanwhile, had fought a series of wars with the Venetians, as a result of

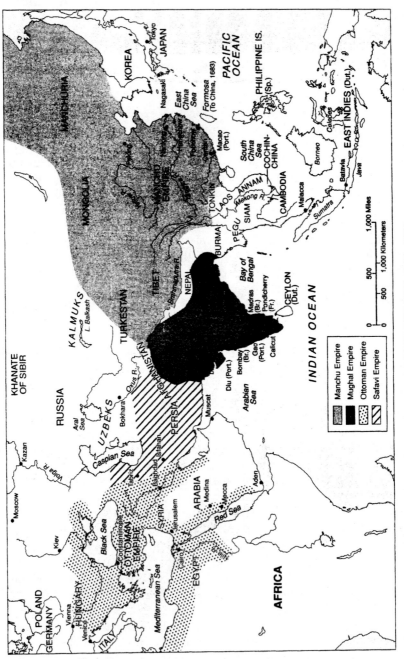

**MAP 5.1** *THE FOUR GREAT ASIAN EMPIRES OF THE PERIOD 1600–1700.*

which the Venetians had become dependent upon Ottoman good will. The Venetians, however, also depended on their relations with the Mameluk Empire, which controlled the flow of Asian spices into the Mediterranean. The Ottoman government, influenced by its own merchant community, was uneasy about possible alliances between either the Mameluks or the Venetians and Shah Ismail. The Turks were also attracted by the potential for profit implied by control of the trade in Asian commodities.

The appearance of Portuguese warships in the Indian Ocean aggravated this situation and gave the Ottomans a pretext for interfering in Mameluk affairs. In 1507 the Mameluks sent their fleet to intercept the Portuguese off the coast of India. The Portuguese were defeated in the first battle, but subsequently they caught the Mameluk fleet in a vulnerable situation and destroyed it. This allowed them to capture Hormuz in 1508, giving them control of the Persian Gulf. The Mameluks, however, defeated a Portuguese attack on Aden in 1513 with Ottoman help. As a result, the Portuguese never controlled the Red Sea as well as they wished.

As we will see later, Portuguese strategy in the Indian Ocean was often self defeating. They mixed commercial goals with religious ones carried over from their attempts to conquer and Christianize Morocco. Powerful individuals in the Lisbon of the 1400s and 1500s were committed to the idea of a crusade against Islam. They were attracted to the Indian Ocean by what they knew of the half mythical Christian Empire of Ethiopia, which they saw as a possible ally in the reconquest of Jerusalem. As a result, the Portuguese in the Indian Ocean exhibited an unbending hostility to the Muslims they encountered. This led the Portuguese to disrupt the Muslim pilgrim trade and to consider a campaign to conquer Mecca as a prelude to a Crusade that would free Jerusalem from Muslim rule.

The governments in Cairo and Constantinople were well informed of Portuguese actions, but the Mameluks were unable to rebuild their navy. This gave the Ottoman government an opening to intervene in Egyptian affairs. The ill-fated Mameluk fleet of 1507–1508 had been fitted out with Turkish help, and between 1508 and 1515 the Turks sent naval supplies, shipwrights, cannon founders, infantry, and a Turkish admiral to the Mameluk navy base on the Red Sea. By 1514 the Mameluk base was an Ottoman military enclave. At the same time, the Ottomans defeated Shah Ismail, driving him back into Iran and forcing him to turn his attention toward the Indian Ocean. This set the stage for the spectacular Turkish campaign of 1516–1517, when Sultan Selim annexed Syria, Iraq, the Holy Land, and Egypt to the Ottoman Empire.

Over the next 50 years the Turks maintained a strong sphere of influence in the Indian Ocean. Turkish merchants were as eager as European ones to profit from the trade between Asia and the Middle East. The Turks possessed a diplomatic advantage because they now protected the Caliph, Mecca, and the pilgrim traffic. Thus, while the Portuguese controlled Hormuz and access to the Persian Gulf, they could not completely monopolize trade along the coast between India and the Red Sea. The Turks, meanwhile, could use supply bases along the shoreline and developed an alliance with the merchant state of Gujerat on the coast of India. They also enjoyed good relations with other Muslim-ruled countries and in the 1530s and 1540s the Ottoman navy maintained 40 to 50 warships in the Indian Ocean.

Turkish anxiety about the Portuguese presence in the Indian Ocean was vindicated in 1542, when their expansion into the Indian Ocean had a setback similar to those at Vienna in 1529, Malta in 1565, and Lepanto in 1571. As they consolidated their power in the Red Sea, the Turks attempted to spread Islam into the Christian Ethiopian Empire. In alliance with one of the Muslim states on the African coast of the Red Sea, the Turks were sponsoring a war of conquest in Ethiopia. The Portuguese supported the Christian Ethiopian resistance, and in 1542 a Portuguese expedition arrived at Massawa on the Red Sea and turned the tide in favor of the Christian allies.

From time to time, however, Turkish power was projected even farther afield. In Southeast Asia the Portuguese continued to control Malacca, which dominated the straits between Sumatra and Malaya. In the middle of the 1500s, however, their monopoly was weakened by the Muslim state of Acheh, on the northern tip of Sumatra. With a respectable navy of its own, Acheh diluted Portuguese control of the straits and facilitated contraband with Bengal, Burma, and Madras on the east coast of India. In 1568 the Portuguese attempted to capture Acheh, only to discover that the local navy was supported by a powerful Turkish fleet. Thanks to effective intelligence, the Turks were able to dispatch the fleet in time, avoid Portuguese squadrons, and limit Portuguese power in Asian trade.

Thus, if the Portuguese were drawn into the Indian Ocean to create a commercial empire, so were the Turks. Despite Portuguese efforts to divert the spice trade to their route around Africa, by the 1530s the flow of Asian commodities through the hands of Indian Ocean merchants to Middle Eastern markets had returned to its normal proportions. In many areas the Portuguese exacted fees and tariffs, but the Turks maintained enough autonomous trade routes and markets to provide effective competition. Moreover, thanks to Turkish power in the Mediterranean, the Venetian "empire" there had become *de facto* the marketing agent through which Ottoman middlemen distributed Asian products in Europe. This led to an oversupply of exotic goods in Europe and eroded the profitability of the Portuguese spice trade. The Ottoman recapture of this Mediterranean–Middle Eastern market for Asian commodities was, in fact, one of the factors that contributed to corruption within the Portuguese system. While Portuguese officials and merchants provided cargoes for the ships of the *Estado do India* (the Portuguese State or Kingdom of India) bound for Lisbon, they also sold the same commodities to Asian merchants, evaded Portuguese taxes, and helped to keep open the traditional east-west routes through the Middle East. The effect was to vitiate the Lisbon monopoly and weaken the profits of the official trade to the benefit of corrupt or independent Portuguese in Asia.

## THE SAFAVID PRESENCE

The Turks, however, were not without competition within the Muslim Middle East. After the Ottomans defeated Shah Ismail in 1514, the Safavids withdrew from confrontation with Turkey and extended their authority south to the Persian Gulf and Indian Ocean. Shiite rather than Sunni Muslim, the Safavids looked for ways to undermine Ottoman influence. This laid the basis for contact between Persia and Portugal, and later between Persia and England. The tension between Portuguese and Ottoman interests in the region made it logical for the Safavids to deal with the Portuguese, who controlled Hormuz, located at the entrance to the Persian Gulf just off the coast of the Safavid Empire. (See Illustration 5.2.)

This opened another channel through which Asian spices could reach Europe. As soon as the Portuguese took Hormuz, the Safavids began to negotiate terms for importing Asian goods via that port. Initially this was a matter of supplying Persian markets, but when the Ottomans

**ILLUSTRATION 5.2**
*THE SHAH OF THE SAFAVID EMPIRE AT A RECEPTION.*
*This seventeenth-century Persian painting shows the Shah or Emperor of the Safavid Empire at a reception, with dancers providing entertainment.*
Source: Gulru Necipoglu, *Architecture, Ceremonial, and Power: The Topkapi Palace in the Fifteenth and Sixteenth Centuries* (Cambridge: MIT Press, 1991), illustration 139, p. 255. Seventeenth-century mural painting from the Chehel Sutun Palace in Isfahan.

seized the Persian Gulf port of Basra after 1517, the possibility of getting better terms for bringing goods into the Persian Gulf than the Portuguese would grant the Ottomans encouraged Safavid–Portuguese collaboration. Moreover, caravans had been carrying luxury goods across Asia and through Iran for over a thousand years. The sixteenth century saw the development of the increasingly powerful state of Muscovy, later known as the Russian Empire. By the second half of the sixteenth century, caravans loaded with Asian imports were making their way from Hormuz northward through the Safavid Empire to the Caspian Sea. From there they travelled by boat to Russia and reached the Baltic along routes developed by the Scandinavians centuries before.

Indeed, this development inspired an improbable attempt by the English to circumvent Portuguese, Turkish, and Venetian control of the spice trade during the reign of Elizabeth I (1558–1603). The English position was weak. They could not confront Spain and Portugal militarily in the Atlantic and lacked the capital to mount the large fleets that had a hope of getting through. Aware that Muscovy traded with Persia, a group of Englishmen created the Muscovy Company. This company fitted out ships that sailed around Scandinavia to Archangel on the White Sea in hopes of obtaining goods from Asia. The quantity of Asian goods that reached England by this route was small, but it represented an element of the east–west trade that evaded both Portuguese and Turkish control.

## THE RISE OF THE MUGHAL EMPIRE IN INDIA

As Ottoman and Safavid power shaped affairs in the western part of the Indian Ocean in the first half of the 1500s, the situation in India changed even more dramatically. India entered the 1500s as a mosaic of independent countries, most of them with Hindu populations and many of them with Muslim ruling classes. The two largest entities were both inland states: the Hindu Vijayanagara Kingdom in the south and the Muslim Sultanate of Delhi in the Ganges valley in the north.

In 1526 India was invaded in one of last of the imperial takeovers by mobile military elites derived from the nomadic migrations out of central Asia. Known as the Mughals, this tribe had ruled a small kingdom in central Asia during the 1400s. In the early 1500s they were forced out of their kingdom and were using the area around Kabul in Afghanistan as a base from which to fight back. Under their leader Babur, they began to raid northern India and, in 1526, Babur led a full-scale army into the Sultanate of Delhi. Using modern musketry and artillery, Babur defeated two much larger armies and established the Mughal Empire, with its capital at Agra, near modern Delhi. After a period of instability, Babur's grandson Akbar took control in 1560 (at age 17) and proved a political genius of the first rank. Akbar reorganized the government, drew prominent Hindus into his administration, and set up a system of semi-military local government similar to that of the Ottoman Empire. He also encouraged compromises that eased the tension between Muslim and Hindu factions. (See Readings 5.1 and 5.2.)

---

READING 5.1

*The political and religious attitudes of the earlier Muslim Sultans of Delhi are seen in the reign of Firuz Shah (1351–1389). Firuz Shah presents himself in his autobiography as a thoughtful and benevolent ruler, but this did not include our idea of tolerance. The modern tension between Hindus and Muslims in India clearly has very old roots.*

In the reigns of former kings the blood of many Musulmans had been shed, and many varieties of torture employed. . . . Through the mercy which God has shown to me these verities and terrors have been exchanged for tenderness, kindness, and mercy. . . . By God's help I determined that the lives of Musulmans and true believers should be in perfect immunity, and whoever transgressed the Law should receive the punishment prescribed by the Book and the degrees of judges. . . . The sect of *Shi'as* . . . had endeavored to make proselytes. . . . I seized them all and I convicted them of the errors and perversions . . . . There was in Delhi a man named Tukn-ud-din, who was called Mahdi, because he affirmed himself to be the Imam Mahdi who is to appear in the latter days, and to be possessed of knowledge by inspiration. . . . When he was brought before me I investigated the charges of error and perversion brought against him, and he was convicted of heresy and error. . . . I ordered that this vile fellow's rebellion and wickedness should be communicated to all societies of learned men, and be made public . . . and that the guilty should be brought to punishment. They killed him with some of his supporters and disciples, and the people rushing in tore him to pieces and broke his bones into fragments.

The Hindus and idol-worshippers . . . now erected new idol temples in the city and the environs in opposition to the Law of the Prophet which declares that such temples are not to be tolerated. Under Divine guidance I destroyed these edifices, and I killed those leaders of infidelity who seduced others into error. . . .

From William McNeill and Jean Sedlar, *China, India, and Japan: The Middle Period* (New York: Oxford University Press, 1971), pp. 154–157.

---

Under Emperor Akbar (1556–1605) the Mughal Empire became a formidable military power and a major factor in the Asian economy. In its first decades the Empire had no maritime outlet, but by 1576 Akbar had conquered both the Gujerat on India's west coast and Bengal on India's east coast, giving the Mughal Empire access to the sea on both sides of the subcontinent. While at one point in the 1650s the Mughal Emperor Shahjahan owned a fleet of large merchant ships that operated from the Gujarati port of Surat, the Mughal empire generally left maritime trade in private hands. As did the Ottomans, the Mughals incorporated mercantile societies like the Gujeratis into their empire. (See Map 5.2.) The Mughals managed the maritime interests of their empire by allowing merchants from all countries to trade in Indian ports and by playing off the European and Asian maritime powers operating in the area against each other. The Empire's high card in this game was the vast and wealthy Indian market. It was also a source of sophisticated exports much in demand in China, the Middle East, and Europe, especially a wide variety of cotton textiles. None of the Asian or European merchant communities in the

## READING 5.2

*The Mughal Empire was consolidated by the Emperor Akbar in the second half of the 1500s. Although he was a Muslim, consolidation rested on Akbar's willingness to practice toleration of other religious sects, a policy that ran against the traditional hostility to non-Muslims that had characterized the preceding Sultanate of Delhi. The following is excerpted from a history of Akbar's reign by a Muslim historian of the era (he lived 1540–1615) who was hostile to the policy of toleration.*

Crowds of learned men from all nations, and sages of various religions and sects came to the Court, and were honored with private conversations. . . . Everything that pleased [Akbar], he picked and chose from any one except a Moslem, and anything that was against his disposition, and ran counter to his wishes he thought fit to reject and cast aside. . . . and by a peculiar acquisitiveness and a talent for selection, by no means common, [he] made his own all that can be seen and read in books.

. . . Learned monks also from Europe, who are called Padre, and have an infallible head, called Papa [the Roman Catholic Pope], who is able to change religious ordinances as he may deem advisable for the moment, and to whose authority kings must submit, brought the Gospel, and advanced proofs for the Trinity. His Majesty firmly believed in the truth of the Christian religion, and wishing to spread the doctrines of Jesus, ordered Prince Murad to take a few lessons in Christianity under good auspices, and charged Abu-l-Fazl to translate the Gospel. . . .

Fire-worshippers also came from Nousari in Gujrat, and proclaimed the religion of Zardusht [Zoroastrianism]. . . . They also attracted the Emperor's regard. . . . Every precept which was enjoined by the doctors of other religions he treated as manifest and decisive, in contradistinction to this Religion of ours, all the doctrines of which he set down to be senseless, and of modern origin, and the founders of it as nothing but poor Arabs. . . .

---

Excerpted from Al-Badaoni, *Muntakhabu-T-Tawarikh*, trans. W. H. Lowe (New York: Reed, 1973), no page given, as presented in Schwartz, Wimmer, and Wolff, *The Global Experience*, Vol. II, pp. 57–59.

Indian Ocean dared challenge Mughal authority, and all were required to trade with India on the terms established by the Mughal government.

Akbar is an interesting figure for many historians. He apparently never learned to read, but was very interested in learning and religion. This interest meant that several Jesuits were able to visit the Mughal court, where they sought to convert Akbar to Christianity. Akbar, however, debated religion not only with Christians, but with Muslim theologians, Hindus, Jainists, Parsis (Zoroastrians), and Sikhs. He developed a personal religion, *Din-I-Ilahi* or "Divine Faith," which was derived from Islam's mystical Sufi side, and from similar elements in the other religions he studied. Despite an obvious evolution in his religious beliefs, the Jesuits were disappointed that Akbar never seriously considered the conversion they hoped for, while his successors were much more orthodox in their Muslim beliefs and policies.

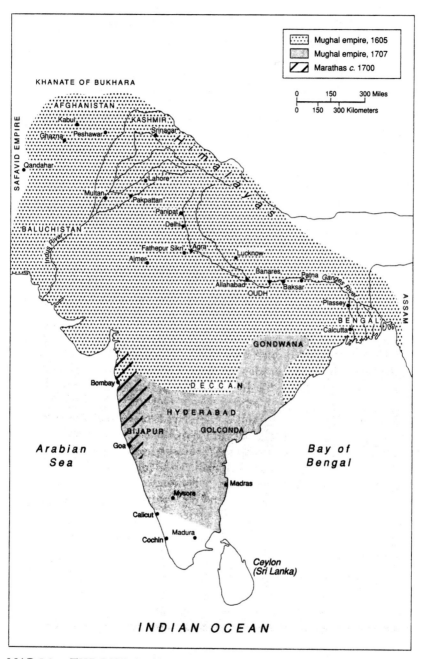

**MAP 5.2**   *THE RISE OF THE MUGHAL EMPIRE TO ITS HEIGHT IN 1707.*

As the Mughal Empire became better organized and prosperous, the cities of northern India constituted a growing market for Indian Ocean commodities. This made the Gujerat strategically important since, in addition to fostering the east–west trade and pilgrim traffic of the Indian Ocean, its merchants profited from the growing import–export trade of a prosperous Mughal Empire. At the same time, Akbar's conquest of Bengal opened the Ganges River as a route for Indonesian spices and Chinese manufactures entering Asia on the way to Persia, Russia, and Europe. Large boats could sail hundreds of miles up the Ganges toward Delhi and the internal markets of India. This explains why, as we will see, the Bay of Bengal attracted many Portuguese. As part of the attempt to control long-distance trade in the Indian Ocean, the *Estado do India* defined several official trade routes (*carreiras*) in the Bay of Bengal, and contracted with merchants to service them in the King's name. While much of the trade into the Bay was seeking markets in Burma and India, Akbar also encouraged overland transit trade. Asian products thus made their way up the Ganges, then travelled by caravan through Afghanistan and Persia to the Caspian Sea. There Indian overland trade joined with the caravan routes to the Mediterranean and Eastern Europe. This created yet another intercontinental route for Asian spices that competed with the Portuguese attempt to create a monopoly based on their route around Africa. By the late 1500s the Eurasian spice trade was operating along a vast network of routes that connected Europe with Asia. These routes were mediated not only by the Portuguese, but by the Ottoman, Safavid, and Mughal Empires.

Interestingly, much of this overland trade was actually organized by an ethnically based trade diaspora of the sort seen in other settings. In this case, Christian Armenians from the Caucasus area between the Black Sea and the Caspian Sea provided the organization for this far-flung commercial network. Armenian merchant communities were found in market towns in India, Afghanistan, Iran, and the Ottoman Empire and provided a network of common commercial understandings from Delhi to Constantinople and Moscow. Safavid rulers encouraged this development, creating caravan routes and caravanseries (government inns) on routes from Hormuz to the Caspian Sea and from India to the Ottoman frontier.

Without a doubt, the rise of the Mughal Empire was the most important development in the Indian Ocean between 1500 and 1700. Akbar and his successors ruled an Empire that stretched two thousand miles across northern India from Iran to Burma. Indian merchants dealt with traders from all over the Indian Ocean and with the Portuguese, French, Dutch, and English. The Empire reached its greatest extent under the Emperor Aurangzeb (1658–1707), when its armies moved south and conquered the various Muslim Sultanates and the large Hindu Vijayanagara Kingdom.

These conquests were costly and proved hard to control. Although these wars extended Mughal power a thousand miles to the south and established Mughal authority over the coastal states of south India, they also undermined the prosperity of the Mughal government. At the same time, Aurangzeb greatly intensified Muslim persecution of the Hindu population and forced non-Muslims out of government offices. War and persecution of the Hindu population contributed to religious dissent and a decentralization of power inside the empire that left it vulnerable when confronted by English and French expansion in the mid–1700s.

Whatever the problems of the later Mughal Empire, however, Babur, Akbar, and Aurangzeb were world-class rulers. Their empire was the political and economic center of the Indian Ocean for two centuries after 1526, and they set the framework for later Indian history. We think of modern India as the creation of the British Empire, but the boundaries used by the British were the heritage of the Mughal Emperors who shaped British perception of what we now call India.

## EUROPEAN PARTICIPATION IN THE INDIAN OCEAN REGION

On May 20, 1498, three weather-beaten and (to Indian eyes) odd looking ships appeared at Calicut, the seaport for a small but prosperous sultanate on the western coast of India. The ships were not particularly large, but had heavy, rounded plank hulls and high superstructures. Their sides had square windows, from which protruded cannon. The cannon were similar to ones used in India, but for Indians it was unusual to find them mounted on ships. The ships had sternpost rudders similar to those used in China and the Indian Ocean, but their three-masted rigging and square sails were unfamiliar to the locals. The ships were battered, undermanned, and dirty. Commanded by the Portuguese navigator Vasco da Gama, these ships had just finished a 9,500-mile voyage that had started in Lisbon, Portugal, ten months before. (See Illustration 5.3.)

Da Gama's voyage was the product of a gradual expansion of Portuguese objectives in the later 1400s. Although in the 1480s King João at first sought to consolidate Portugal's Afro–Atlantic position, exploratory voyages continued to probe down the African coast. They were motivated by the dual goals of expanding trade and the search for a way to outflank the Muslims of North Africa. Meanwhile, legends of a Christian empire in Africa (Ethiopia) and wildly optimistic estimates of how far away it was, prompted the king to sponsor the voyage of Bartolomeu Diaz. By May 1488, Diaz had confirmed the existence of a route around Africa, while other Portuguese agents were sent to the Indian Ocean via the Middle East. Following complicated political maneuvering in Portugal, da Gama was chosen to command the first fleet destined to reach India from Europe.

Da Gama rounded the Cape of Good Hope in November of 1497 and worked his way up the African coast. Interested both in trade and in

**ILLUSTRATION 5.3**
*VASCO DA GAMA IN 1524.*
*The first Portuguese commander to reach India, Vasco da Gama returned as Viceroy at the end of his life. This picture was painted in Goa in 1524 shortly before his death.*

Source: Postcard citing the picture as "D. Vasco da Gama, Almirante dos Mares da India e Conde da Vidigueira, 2o Vice-Rei da India, em 1524, faleceu neste mesmo ano, em Goa." Edicao da Museu de Marinha, Lisbon, Portugal.

finding Christians, the Portuguese made something of a nuisance of themselves. The European merchandise they had to offer was crude and inappropriate for tropical markets. Desperate for supplies and bent on getting to India, da Gama and his men employed rather blunt tactics by regional standards. Their first contact with the Indian Ocean trading system was in Mozambique and ended in a three-hour artillery battle, during which an Arab merchant ship was run aground. Da Gama reached Mombassa in early April of 1498, where he precipitated another shootout. The Portuguese then sailed into Malindi, seizing an unarmed Arab ship on the way. When the ruler of Malindi sent an ambassador to da Gama's ship, da Gama promptly held him as a hostage until local authorities provided a pilot to show the Portuguese the route from Africa to India. The spring trade winds then took the Portuguese to Calicut, an Indian city that was an entrepôt for merchandise moving between southeast Asia and the Middle East. After three months of behavior that taxed the patience of the authorities in Calicut, da Gama had refitted his ships, obtained a modest cargo of pepper and spices, and set sail for home. (See Reading 5.3.) Modest though it was, in Europe that cargo paid the entire cost of the expedition and produced a huge profit. The whole episode also created an atmosphere of suspicion and antagonism that shaped subsequent Portuguese tactics. The sigh of relief breathed in Calicut, Mombassa, Malindi, and Kilwa as the Portuguese ships departed was destined to be short-lived.

---

## READING 5.3

*When Vasco da Gama returned from India in 1499, the King of Portugal wrote to Ferdinand and Isabella of Aragon and Castile to give them the news. After observing the meager returns of Columbus' first two or three ventures, King Manuel I can be forgiven the somewhat smug tone of the message. It also conveys a hint of the contradictory nature of Portuguese commercial and religious objectives.*

Most high and excellent Prince and Princess, most potent Lord and Lady!

Your highnesses already know that we had ordered Vasco da Gama, a nobleman of our household, and his brother Paulo da Gama, with four vessels to make discoveries by sea, and that two years have now elapsed since their departure. . . . From a message which has now been brought to this city by one of the captains, we learn that they did reach and discover India and other kingdoms and lordships bordering upon it; that they entered and navigated its sea, finding large cities, large edifices and rivers, and great populations among whom is carried on all the trade in spices and precious stones, which are forwarded in ships (which these same explorers saw and met in good numbers and of great size) to Mecca, and thence to Cairo, whence they are dispersed throughout the world. Of these [spices, etc.] they have brought a quantity including cinnamon, cloves, ginger, nutmeg, and pepper, as well as other kinds, together with the boughs and leaves of the same; also many fine stones of all sorts, such as rubies and others. And they also came to a country in which there are mines of gold, of which [gold], as of the spices and precious stones, they did not bring as much as they could have done, for they took no merchandise with them. . . . [And when the local population] shall have been converted . . . and fortified in the faith, there will be an opportunity for destroying the Moors [Muslims] of those parts. . . .

---

Found in E. G. Ravenstein (ed. and trans.), (London: Hakluyt Society, 1898), pp. 77–79, as presented in Marvin Lunenfeld (ed.), *1492: Discovery, Invasion, Encounter* (Lexington, Mass.: D. C. Heath, 1991), pp. 21–22.

Two years later the Portuguese showed up in the Indian Ocean again, this time with thirteen armed ships and a thousand men. In the next several years a series of Portuguese fleets arrived under the command of Viceroys Francisco de Almeida and Afonso de Albuquerque. The Portuguese quickly learned the structure of Indian Ocean trade, discovered the choke points in that trade, and developed a plan to monopolize its most profitable component, the spice trade. Initially they sought to divert European-bound spices to their route around Africa, thus moving the European spice trade from Cairo and Venice to Lisbon and Antwerp. To succeed, however, they also had to control the spice trade that supplied Middle Eastern markets and, if possible, to control production in Sri Lanka and Indonesia. This meant establishing a sphere of influence that reached across the 10,000 miles of the Indian Ocean. This proved to be a precarious enterprise when based on the resources of a poor European country with less than a million inhabitants, most of whom were farmers. It is doubtful that the Portuguese ever had more than 10,000 to 15,000 men and two dozen war ships in the Indian Ocean at any one time.

Albuquerque's strategy was designed to control the main transfer points for long-distance trade across the Indian Ocean and to create a royal monopoly over that trade. To do so, he laid the foundations for what the Portuguese called the *Estado do India* (State of India), a new kingdom directly under the authority of the King of Portugal. Albuquerque and his predecessors occupied and fortified Kilwa on the African coast and in 1508 captured Hormuz, which controlled the Persian Gulf. To control trade around the tip of India, he captured the Indian port of Goa in 1510 and made it Portugal's Asian capital. Albuquerque went on to capture Malacca (near modern Singapore) in 1511, giving him control of the Sumatra straits and trade between the Pacific and Indian Oceans. The system was extended to its logical extreme with the capture of Ternate in the spice islands. With very limited resources, the Portuguese had laid claim to the right to regulate long-distance trade from Africa to Indonesia.

The perennial question raised about this spectacular bit of expansion is simply "What made it possible?" A part of the answer is similar to the answer to the same question in Spanish America. The Europeans who arrived in the Indian Ocean were ruthless risk-takers with little to lose. They were thousands of miles from home, in a foreign environment. They had limited resources and no backup. Over and over again their best tactic was to move quickly, throw their opponents off guard, and consolidate gains with strong defensive positions.

As we will see, this did not get them far in well-organized countries like the Ottoman Empire, Safavid Persia, Mughal India, Ming China, and unified Japan. But it did give them a way into the complex, interdependent world of the Indian Ocean. Their resources, often no more than eight or ten ships and a few hundred men, were no match against a large kingdom. In the vast Indian Ocean, however, they easily found small countries with military resources on the same scale as their own. They located internal factions, used their military reserves in tactically effective ways, and inserted themselves as the ruling group in small places. They then knit these distant strongholds into a militarized trade diaspora that reflects European experience in the medieval Mediterranean and in the African–Atlantic world.

This is well illustrated by their experience on the coast of east Africa. There, to their surprise, the Portuguese found a string of city-states with sophisticated governments, stone-built cities comparable to their own, and a rich and varied commercial economy. Each port city, however, was the center of a small and jealously independent sultanate with correspondingly small military resources. In that context the Portuguese fleets were formidable and they were able to seize and fortify several east African ports.

The Portuguese also had a tactical advantage based on the capabilities of their warships. The use of sails instead of oars was combined with a heavy, rigid hull construction that allowed gun ports between the ribs of the ship. This made it possible for the Portuguese to mount several cannon on each ship. Such ships were very effective negotiating tools in seaports unprepared for seaborne artillery attacks. These ships were also effective against the galleys of the Mameluk and Ottoman navies, although the advantage was not as great as often asserted. In open sea the galleys remained formidable, and they carried powerful bow-chaser cannon. They could not stay at sea for long periods, however, and the Portuguese learned to attack seaports while the galleys were at distant bases. They also tried to catch the galleys inside harbors, where they could close the entrance and use artillery to destroy the enemy at a distance. The Portuguese won some key early battles against galley fleets, but over the long run they lost as many battles as they won.

Some historians attribute European success to the superiority of European cannon. In fact, artillery was known and used throughout Asia, and many oar-propelled galleys carried cannon. One of the ironies of Portuguese expansion is that when, in 1511, Albuquerque was short of men for the fleet he was sending to Malacca, he solved the problem by hiring Indian gunners for his artillery. By the seventeenth century, confronted with this situation, the shipbuilders of the Gujerat in India were building armed European-style frigates to guard the pilgrim fleets, frigates that were treated with respect by Portuguese and English sea captains.

Thus the secret of the Europeans' initial success was partly in their desperate aggressiveness, partly in the exploitation of a different naval technology, and partly in the availability of local governments too weak to resist. Moreover, the maritime traditions of the Indian Ocean led local authorities to assume that visitors were interested in mutually profitable trade. As we have seen, however, it is one thing to conquer, it is another to maintain authority over the long term. Here the Portuguese record is problematic and assertions about their "success" depend upon how you define the term.

While Goa remained the center of Portuguese authority in Asia, its influence as a center of power within India was limited by religious prejudices. Portuguese authorities were consistently suspicious of and hostile toward the Muslim elites that they met in India. They also persecuted the Christian communities already in India when they arrived. The Portuguese found large numbers of St. Thomas Christians in India, a sect supposedly founded by the Apostle Thomas in the early days of Christianity. Rather than finding a common ground with these fellow Christians, the Portuguese set up the Inquisition in Goa and began to try them for heresy.

The political and commercial "empire" that the Portuguese built in Asia evolved three or four components that often were at odds with each other. The initial enterprise was sponsored by powerful merchants and aristocrats close to the throne. Their twin goals were monopoly control of the spices reaching Europe, and military and political offices in the new empire that would bring status, wealth, and patronage to the families involved. As the empire evolved, Goa became a second Portuguese capital that was the stronghold for this court-based imperial elite. Based on a spice trade controlled by royal officials, with cargoes travelling in huge carracks owned by the crown, this phase of expansion was dominated by the King and his aristocratic cronies. The affairs of the *Estado do India* were also complicated by political tensions in Lisbon between those who sought commercial profit and advocates of the Portuguese tradition of an anti-Muslim crusade. This form of expansion shaped Portuguese affairs in the area between India and Africa, but was less effective farther east.

As the Portuguese reached into Indonesia, they set up strongholds in Malacca, at Colombo in Sri Lanka, and at Ternate in the spice islands. The governors of these posts reported to the Viceroy in Goa, and the crown aspired to control their trade as well. As time went on, however, the crown was unable to maintain an adequate supply of its own cargo vessels. Meanwhile, Portuguese merchants found new sources of profit in servicing the growing trade between various Indian Ocean countries. Finally, as the merchant community in Lisbon grew, new merchants wanted to break the narrow royal monopoly on trade with India.

As a result, more and more Portuguese arrived in Asia and broke away from the authority of the Portuguese crown. At the same time, with royal ships scarce, Portuguese authorities in the eastern Indian Ocean and Indonesia developed a system of royal contracts, or *carreiras*, that chartered private ship owners to carry "royal" commerce between specified trading centers. Officially these contractors were part of the regulated trade otherwise carried aboard the King's ships, and their vessels carried royal agents, but such contracts became a cover for widespread contraband. Many of these contractors were Portuguese ship owners who were learning how to avoid royal control and taxes, and a substantial number were Chinese, Indonesian, or Indian merchants and ship owners.

Alongside the system of contracted trade routes, the Portuguese developed the *cartaz*, or shipping license. Local governors sold licenses to merchants of all sorts, authorizing them to trade between parts of Asia.

As early as 1510 this system was used at Hormuz, where the Portuguese controlled access to the Persian Gulf. In practical terms it was a protection racket, since the license only had value if a Portuguese warship turned up to give substance to the penalties that they threatened to impose on ships sailing without a license. By the second half of the 1500s this system of control leaked like a sieve. Although the part of the *Estado do India* between Africa and Goa remained profitable, the system between Goa and Indonesia was so corrupt that it cost more to maintain than the crown collected in revenue and profit.

A third component of this haphazard Portuguese expansion escaped royal control altogether, but fed the growing corruption of the official structure. Hundreds of Portuguese went to the *Estado do India* and then left its jurisdiction altogether. They settled in ports all over Africa and Asia, learned the local languages, married local wives, and on many occasions converted to Islam, the dominant religion of long-distance trade. These people were thus assimilated to the trading communities of the Indian Ocean, not as agents of an imperial power, but as yet another of the many groups of "outsiders" who had knit together the system of Indian Ocean interdependence. (See Reading 5.4.)

The Portuguese "empire" in the Indian Ocean thus became a complex, loose-jointed entity. It diverted a certain amount of monopoly profit from spices to the Portuguese elite. It collected a certain amount of revenue and tribute that it redistributed to royal officials and favorites. At the political level, royal diplomacy rarely aspired to control Indian Ocean states directly, except in a few fortified seaports. As with the Chinese a century earlier, most treaties with Indian Ocean rulers brought the Portuguese king token amounts of tribute. This allowed the king to present himself in Europe as the nominal sovereign over many African and Asian potentates, a claim that had little substance in the Indian Ocean itself. The Portuguese "empire" also inserted European trade practices and ship technology into the Asian world. Initially the Portuguese impact on regional trade was disruptive, and into the early 1530s royal revenue from regulated commerce was substantial. Within 20 years of the seizure of Goa and Malacca, however, Indian Ocean trade looked a great deal like it had before the Portuguese arrived.

In practice, the only thing that kept the *Estado do India* afloat financially in the later 1500s was the special niche it developed in trade between India, China, and Japan. As we will see in the next chapter, the Portuguese developed formal trade with both Japan and China in the 1540s and 1550s. Europe had few goods that interested these markets and the mainstay of that part of Portuguese trade was the security offered by the King's huge armed carracks. These ships brought silver from Europe, via Goa, to China, along with Asian spices. They also profited from carrying Japanese silver and copper to China. This trade was extremely profitable for the Portuguese Crown and helped to keep the *Estado do India* in Goa from becoming a financial drain on the government in Lisbon. This changed quickly with the arrival of the Dutch and the expulsion of the Portuguese from Japan.

## READING 5.4

*Both the limits of Portuguese control in the Indian Ocean, which echo the situation in the Kongo, and the scope of the Jesuit project in Asia are captured in the following passage. It is from a letter from India to Rome written by Saint Francis Xavier in about 1549.*

... In the first place, the whole race of the Indians, as far as I have been able to see, is very barbarous; and it does not like to listen to anything that is not agreeable to its own manners and customs, which, as I say, are barbarous. It troubles itself very little to learn anything about divine things and things which concern salvation. Most of the Indians are of vicious disposition, and are adverse to virtue. ... We have hard work here, both in keeping the Christians up the mark and in converting the heathen. ... You know very well what a hard business it is to teach people who neither have any knowledge of God nor follow reason, but think it a strange and intolerable thing to be told to give up their habits of sin, which have now gained all the force of nature by long possession. ...

The experience which I have of these countries makes me think that I can affirm with truth, that there is no prospect of perpetuating our Society out here by means of the natives themselves, ... so that it is quite necessary that continual supplies of ours should be sent out from Europe. We have now some of the Society in all parts of India where there are Christians. Four are in the Moluccas, two at Malacca, six in the Comorin Promontory, two at Coulan, as many at Bazain, four at Socotra. The distances between these places are immense; for instance the Moluccas are more than a thousand leagues [4,000 miles] from Goa, Malacca five hundred [2,000 miles] ....

The Portuguese in these countries are masters only of the sea and of the coast. On the mainland they have only the towns in which they live. The natives themselves are so enormously addicted to vice as to be little adapted to receive the Christian religion. ... Certainly, if the Portuguese were more remarkable for their kindness to the new converts, a great number would become Christians; as it is, the heathen see that the converts are despised and looked down upon by the Portuguese, and so, as is natural, they are unwilling to become converts themselves. ...

---

Excerpted from selection in Kevin Reilly (ed.), *Readings in World Civilizations*, Vol. 2, *The Development of the Modern World* (New York: St. Martin's Press, 1995), pp. 65–66.

By the end of the 1500s the Indian Ocean world that the Portuguese had found in 1497 had changed substantially, and the changes were even more pronounced after 1600. Soon after 1600 the Portuguese lost control of the Japanese silver trade, which had subsidized the *Estado do India* in Goa. In 1612 the expanding Kingdom of Burma captured the Portuguese port of Syriam, a key link in the booming trade between Southeast Asia and the Mughal Empire. In 1622 the situation worsened when the Safavid Empire conquered Hormuz from the Portuguese with English help. This did not eliminate the Portuguese from the Persian Gulf, but it allowed the Safavids to increase their role in Indian Ocean trade. The Portuguese were further weakened when their port on the south side of the Persian Gulf was seized by the Shah of Oman.

The last event highlights the rise of a strong regional state at the mouth of the Persian Gulf, the Sultanate of Oman. Aside from Portuguese loss of control in the Gulf, this development was important for their position in east Africa. Oman had historic cultural and commercial ties with east Africa, and supported the east African states in a campaign against Portugal. This project was finished in 1698, when the Portuguese were evicted from their key fort in Mombasa, leaving them without a single base in east Africa north of Mozambique.

European history texts usually explain the decline of Portuguese power by saying that the Dutch and English were more effective competitors, and they are not entirely wrong. Nevertheless, the decline of the Portuguese "empire" was equally the result of action by emerging Asian states such as Japan, Burma, Mughal India, Safavid Persia, the Sultanate of Oman, and the Ottoman Empire. Ironically, the long-term survival of a Portuguese presence in Asia was due to the degree to which they had assimilated to Asia and had become useful to local elites. As of 1700, Asia was still more important to Europe than Europe was to Asia.

## GLOBALIZING THE CROSSROADS: INTIMATIONS OF EUROPEAN IMPERIALISM

### ENTER THE ENGLISH

The next chapter in the evolution of the Indian Ocean as a world crossroads was contributed by the Dutch and the English. From an Asian perspective this simply involved more Europeans, some with better guns, some with better merchandise, and some with better manners. It also offered Indian Ocean countries the opportunity to play potential enemies against each other. Unlike the Portuguese, and perhaps because the Portuguese were already entrenched in some areas, the Dutch and English approached the Indian Ocean and Indonesia in distinctive ways. The Dutch concentrated on Indonesia and the spice trade, the English on India and the quality handicrafts and textiles manufactured there.

Of the two, the English had the smaller impact before 1680, even though later they became the most important European power in the region. England was a secondary part of the European economy well into the 1600s, and English entrepreneurs were in no position even to speculate about direct trade in Asian products until Elizabeth I (1558–1603). Before then, English trade consisted primarily of selling raw wool and rough cloth to the Netherlands in return for manufactures and luxuries. Those luxuries obviously included Asian products brought to Europe by the Portuguese and distributed from Antwerp. Until late in the 1500s the English lacked the resources to challenge Spanish and Portuguese control of the Atlantic. This explains their improbable attempt to connect with Asia via Russia and the Muscovy Company beginning in the 1550s. Because they were not major players in the international trade of the 1500s, few Englishmen had been involved in Asian expansion and thus England had little accurate information about Asia. As an underdeveloped country, England had little that it could trade for Asian goods and limited ability to acquire the silver demanded by Asian economies.

The English fitted out two or three small Indian Ocean ventures in the 1590s, one of which disappeared without a trace. These expeditions followed the Portuguese track around the Cape of Good Hope to India. They managed to evade Portuguese ships and arrived at the Mughal port of Surat on the Gujerat coast, well north of Portuguese Goa. There they operated as freelance traders, minded their manners, and acquired a modest cargo. Their good behavior reflected in part the military weakness of a small commercial venture. They succeeded in part simply because the Mughals wanted them to. Surat was by then part of the Mughal Empire. The Mughals did business with the Portuguese, along with other trading communities, but resented their hostility to Islam and their relations with the Safavid Empire. At the same time, the Turkish presence in the region had declined. As Europeans, the English were not particularly welcome, but as English they offered the Mughal Emperor a foil against the Portuguese.

Attracted by the prospect of large profits, in 1600 an English syndicate pulled together several small ventures and obtained a charter for the first English East India Company. A modest enterprise compared to what it later became, the first East India Company was chartered for only a few years. It raised enough capital to send modest fleets to India, and paid handsome profits. During the first half of the 1600s the English chartered a series of these short-lived companies. They traded with India on a regular basis, but did not create a permanent base there. They established resident agents, first at Surat and, after 1639, in Madras on India's east coast, but it was not practical for an enterprise that periodically liquidated its assets and returned them to stockholders to maintain large permanent forts and warehouses. The English East India Company also obtained privileges at Hormuz from the Safavid Empire and developed connections in the Bay of Bengal, where Portuguese control had been weakened by Mughal and Burman power. Thus the first English expansion to Asia was based on their willingness to operate within established Asian trading structures and on their ability to find regions where Asian governments had neutralized Portuguese influence.

This began to change in the 1650s. In the wake of the English Civil War (1642–1649), England rapidly developed an aggressive commercial policy and a more sophisticated commercial elite. The East India Company was reorganized and capitalized on a much larger scale. Its new charter resembled that of a modern corporation and gave the Company an indefinite life span. Its scale of operations expanded as the reorganized Company developed a bureaucracy and accounting office in London and permanent facilities in India. In 1661 the Mughal Emperor granted them a permanent base at Bombay, and in 1690 the Company got the same privilege in Calcutta. By this time the English economy was extremely dynamic. Thanks to its plantation colonies in the Caribbean, the English had large amounts of sugar and tobacco that they could sell in Europe to pay for the American silver they needed to trade in India.

While the English did import spices, their main Asian imports were textiles. The demand for Indian textiles represented one of the first important departures in the structure of Indian Ocean commerce. English demand became so strong that, for the first time, an important regional economy in the Indian Ocean came to depend upon unbroken trade with European markets and on a trade system controlled by Europeans. Hundreds of Indian villages specialized in the production of textiles for export in quantities far greater than could ever be sold within the Indian Ocean economy. Whole regions now depended on earnings generated by exports to Europe in order to buy their food and other essentials. Thanks to English commerce, the interdependence that long defined the Indian Ocean as a region had been transcended. Until the emergence of this situation, Asian exports to Europe were not large enough or specialized enough to create this kind of dependence.

At the same time, unlike the Portuguese, the English East India Company encouraged the development of a private English commercial community and merchant marine in Asian waters. Thus, while the Company's own ships concentrated on the trade between India and England, English merchants and shippers played a growing part in the transport of goods between different Asian countries. Whereas Portuguese authorities considered it illegal for their agents to do business outside the official monopoly, the English East India Company encouraged it. As a result, some parts of the intra-Asian trade were dominated by the English as early as 1700. (See Map 5.3.) The situation was not yet obvious, but in subsequent decades it made more and more of Asia vulnerable to decisions made in Europe, by people uninterested in the overseas impact of those decisions.

## AND THE DUTCH

The Dutch also arrived around 1600, and had a much greater initial impact. It was only around 1700 that Dutch influence declined as it succumbed to the same factors as had Portuguese power a century earlier. This decline after about 1670 was, in the European context, the counterpart to the growing power of England.

Compared with the English, the Dutch were economically powerful and commercially sophisticated by 1600. With their independence from Spain, which was declared in the 1560s, the Dutch had captured the central role in European trade that Antwerp had held in the 1400s and early 1500s, and they were eager to become Europe's clearing house for Asian imports. The fact that the Dutch had been under Spanish rule and were already deeply involved in long-distance commerce meant that, unlike the English, they began overseas expansion with a great deal of practical expertise.

Until Dutch independence, Antwerp had been the major seaport of the Low Countries and the Portuguese had used Antwerp as the clearinghouse for marketing their spices to the rest of Europe. During the Dutch War of Independence, Antwerp was cut off from overseas trade and many

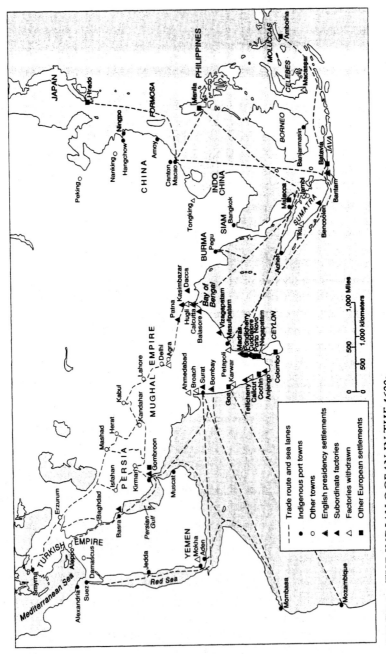

**MAP 5.3   THE INDIAN OCEAN IN THE 1600s.**
*This map shows maritime and overland trade routes, main cities, and European settlements. Although Europeans were established in Asian and Indian Ocean trade, in 1700 they were only beginning to dominate parts of the system.*

Within the map:

JAPAN
Mt. Hirado
Ningpo
Nanking
Hangchow
Amoy
Peking
CHINA
Canton
Macao
FORMOSA
PHILIPPINES
Manila
MOLUCCAS
Amboina
CELEBES
Macassar
BORNEO
Banjarmasin
JAVA
Batavia
Bantam
INDO CHINA
Tongking
SIAM
Bangkok
Pegu
BURMA
Bay of Bengal
Malacca
SUMATRA
Jambi
Achin
Bencoolen
Patna
Kasimbazar
Dacca
Hugli
Calcutta
Balasore
Vizagapatam
Masulipatam
Madras
Pondicherry
Cuddalore
Porto Novo
Negapatam
CEYLON
Colombo
Petapoli
Karwar
Tellicherry
Calicut
Cochin
Anjengo
Goa
Bombay
Surat
Broach
Ahmedabad
Delhi
Agra
MUGHAL EMPIRE
Lahore
Kandahar
Kabul
Herat
Mashad
Isfahan
Kirman
PERSIA
Gombroon
Muscat
Kandahar
Baghdad
Basra
Persian Gulf
YEMEN
Mokha
Aden
Jedda
Suez
Red Sea
Damascus
Aleppo
Erzurum
Smyrna
TURKISH EMPIRE
Alexandria
Mediterranean Sea
Mombasa
Mozambique

Legend:
- – – Trade route and sea lanes
- ● Indigenous port towns
- ○ Other towns
- ▲ English presidency settlements
- ▲ Subordinate factories
- △ Factories withdrawn
- ■ Other European settlements

0   500   1,000 Miles
0   500   1,000 Kilometers

of her merchant families migrated to Amsterdam, bringing with them their capital and commercial connections. Furthermore, the Portuguese had always been short of sailors and navigators to man their East India ships, and they recruited sailors from any country. When the Dutch rebelled against the Spaniards, therefore, they inherited many sailors, navigators, pilots, and merchants who had been to Asia on Portuguese ships and knew how its trade was organized.

The first preliminary Dutch voyage took place in 1597. The trade was so profitable that in 1601 fourteen companies dispatched 65 ships to Asia, a situation that threatened to drive up prices in Asia and glut the market in Europe. (See Illustration 5.4.) To regulate this trade, in 1602 the

**ILLUSTRATION 5.4**

A DUTCH *FLUIT OR "FLYBOAT" OF THE 1600s.*

*The Dutch were the most commercially successful European seafarers of the 1500s and 1600s. While Europe's Asian trade depended on large armed ships called East Indiamen, the backbone of the Dutch commercial fleet was the fluit or "flyboat." Midsized, fat, and slow, it carried large cargoes with small crews. It was the European equivalent of the Arab dhow, the Indonesian freight canoe, and the Chinese junk. (See Illustrations 5.2 and 6.1.)*

Source: Mark Kishlansky, Patrick Geary, Patricia O'Brien, and R. Bin Wong, *Societies and Cultures in World History, Vol. B, 1300–1800* (New York: HarperCollins, 1995), p. 542. Engraving by Salomon Savery, mid-seventeenth century, Nederlandsch Historisch Scheepvaart Museum, Amsterdam.

Dutch organized the Dutch East India Company. Like its English counterpart, this company was different from a modern corporation, since it did not have a permanent charter. It had seven governing boards, one in each province. Each provincial board sent representatives to a 17-member board of directors, but the wealthiest provinces controlled most of the directorships. Unlike a modern corporation, the Company was authorized to wage war on behalf of the Dutch government if necessary. Its initial charter ran for 20 years, and its initial capitalization was far greater than the English ever dreamed of raising in the early 1600s.

From the start the Dutch could afford to send large, well-manned, and well-armed fleets. The initial approach, like that of the English, was to arrive in Asian ports as merchants and trade in established markets. By 1605, however, they were looking for a permanent base and at one point tried unsuccessfully to capture Malacca from Portugal. As they moved from open trade to monopolistic control of the spice trade, the Dutch adopted a strategy different from that of the Portuguese. Instead of intercepting trade at the Indian Ocean choke points, many of which the Portuguese still controlled, the Dutch opted to intercept the spice trade at its point of origin, regulating production rather than distribution.

This required a permanent base, and they saw an opportunity in the small Javanese port kingdom of Jakarta. It was a situation analogous to the one that the Portuguese earlier exploited in east Africa. The diverse nature of Indonesia and its numerous islands hampered development of large and stable governments. On the surface, Java in 1600 was dominated by the Kingdom of Mataram, and all the local rulers had refused to grant the Dutch permission for a fortified base. Mataram, however, was weakly led and the Dutch commander was able to exploit the unstable situation on Java by seizing and fortifying the tiny Sultanate of Jakarta without resistance. Renamed Batavia, Jakarta–Batavia became the major naval base, ship-building center, and entrepot for the Dutch East India Company.

With Jakarta–Batavia as a base, the Dutch could avoid the established Portuguese and English routes across the Indian Ocean. They had little choice but to follow the Atlantic route to South Africa pioneered by the Portuguese, but from there they used a bolder tactic. From the Cape of Good Hope they sailed east across the southern Indian Ocean, following prevailing winds until they neared Australia. They then turned north toward the straits between Java and Sumatra, which were near Batavia. This route allowed the Dutch to keep clear of Mughal, Portuguese, and English centers of power. It also meant a daring 6,000 mile trip in open seas along the edge of the Antarctic iceberg zone.

Jakarta–Batavia became the center of a commercial system with spokes radiating out in several directions. One spoke extended eastward in the spice islands, where the Dutch built a series of forts and expelled the Portuguese. Another reached north to Macao and Canton on the Chinese coast, went on to a Dutch base on Taiwan, and ended at Japan. As we will see, by 1650 the Dutch had replaced the Portuguese as Japan's commercial contact with the rest of the world. A third spoke ran westward. The Dutch took Malacca from Portugal in 1641 and, helped by the

Mughal policy of trade with all comers, they soon had factors and forts on the southern coast of India. By 1658 they controlled most of Sri Lanka (Ceylon), the main source of cinnamon.

Many aspects of Dutch trade were similar to those of other Europeans in Asia. Where they lacked military control they traded with Asian countries as equals and played an important role in carrying goods from one Indian Ocean port to another. In terms of overall Asian geography and the volume of goods carried, this was by far the largest part of Dutch activity. We have already seen that by the later 1600s the English had displaced Asian merchants and shippers in some areas. As Dutch activity in Indonesia increased, the same thing happened there, and by 1700 local shipping by Asian merchants and ship owners played a much reduced role in regional trade. (See Reading 5.5).

The European demand for Asian goods delivered to Amsterdam also created in parts of Indonesia the same dependence on European markets that we saw emerging in parts of India. The Dutch not only exported textiles from India, but forced spice-producing regions into dependence on the export of spices to Europe. Some spices require very specific conditions and can be grown only on certain islands. As they specialized in particular exports, such islands came to depend on imported food and essential items. If European demand for their exports declined, such societies faced economic crisis.

Finally, the Dutch led the way with a more oppressive form of colonialism. As part of their effort to control the production of spices, they systematically attacked competing producers and destroyed the trees and bushes on which the spice crops grew. To cut costs, they started their own plantations, first in Java and Sri Lanka, but later in a number of spice islands where they had imposed military control. It was not long before such plantations were using slave labor on a commercial scale. In the overall scale of things, as of 1700 these Dutch initiatives were still marginal to Asian affairs, but they point to another way in which the relationship between Asia and Europe was about to change. The Indian Ocean would remain a major global crossroads, but the traffic signals at the intersection would increasingly be controlled from London and Amsterdam.

By the end of the 1600s, therefore, the Indian Ocean was becoming a global crossroads on an even bigger scale than it was between 1200 and 1500. Until well after 1600 the complex trade structures of the region reflected primarily supply and demand within the region, supplemented by trade with China, Africa, and the Mediterranean. The 1500s and 1600s saw the emergence of three great Muslim empires as well as effective governments in Burma, Siam, and Viet Nam. This increased the volume and complexity of trade within the Indian Ocean and opened a variety of connections between South Asia, the Middle East, Russia, and Europe. In conjunction with the unprecedented expansion of the Chinese economy (see Chapter 6) and the remarkable system of long-distance maritime trade created by Europeans, these changes increased the relative importance of trade that extended outside the Indian Ocean basin.

## READING 5.5

*In the eighteenth century, even after the Portuguese, Dutch, and English es-
tablished themselves in the Indian Ocean trading system, some trade in the region was still carried on by Asians. The excerpt below, from the end of the
1700s, documents the persistence of Asian merchant traditions, but also suggests a narrowing of the scope of local merchant activity. It also suggests the
nature of the arrangement that had evolved between European traders and local rulers to control the spice trade.*

A Malay, a native of Bayang in the kingdom of Menangkabau, who was distinguished by the appellation of Nakhoda Makuta, undertook a trading voyage
to Java, and continued for some time to navigate from one port to another of
that country. Visiting afterwards an island called Karimata, situated between
Pasir and Banjar (Borneo), which he found to be the resort of a considerable
number of Malays, who were drawn thither, as well for its being suited to the
purposes of commerce, as on account of gold mines at that time worked by the
natives; and observing it to be a place where the people lived undisturbed in
their industrious pursuits, he formed the resolution of making it his future residence . . . [Forced to move to Tayan in Borneo he built a] praw [ship], for
which he provided a cargo as soon as she was ready for sea, and when a fortunate hour presented itself, he set sail, with his family and household, for a trading voyage to the country of Lampong. . . . [There a native chief whose title
came] from the sultan of Bantam [in Java] . . . said "fix your abode in my country, and cease to lead a wandering life . . . there is ample scope for trade between this place and Bantam."

His . . . son was sent to visit several countries . . . [for] seven years . . . and
he said to him "Content yourself with making trips between this port and
Bantam," . . . The value of pepper in this part of the country, if the advances of
money are made in the preceding year, that is six months, before, is six (Spanish) dollars for the *bathar* (500 lbs.), or seven dollars, if the purchase be made
at the place of weighing for money paid down. . . . Now this pepper, when
safely transported to Bantam, is resold to the sultan for twelve dollars the
*bathar*; and be the quantity what it may, he never fails to take it off. By him it
is again disposed of to the Dutch Company at twenty dollars, according to an
agreement that has long subsisted between them. The Company cannot purchase it in the first instance from the chiefs of the country, nor from the Malay
traders, without the consent of the Sultan, and if these should be detected in
the sale of it, they would become liable to capital punishment; the pepper having ever been considered as at the exclusive disposal of the prince.

From *Memoirs of a Malayan Family: Written by Themselves*, trans. W. Marsden
(London: Oriental Translation Fund, 1830), pp. 1–7, excerpted from Stuart
Schwartz, Linda Wimmer, and Robert Wolff, *The Global Experience, Vol. II*
(New York: A-W-Longman, 1997), pp. 73–75.

By 1700 this had reached the point where important regions around
the Indian Ocean depended on European markets and commerce for income that was essential to their economic well-being. This dependence
was a sign of future changes in the balance of power between Europe and
Asia and also a sign of the increasingly complex way in which the Indian
Ocean was the crossroads of the world. To appreciate the scope and complexity of some of these developments, however, we must look at the parallels in China and the western Pacific between 1200 and 1700.

# 6

## AMBIGUOUS EXPANSION

# China, Japan, and the Western Pacific

## PERCEPTIONS

One of the paradoxes of world history is that China, the largest and most coherent culture and empire of the era 1200–1700, does not have an image as an expansive society. It has been stereotyped as inwardly oriented and disdainful of the rest of the world. On a smaller scale, a similar stereotype has been attributed to Japan. In fact, from 1200 C.E. onward China established a presence throughout southeast Asia and the Indian Ocean. Its ruling elite, along with that of Japan, was aware of and borrowed selectively from the culture and technology of the rest of the world.

As we saw in Chapter 1, between 1207 and 1279 the Mongols established themselves as the rulers of China. Calling themselves the Yuan Dynasty, the Mongols united an empire that had been divided during most of the thousand years since the fall of the Han Dynasty. Epidemics, unstable weather, and political disunity in the mid-1300s led to the rise of the native Ming Dynasty. The first Ming ruler, a peasant rebel named Zhu Yuanzhang, began his career as "enforcer" for one of the regional warlords who challenged Mongol authority around 1350. By 1368 Zhu had taken his patron's place, unified several regional rebellions, driven the Mongols from the throne, and assumed the title of Hongwu Emperor.

The first Ming Emperors maintained the Mongol policy of overseas expansion, extending Chinese influence throughout Indonesia and Southeast Asia. This era (1368–1434) was marked by internal politics in which the new rulers used officials and servants from outside the scholar-gentry bureaucracy and sought to reform that bureaucracy. This is an important point because the scholar-bureaucrats opposed foreign contacts and sought to control access to the emperor. According to the standard narrative, after 1430 the Ming emperors shifted their attention to internal matters and deliberately withdrew from Southeast Asia. This withdrawal from overseas expansion is often explained by pointing to the pressure from nomadic tribes on China's northern frontier. It is also explained, however, by the fact that the scholar-gentry bureaucracy, with its emphasis on Confucian ideas and its suspicion of royal officials who were not from their own ranks, gained control of the education and environment of the heirs to the throne. As a result, the court gradually became self-involved and incapable of responding to new challenges. This trend culminated in 1644, when the nomadic Manchu, taking advantage of an internal rebellion, seized the imperial government. Calling themselves the Qing (Ching) dynasty, the Manchus ruled China until the Revolution of 1911.

The short version of Japan's story is a bit different, but contains similar stereotypes. Japan was heavily influenced by Chinese culture between 100 C.E. and 900 C.E., but by the seventh century had developed its own tradition of imperial authority. By the eleventh century, however, that authority was being challenged by a provincial warrior elite. This brought a long period of feudal disunity and disorder that lasted into the 1500s. Much like Europe at the same time, medieval Japan was dominated by regional warlords. In the 1540s an astute and ruthless warlord named Nobunaga began a gradually successful struggle to unify Japan. The result was the reaffirmation of a long-standing dual political structure in which the Emperor was powerless but symbolically important, while real power was controlled by his chief minister, the Shogun. Concerned that outside influences were threatening Japan's traditions and hard-won political unity, Shogun Ieyasu banned Christianity in 1614. Between 1616 and 1643 the Japanese evicted most Europeans and restricted Japan's outside contacts. This, at least, is the standard story of how Japan became the "hermit empire" that was forced by the Americans to open up to outsiders in 1854.

These simplified narratives of self-isolation are only partly true. They mask complex stories that include Chinese expansion comparable in scale to that of the Ottoman Turks or the disorganized Europeans and they hide continued Japanese awareness of outside developments. We characterized Ottoman expansion (Chapter 2) as centrally organized political and military aggression, while the tropical Atlantic (Chapter 3) saw haphazard exploitation driven by a combination of crusading ideology, noble land hunger, and capitalist profit seeking. The three American empires (Chapter 4) were assembled with heavy reliance on religious factors, although the Spanish–American one was also shaped by European politics and commerce.

By comparison, China was the center of a process best characterized as cultural expansion. The other driving forces inherent in expansion (political power, economics, and religion) played their parts, but the outcome in this case was the persistent expansion of the geographic area that was identified with Chinese culture, accepted a Chinese presence, or was politically and economically oriented to China. Long before the period that concerns us (1200–1700), this process implanted Chinese culture in parts of central Asia, in what is now southern China, and on various offshore islands. Chinese expansion after 1200 must be seen in the context of that earlier process. Thus the concept of cultural expansion offers the best framework for talking about the largest player in the Asian arena.

To follow this logic, we must think of the western Pacific and east Asia as the stage for several interconnected narratives, some of which involved Europeans. A handful of Europeans reached China in the later Middle Ages, but they were not significant from an Asian perspective until after 1510. Prior to 1700 these Europeans were the most novel, if not the most important, component in the mix. Even then, however, they were one of many participants in a dynamic regional scenario.

## CHINA AND CULTURAL EXPANSION

Unlike the other great empires that we have mentioned, by 1200 C.E. China had a thousand-year-old tradition of centralized and bureaucratized imperial government. This does not mean that China was always a single empire, however. The empire was reunified for a time under the great Tang Dynasty (618–907), but under the Song dynasty (960–1279) China was divided into three independent empires. As we saw in Chapter 1, the Mongols began their conquest of China by first capturing the two smaller Chinese states north and west of the Song Empire itself.

Despite a thousand years of political disunity, however, any would-be emperor of China was guided by cultural conditioning that caused most Chinese to think of a unified empire as normal. This meant that the Mongols, Chinese, and Manchus who seized the throne did not have to create the traditions of legitimacy, religious support, and bureaucratic administration that empires need to survive beyond initial conquest. Any new Chinese ruler could draw upon the general assumption that central rule was normal, the recognized primacy of the throne, a trained bureaucracy committed to the state, and a working relationship between spiritual and royal authority. (See Reading 6.1).

The most remarkable of these institutions was the scholar-gentry bureaucracy, a class of professional administrators referred to in older history books as Mandarins. Dating from the Han Dynasty (202 B.C.E.–220 C.E.), the scholar bureaucracy became a dominant factor in Chinese government in the Tang period. This institution recruited administrators through a system of examinations in literature, philosophy, and history, but which had no military component. It was a civilian organization that drew recruits from outside the old aristocracy and provided a hierarchy of officials that reached from the imperial court to local towns. The presence of this bureaucracy meant that in 1200 China already had a key component of stable empire, one that the Turks, Incas, and Spaniards

READING 6.1

*Imperial power in China normally passed from father to son, and some dynas-*
*ties lasted over two centuries. Ultimately, however, the imperial concept and*
*function was more important to legitimacy than direct succession. The strength*
*of this imperial concept is suggested by this selection from an essay written by*
*the historian Ssu-ma Kuang between 1071 and 1085 [during the Song dy-*
*nasty]. You might compare it with the logic of the Requirement or with Euro-*
*pean concepts of political legitimacy.*

Your servant Kuang observes: Heaven gave birth to the multitudes of people.
But conditions make it impossible for them to govern themselves, so that they
must have a ruler to govern over them. Anyone who is able to prevent violence
and remove harm from the people so that their lives are protected, who can re-
ward good and punish evil and thus avoid disaster—such a man may be called
a ruler. . . . But he who united all these countless states and who set up laws
and issued commands which no one dared to disobey was called a king. . . .
Are we to consider [only] those states legitimate which received the throne
from the hands of their immediate predecessor? . . . Should we consider as legitimate those [usurpers] who occupied parts of China proper? . . . Or are we
perhaps to make virtuous ways the criterion of legitimacy? . . . Thus from ancient times to the present these theories of legitimate dynasties have never possessed the kind of logic sufficient to compel men to accept them without question. . . . Chou, Ch'in, Han Chin, Sui, and T'ang each in turn unified the nine
provinces and transmitted the throne to its descendants. And though their descendants in time grew weak and were forced to move their capitals, they still
carried on the undertaking of their ancestors, continued the line of succession,
and hoped to bring about a restoration of power. Those with whom rulers
contended for power were all their former subjects. Therefore your servant
has treated these rulers with all the respect due the Son of Heaven. . . .

From Ssu-ma Kuang, "A Discussion of Dynastic Legitimacy," in *The Comprehen-*
*sive Mirror for Aid in Government*, written between 1071 and 1085, excerpted
from selection in Mark Kishlansky (ed.), *The Sources of World History: Readings*
*for World Civilization*, Vol. I, (New York: HarperCollins, 1995), pp. 166–167.

---

had to create. An autonomous extension of royal authority, during the
Ming era (1368–1644) this class of educated bureaucrats merged with the
wealthy landed class.

The Chinese had also achieved a durable relationship between religion and political power based on Confucian beliefs. An ethical code that
emphasized reverence for precedent, ancestors, and paternal authority,
Confucianism provided spiritual authority for the emperor without the
need for religious conformity among his subjects seen in Europe. This allowed Confucianism, Taoism, Buddhism, Islam, and eventually Christianity to coexist within China.

The third key element of empire was the throne itself. The position
of Emperor was hereditary within a ruling dynasty, but the office had a
legal and conceptual existence that transcended the occupant or his family. This allowed the empire to adjust to changes in dynasty, whether
caused by invasion or rebellion. Practically speaking, new emperors were
legitimate only partly because of inheritance. It was equally important

that whoever occupied the throne fulfilled the role of emperor within a conceptual scheme in which, as Son of Heaven, the emperor enacted rituals that defined the well-being of the empire. Usurpers had internal opponents, but if they fulfilled certain roles, the elites of the empire could be persuaded to acquiesce in their authority. Even the Mongol Yuan dynasty, which has a bad historical reputation, maintained its authority until natural crises encouraged local rebellion and reduced the revenues that made government effective. (See Reading 6.2).

Chinese "expansion" had several facets. Its most striking phase took place under the Mongol and early Ming emperors. Between 1274 and 1435 China maintained policies that projected Chinese power into Southeast Asia, Indonesia, and the Indian Ocean while also importing art, science, and technology from other societies. The Mongols invaded and briefly ruled parts of Vietnam, Burma, and Korea. They also attacked Japan and Indonesia. In Indonesia they sought to control trade and intervened in local politics to promote local rulers whom they favored. Several Mongol naval expeditions were badly defeated, but their policy was continued in a less assertive way by the Ming dynasty. The successor to the Hongwu Emperor, the Yunglo Emperor (1403–1424), in fact expanded Chinese activity far beyond that of his Mongol predecessors. Between 1405 and 1424 Chinese maritime expansion reached its high point when Admiral Zhenghe (Cheng Ho) led a series of huge imperial fleets into the Indian Ocean. The project lost momentum with the death of Yunglo in 1424, but one last voyage took place in the 1430s before the policy was suspended. At least two of these fleets travelled as far as the Persian Gulf, the Red Sea, and Africa. One of the two returned to India via the lonely route that follows the prevailing winds of the southern Indian Ocean, anticipating the route of the Dutch East India ships two centuries later.

The first of these Chinese expeditions included 62 ships, 15 to 20 of them huge "treasure ships," and 28,000 soldiers, sailors, diplomats, and imperial officials. The larger ships, six times as long as Vasco da Gama's largest vessel in 1498, were comparable in size to the three-decked European ships of the line in the eighteenth century (see cover illustration). These expeditions are hard for Westerners to categorize because they were not clearly examples of exploration, conquest, or control of trade. The Indian Ocean had long been a setting for long-distance commerce that included China. It was known territory, and thus these voyages were not explorations. Nor, unlike Mongol ventures in Indonesia and Vietnam, did these expeditions attempt overt conquest.

Chinese visits took the form of diplomatic exchanges with the countries they reached. At the same time, however, Chinese officials did not perceive these contacts as exchanges between equals and they were not above using, or threatening to use, force to promote the accession of rulers whom they preferred. The money, gifts, and ambassadors proffered by local governments were characterized in Chinese documents as tribute or hostages. Most visits by these fleets were peaceful, but it was a peace enforced by several thousand Chinese troops with advanced military technology. When, on occasion, the Chinese intervened militarily, it was in support of regimes willing to acknowledge Chinese authority. The elaboration of this sphere of influence over the Indian Ocean ended after the death of the Yunglo Emperor in 1424, and the last great voyage took place in 1431–1435. Only a few Chinese documents about these voyages survived the scholar-bureaucrat campaign against outside influences, but archaeologists have uncovered traces of Chinese commerce from Malaysia to Kenya.

The abrupt end of this form of Chinese expansion has long puzzled historians, but it offers an insight into the institutions that unified the Chinese Empire, and into the limits faced by emperors who sought to change policies favored by men entrenched in those institutions. The problem is personified by China's greatest admiral, Zhenghe (Cheng Ho). The person who organized China's remarkable Indian Ocean voyages, Zhenghe was both a Muslim and a eunuch. As a Muslim he came from a part of Chinese society outside the world of the scholar-gentry bureaucrats. To the latter, he represented the unwelcome Muslim influence introduced by the Mongol Yuan Dynasty. As a eunuch, Zhenghe was linked with the eunuchs who ran the imperial household. These household eunuchs were a threat to scholar-gentry power because they had access to the emperor that the scholar-gentry bureaucrats could not control.

This combination of talent and outsiderness explains why the first Ming emperors used men like Zhenghe in their government. The leaders of the new dynasty wanted to revitalize China. To do so, they had to break with traditions that reinforced the scholar-bureaucrat elite. A talented Muslim administrator and admiral, who was also a eunuch, Zhenghe exemplified the political allies that offered the new dynasty a way to implement policies opposed by the scholar-gentry class. An effective emperor needed diverse sources of information about his empire, not just information filtered by bureaucrats who sought to direct imperial policy in a particular direction. The palace eunuchs, although they had their own agendas and a bad reputation for isolating the emperor, at times provided him with an alternative source of information.

In the longer run, the Ming Emperors had to live with an entrenched officialdom, without which no ruler could run a huge Empire. (See Map 6.1.) The authority of the scholar-gentry bureaucrats, however, depended on a three-part arrangement between themselves, the ruler, and a paternalistic form of Confucianism. They were suspicious of officials who practiced other faiths, feared that outside contact would undermine tradition, and resented the palace eunuchs. The scholar-gentry bureaucrats worked to undermine the autonomy of the first Ming rulers, and, by the 1430s, they had succeeded. They took over the education of successors to the Yunglo Emperor, with the result that later emperors reversed many of his policies after he died in 1424. Outsiders like Zhenghe were no longer appointed to important government posts. The new regime stopped the great voyages and forbade construction of the large ships that were the core of the fleets—a decision that has come to symbolize Chinese cultural introspection.

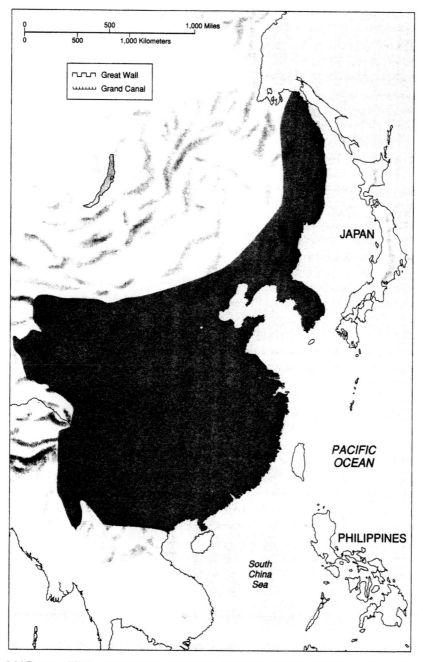

**MAP 6.1** *THE CHINESE EMPIRE UNDER THE MING DYNASTY (1368–1644).*

Despite the end of overt maritime expansion, however, China remained one of the world's major centers of economic, demographic, and cultural expansion. This dynamism had two contrasting aspects: it made China a magnet for world trade, but it also left the imperial government unable to respond to new challenges. The driving force behind this expansion came from within China, and, in the 1600s, brought the end of the Ming dynasty at the hands of Manchu—one of the last great examples of conquest by mobile military elites.

Between 1400 and 1600 the domestic economy of China, like those of Ottoman Anatolia and Western Europe, was remarkably dynamic. More stable weather, the weakening of the plague, improved transportation, and a wider range of food crops helped the population to grow from 80 million people in the wake of the plagues of the 1300s to 120 million people by 1600 and 300 million in 1800. While the figure for 1600 is small by modern standards, it was twice that of the Ottoman Empire and ten times that of Spain.

Chinese economic growth was assisted by external factors, but was self-generating. It grew out of the interaction between agriculture and the burgeoning cities, several of which were larger than any in the Western world. Indeed, Turkish Constantinople (Istanbul) was the only Western city that approached Beijing, Canton, and other Chinese cities in size. New American crops, such as corn, peanuts, sweet potatoes, and new types of beans, filled empty niches in China's agricultural ecology and brought greater output from existing farmland. Economic expansion was encouraged by the Chinese government. The scholar-gentry bureaucrats oversaw the construction of roads and canals and the improvement of rivers for navigation. Their most spectacular achievement was reconstruction of the 1,200-mile long Grand Canal between northern and southern China. Over a hundred feet wide, the Canal, and the highway that followed its route, linked China's river systems into a single transport network and moved thousands of tons of food, fuel, and manufactured goods every year. (See Reading 6.3).

Economic dynamism, however, intersected with the self-interest of the scholar-bureaucrats in a way that caused the government to lose touch with its tax base and with important parts of society. As a result, state revenues did not grow with the economy and the potential for self-sustaining economic growth was stifled. These outcomes reflect scholar-bureaucrat control of the throne, their adherence to a conservative kind of neo-Confucianism, an alliance between scholar-bureaucrats and landowners, and social barriers that made it difficult for successful business families to acquire political influence.

Part of this process involved manipulation of the neo-Confucian restatement of Confucianism to reinforce bureaucratic control of the throne. The neo-Confucian synthesis of the Song period (960–1279) combined Confucian respect for precedent and paternal authority with the idea that this world was the imperfect reflection of an ideal Heavenly World—an addition that shows the influence of Buddhism. The scholar-bureaucrats of the 1500s and 1600s promoted a version of this worldview in which the Emperor, as the Son of Heaven, was the vital mediator between ideal and real worlds. As a result, later Ming emperors were enveloped in rituals, each of which was presented as vital to the well-being of the Empire. Such rituals signaled when it was time to sow the fields, begin the harvest, and undertake other parts of the annual cycle of life. Because the Emperor projected the ideal world into the real one through such rituals, mistakes in their enactment were omens of disaster. Thus the scholar-bureaucrats isolated the Ming emperors within a world of symbolic ritual separate from actual government.

Simultaneously, scholar-bureaucrat families strengthened their association with an increasingly powerful landed nobility through marriage and preferential treatment, evolving into a landed scholar-gentry class. This gave wealthy landowners access to status as scholar-bureaucrats, while bureaucratic families got access to landed wealth. Together, bureaucrats and landlords gave substance to the term scholar-gentry that is applied to the bureaucracy which controlled government and blocked tax reform. Tax reform would have strengthened imperial government, but implied taxing the landed wealth of the emerging scholar-gentry alliance. Thus, while the Chinese economy prospered, government revenue was static. Static tax revenue and the selfishness of the controlling scholar-gentry class thus prevented an effective response to Manchu pressure from the north after 1600. (See Illustration 6.1.)

**ILLUSTRATION 6.1**
*CARICATURE OF THE MANDARIN-SCHOLARS.*
*This caricature of the Chinese Mandarin-scholars was drawn by the Chinese artist T'ang Yin, who lived 1470–1524. It does not show quite the same respect for these learned officials that we find in Mateo Ricci's commentary.*
Source: Wen C. Fong and James C. Y. Watt, *Possessing the Past: Treasures from the National Palace Museum, Taipei* (New York: Harry Abrams, the Metropolitan Museum of Art, and the National Palace Museum, Taipei, Taiwan, Republic of China, 1996), p. 387. By T'ang Yin, *The Lofty Scholars*, detail. Handscroll, ink on paper, 23.7 x 195.8 cm.

### READING 6.2

*Matteo Ricci was another Jesuit who spent much of his life trying to convert Asia to Christianity. He lived in China between 1583 and 1610 and had close associations with the imperial court. Here he comments firsthand on the nature of legitimacy and imperial succession in China and on the nature of the scholar-gentry bureaucracy.*

Chinese imperial power passes on from father to son, or to other royal kin, as does our own. . . . More than once, however, it has happened that the people, growing weary of an inept ruler, have stripped him of his authority and replaced him with someone pre-eminent for character and courage whom they henceforth recognized as their legitimate King. . . . There are no ancient laws in China under which the republic is governed in perpetuum. . . . Whoever succeeds in getting possession of the throne, regardless of his ancestry, makes new laws according to his own way of thinking. His successors on the throne are obligated to enforce the laws which he promulgated as founder of the dynasty, and these laws cannot be changed without good reason. . . .

Relative to the magistrates in general, there are two distinct orders or grades. The first and superior order is made up of the magistrates who govern the various courts of the royal palace, which is considered to be a model for the rule of the entire realm. The second order includes all provincial magistrates or governors who rule a province or a city. . . . Another remarkable fact and quite worthy of note as making a difference from the West, is that the entire kingdom is administered by the Order of the Learned, commonly known as the Philosophers [Scholars]. The responsibility for orderly management of the entire realm is wholly and completely committed to their charge and care. The army, both officers and soldiers, hold them in high respect and show them the promptest obedience and deference, and not infrequently the military are disciplined by them as a schoolboy might be punished by his master. Policies of war are formulated and military questions are decided by the Philosophers only, and their advice and counsel has more weight with the King than that of the military leaders.

Excerpted from Mateo Ricci, *Journals*, written between 1583 and 1610, as presented in Kishlansky, *Sources of World History*, Vol. I, pp. 269–273.

At the same time, Chinese values marginalized parts of the society that might have revitalized the state—a situation reinforced by the scholar-gentry alliance. China always had a large army, but the civilian nature of the bureaucracy meant that military skills and military command enjoyed relatively little status. This left the army open to constant interference. The same value system assigned a low status to merchants and industrialists. While farm labor was honorable, trade and commerce were not, making it difficult for successful businessmen to influence politics unless they abandoned trade and joined the landed elite. Both the army and the merchants helped remake government in other societies. As the Chinese elite recognized, they also posed a threat to the cohesion of the empire as they knew it, and the caution of the controlling elites was not without justification. Yet it remains that the Ming government as it

## READING 6.3

*In the 1500s the imperial government of China was preoccupied with the em-
pire's north and west frontiers and invested heavily in a marginally profitable
trade on that frontier. That trade was part of a policy intended to restrain new
nomadic invasions. At the same time, southern and eastern China was booming and, despite official policies, engaged in a growing foreign trade with Indo-
China, Indonesia, and, as time went on, Europeans. The following observations come from an "Essay on Merchants" written in the later 1500s by a Ming
official named Zhan Han.*

South of the capital is the province of Henan, the center of the empire. Going
from Kaifeng, its capital, to Weizhong, one can reach the Yangzi and Han
rivers. Thus, Kaifeng is a great transportation center; one can travel by either
boat or carriage from this spot to all other places, which makes it a favorite
gathering place for merchants. The area is rich in lacquer, hemp, sackcloth, fine
linen, fine gloss silk, wax, and leather. . . . In general, in the southeast area the
greatest profits are to be had from fine gauze, thin silk, cheap silk, and sackcloth. . . . The profits from the tea and salt trades are especially great, but only
large-scale merchants can undertake these businesses. Furthermore, there are
government regulations on their distribution, which prohibit the sale of tea in
the northwest and salt in the southeast. . . . This law is rigidly applied to all areas where salt is produced during the Ming dynasty. Yet there are so many private salt producers there now that the regulation seems too rigid and is hard to
enforce. . . .

   As to the foreigners in the southeast, their goods are useful to us just as
ours are to them. To use what one has to exchange for what one does not have
is what trade is all about. Moreover, these foreigners trade with China under
the name of tributary contributions. That means China's authority is established and the foreigners are submissive. Even if the gifts we grant them are
great and the tribute they send us is small, our expense is still less than one ten-
thousandth of the benefit we gain from trading with them. . . . Some people
may say that the southeast sea foreigners have invaded us several times so they
are not the kind of people with whom we should trade. But they should realize
that the southeast sea foreigners need Chinese goods and the Chinese need
their goods. If we prohibit the natural flow of this merchandise, how can we
prevent them from invading us? I believe that if the sea trade were opened, the
trouble with foreign pirates would cease. . . . Whereas the northwest foreign
trade ensures only harm, the sea trade provides us with only gain. How could
those in charge of the government fail to realize the distinction?

Written by Zhang Han, a Ming official who lived 1511–1593. Trans. Lily Hwa.
Published in Patricia Ebrey (ed.), *Chinese Civilization: A Source Book* (New
York: Free Press, 1993), pp. 216–218.

was constituted was unable to make an effective response to the Manchu
invasion.

   As a result, while China boomed economically, the expanding class
of wealthy merchants had difficulty influencing the government. Those
who controlled politics considered it demeaning to use merchants in government or even to consult them about policy. Wealthy merchant families
often bought land and offices for their offspring, but this only partly

bridged the gap between the scholar-gentry class and the world of urban-ized commerce. Thus, while the economy expanded and Chinese society became more complex, a persistent gulf existed between the elites who controlled imperial government and the most dynamic part of Chinese society.

This makes it easier to understand how, despite official withdrawal from maritime expansion, China continued its process of cultural expansion into Southeast Asia. We know that Chinese traders and pirates were active there before the Mongols took over China. Mongol and early Ming expansion promoted, but did not begin, the spread of Chinese communities in Vietnam, Malaysia, Thailand, Indonesia, and the Philippines. Thus, while the Emperor ended Zhenghe's expeditions after 1435 and prohibited construction of large ships, such actions did not stop Chinese trade with the rest of the world.

A booming and wealthy society, China developed an appetite for imported goods and for silver to provide coinage for the expanding economy. The rest of the world, meanwhile, had a growing appetite for Chinese manufactures. Throughout the early modern era, hundreds of Chinese merchant ships travelled between China, the Philippines, and Southeast Asia. (See Illustration 6.2.) Despite policy in Beijing, officials in the maritime provinces quietly took their share of the profits and allowed trade to continue. Chinese silks and porcelains reached markets all over the Ottoman Empire, India, East Africa, and Europe. China, meanwhile, imported Indonesian and South Asian pepper, spices, and cotton, the same goods that drew Europeans to the Indian Ocean. Commercial activity was paralleled by the spread of Chinese cultural influence. In Siam the ruling elite had close connections with the Chinese merchant community there and was strongly influenced by Chinese art, religion, and political thought. In Vietnam the government consciously borrowed ideas and techniques from the scholar-bureaucracy of the Chinese Empire.

China, meanwhile, imported large amounts of silver by way of three routes. As we have already seen, much of the silver came from Spanish America in European ships that reached Asia by way of Africa. China's second source of silver was its trade with Japan: a complicated situation, since trade with Japan was technically illegal and Japanese traders in China were regarded as pirates. This attitude was partly justified, since during most of the 1500s Japan was torn apart by civil war and Japanese ships in China were as likely to act as raiders as they were to seek trade. Once the Portuguese established contact with China and Japan, however, they became important intermediaries between the two. The huge Portuguese carracks provided safe, neutral transport for Japanese silver Portuguese trade in China was officially recognized and the exchange provided Japanese warlords with Asian goods and military supplies as they fought over control of Japan.

The third source of silver came by way of the Philippine Islands. The Spaniards had established a claim of sorts to the Philippines in 1520

**LLLUSTRATION 6.2**
*A TRADITIONAL CHINESE SEAGOING JUNK.*
*While not as large as the "treasure ships" of the Zhenghe expeditions, this kind of
Chinese cargo ship often had greater cargo capacity than their European counter-
parts. The junk here is comparable in size to the ships used by the European East
India companies. During the Ming era (1365–1640) they travelled throughout the
South China Sea to the Philippines and Indonesia and were sometimes seen even
farther afield.*

Source: Culver Pictures, Inc., New York.

as part of the world voyage of Ferdinand Magellan and Juan Sebastian Elcano (1519–1521). Drawn by the prospect of trade with China, in the
1560s they established small bases in the Philippines, taking advantage of
the small size of the local sheikdoms. Spain made Manila the capital of its
Philippine holdings in 1571, using it as a base for access to Chinese trade.
American silver regularly crossed the Pacific from Acapulco, Mexico, in
the so-called "Manila Galleons." This American silver, along with silver
brought to Manila from Japan by Japanese merchants, was then sent to

the Chinese markets in Chinese ships. A large Chinese merchant community grew up in Manila to provide this final link between Spanish markets and the Chinese economy.

The effect of this mixture of trade and emigration was to establish a Chinese presence that touched all of maritime Southeast Asia. The intensity of that presence varied, but Chinese settlers and traders were a routine aspect of any port town in Southeast Asia. It was a trade diaspora similar to those seen in earlier chapters, but with a major difference. Rather than a diaspora by a small and distinctive cultural community, it was a diaspora that was also an extension of the largest centrally governed society in the world.

Thus, while China appears introspective and isolated at an official level, the appearance is deceptive. The elites that controlled the government remained at a social distance from the dynamic aspects of their own society, a price they paid to maintain control of the throne and avoid taxes. The commercial parts of the society were far more dynamic. They coordinated the expansion of China's domestic economy, integrated China into world trade, and sustained a process of cultural expansion throughout Southeast Asia.

The Chinese situation, in which political power and economic life offer contradictory images of Chinese expansion, was the central feature of trends in the Pacific Basin as late as 1800. China had the wealthiest and most sophisticated culture in the world, and had by far the largest population under one government. It was the reference point for all other political, economic, and cultural activity in the Pacific world.

## THE ARRIVAL OF THE EUROPEANS

Thus, while the rest of this chapter looks at three other cases of expansion in the Far East, each with its own dynamic, all three were linked to China. One was the development of a permanent European trade diaspora in Asia, manned first by the Portuguese, then expanded by the Spanish and Dutch. A second was the reemergence of Japan as an active presence in the region. The third was a remarkable attempt to convert China to Christianity. While the attempt failed, it is an example of the tremendous increase in Eurasian cultural exchange that paralleled the rise of commercial interdependence.

An occasional Mediterranean merchant or traveller visited China before 1500, following trade routes used by Central Asian peoples for centuries. Nestorian Christians, a sect growing out of a fifth-century schism in Christianity, reached China in the seventh and eighth centuries as they spread throughout medieval Asia. Thus, when Marco Polo visited China (1275–1292 C.E.), he found a centuries-old Nestorian Christian bishopric in Beijing. Living in China for 17 years during Mongol rule, Marco Polo was not only treated with respect, but also served as a minor official of the Chinese government. Similarly, the Moroccan traveller Ibn

Battuta visited China in 1346 and reported several religious communities coexisting within Chinese cities.

By 1500 Europeans had learned how to reach India and China by sailing around Africa, and were beginning to develop direct trade. These European activities, however, were merely an addition to the established flow of Indian Ocean commerce. Chinese and Arab merchant ships had travelled the entire distance between China and Arabia as early as the eleventh century. We saw in the last chapter that as Indian Ocean trade expanded, shipping became more efficient when organized as overlapping regional networks. This focused trade on certain strategically located entrepots, allowing shippers to avoid long periods when their ships were idle. Market centers and warehouses developed at these natural exchange points at the entrance to the Red Sea, in Hormuz on the Persian Gulf, near the straits between Ceylon and India, and in the straits between Sumatra and Malaysia. This left the trade of the western Indian Ocean dominated by Arab and Gujerati merchants, the trade between India and Indonesia by Muslim and Hindu merchants, and trade in the western Pacific by Chinese, Indonesian, and Japanese merchants.

The first Portuguese Europeans found their way to India in 1498 under the command of Vasco da Gama. By 1511 they had captured Malacca on the Sumatra Straits and in 1514 they reached the Spice Islands in eastern Indonesia. The Portuguese reached China in 1519–1521, but their behavior was obnoxious to the Chinese and the Chinese coast guard easily drove them away, leaving the Portuguese to concentrate on the Indonesian spice trade. Only in the 1540s did they open contraband trade with one or two Chinese coastal provinces, and they did not get formal permission to use Macao as a base until 1557. The tentative nature of initial European contacts with China can be attributed to Chinese isolationism and Portuguese obtuseness, but it also reflects the lack of Chinese interest in the limited range of European products on offer. Nevertheless, by the time the Portuguese first reached Japan in 1543, they were an established part of the Asian trading world.

In the longer run the Portuguese survived in East Asia, not as a military power, but because they provided efficient transport and trade between various Asian countries. Their big royal ships were well armed and safe from pirates. In the absence of the large Chinese junks that served this function in the 1300s and early 1400s, the Portuguese took over part of the task of supplying Indian manufactures and Indonesian spices to the expanding Chinese economy. The Portuguese used the profits from this Asian trade to buy Chinese goods for resale in European and South Asian markets. This became easier as American silver entered European commerce and was re-exported to China by way of Seville, Lisbon, and Goa. The Portuguese were far from taking over China's foreign trade, but they created an economic niche for themselves as carriers of valuable commodities and precious metals.

The European presence in East Asia in the form of the Portuguese was soon augmented by the arrival of the Spaniards. They appeared briefly in the form of Magellan's around-the-world expedition in 1519–1521. Magellan arrived in the Philippines in 1520 and immediately intervened in the strife between local sheikdoms, much as his predecessors had done in the Canary Islands and Santo Domingo. Magellan chose sides badly and was killed in battle, but the expedition continued under the command of Juan Sebastian Elcano. Once Spain's control of America was secure, and American silver was seeking profitable markets, the Spaniards renewed their interest in the Philippines. Between 1565 and 1571 a Spanish fleet took control of the northern islands and established a Spanish capital in Manila. With blithe disregard for Indonesian and Philippine geography and local interests, Spain and Portugal agreed that the Philippines fell on the Spanish side of a global partition mediated by the papacy.

Arriving in Asia with limited resources, the Spaniards were excluded from the Indonesian spice trade by established Portuguese and Chinese interests. At the same time, the Spanish government in Madrid was skeptical of trade between America and Asia because it threatened to divert American silver away from Spain. The Crown wanted such trade to pass through its tax system, while merchants in Seville wanted to keep the profits of the American trade under their control. The solution worked out after 1571 was the Manila (or Acapulco) Galleon. Once a year a single huge galleon sailed from Acapulco across the thousands of miles of open Pacific to Manila carrying American silver. This trade explains why such remote Pacific islands as Guam and the Marianas Islands acquired a layer of Hispanic culture.

In the Philippines, confronted by the Portuguese presence in the western Pacific and by official Chinese suspicion of Europeans, the Spaniards developed a trading arrangement with a growing community of Chinese businessmen in Manila. Chinese merchants thus "laundered" Spanish silver on its way to the Chinese market, and provided the Manila galleons with hundreds of tons of Chinese porcelain, silks, lacquer ware, and luxury goods destined for Mexico, Peru, and Seville by way of Acapulco. This arrangement became routine after 1580, when Philip II of Spain added the Portuguese throne to his empire. To avoid alienating interests in Portugal, however, Philip avoided Spanish initiatives in Asia that would have disturbed the Portuguese sphere of influence and allowed Portuguese Macao to control the China-Japan carrying trade.

## THE UNIFICATION OF JAPAN

Meanwhile, the Portuguese developed a relationship with Japan beginning in the 1540s. In the 1550s and 1560s the chronic civil war among Japan's warlords took on a new dimension (See Reading 6.4). Oda Nobunaga, who controlled parts of Japan near modern Tokyo, began a successful campaign that resulted in the unification of Japan by 1600. In the process,

---

READING 6.4

*The first systematic description of Japan by a European was written in 1552 by
Saint Francis Xavier (1506–1552), one of the first Jesuit missionaries to reach
that country. At that time Japan was in the midst of chronic civil war and his
comments are as good an introduction as those of any modern historian. Below
are excerpts from the letter he sent to Rome from India in January, 1552, after
he returned there from Japan.*

Japan is a very large empire entirely composed of islands. One language is spo-
ken throughout, not very difficult to learn. This country was discovered by
the Portuguese eight or nine years ago. The Japanese are very ambitious of
honors and distinctions, and think themselves superior to all nations in military glory and valor. They prize and honor all that has to do with war, and all
such things, and there is nothing of which they are so proud as of weapons
adorned with gold and silver. They always wear swords and daggers both in
and out of the house, and when they go to sleep they hang them at the bed's
head. In short, they value arms more than any people I have ever seen. They
are excellent archers, and usually fight on foot, although there is no lack of
horses in the country. They are very polite to each other, but not to foreigners,
whom they utterly despise. They spend their means on arms, bodily adorn-
ment, and on a number of attendants, and do not in the least care to save
money. They are, in short, a very warlike people, and engaged in continual
wars among themselves; the most powerful in arms bearing the most extensive
sway. They have all one sovereign, although for one hundred and fifty years
past the princes have ceased to obey him, and this is the cause of their perpetual feuds.

---

Published in William McNeill and Misuko Iriye (eds.), *Modern Asia and Africa*
(New York: Oxford University Press, 1971), p. 20.

Nobunaga exploited every opportunity to strengthen his position. The
Europeans were involved in this unification process in three ways.

Sixteenth-century Japan was not only disunited, but was underdeveloped by Chinese standards. Nobunaga was eager to build up his military forces. One way to obtain the required income and supplies was
through foreign trade. At the same time, he was a shrewd military tacti-
cian who was open to innovation. Japan's main exports at that point were
silver and copper. Japanese merchants had long had contacts in Southeast
Asia and Vietnam, but the internal disruption of the sixteenth century
hampered Japanese trade. Inevitably, China was the largest market for
Japan's silver and copper. At the official level, however, China rebuffed
Japanese contacts and, with some justification, treated Japanese merchants and shippers as smugglers and buccaneers, on occasion mounting
naval campaigns against Japanese "pirates." Nobunaga's solution was to
allow Portuguese trade with Japan. Although not eliminating other
Japanese trading (and raiding), the Portuguese carracks provided safe
transport for Japanese silver. By passing the silver through Portuguese
hands, it was effectively "laundered" for the Chinese market, much as

Spanish-American silver was laundered by the Chinese merchants in Manila. As agents for the Japanese, the Portuguese bought and delivered Chinese cloth, porcelain, and iron. The profits and resources provided by this trade were important in helping Nobunaga strengthen his position in the civil war, and by his death in 1582 he had brought half of Japan under his control.

Nobunaga and other Japanese warlords also understood the potential of European guns (See Reading 6.5). Nobunaga not only acquired European muskets from the Portuguese, he also set Japanese craftsmen to duplicating them. Japanese production of guns and gunpowder allowed Nobunaga to build up a corps of several thousand musketeers who played a crucial role in the unification of Japan.

---

### READING 6.5

*The following letter was sent by the Japanese Lord of Bungo to Dom Belchior Carneiro and the Jesuits in Macao in 1568. A major player in the Japanese civil wars, the Lord of Bungo controlled an important fief on the Japanese island of Kyushu. A rather pragmatic attitude toward Christianity pervades his letter.*

I am saddened to hear . . . of your illness. I had looked forward to your visit to our province as I had heard about your person and about the fact that through your suggestion the governor-general [of Goa] had sent me some guns. It was unfortunate that they were lost somewhere during the voyage from Malacca, but I owe you an expression of gratefulness just as if they had arrived. I have not had the fortune of obtaining those guns, and I have not abandoned the hope to procure some guns. My faith in God and the protection I have extended to Christians and Portuguese in my province should sufficiently indicate that I am the servant and friend of the King [of Portugal]. I swear to maintain this relationship while God gives me life and to carry out what you would require of me. Therefore, I hope that you will write a letter to the governor-general and inform him that I am entitled to be given guns as presents. I ask for them as we live on the coast, sharing borders with our enemy, and they are needed for self-defense. If I succeed in defending my province and enabling it to prosper, the church, missionaries, Christians, as well as all the Portuguese who come will prosper.

In William McNeill and Misuko Iriye (eds.), *Modern Asia and Africa* (New York: Oxford University Press, 1971), pp. 29–30.

---

Nobunaga, and his successor Hideoshi (1582–1598), paid a price for European collaboration. Part of the price was acceptance of Christian missionaries into Japan, and the Jesuits and the Franciscans were soon established there. Prolonged violence and civil war in Japan had produced social and spiritual unrest among the poor, and the Christian missionaries offered a faith that responded to their anxieties. Their success was striking and the missionaries themselves estimated that in 1610 Japan had over 200,000 Christian converts.

Beginning in the 1590s, however, the situation inside Japan began to change, and with it the fortunes of European visitors. Hideoshi completed the unification of Japan and established effective central rule, which meant that he had less need of help from outsiders. Moreover, the Europeans themselves had became a problem for Japanese authorities. The Jesuits and Franciscans had different approaches to Christianization. The Jesuits concentrated on converting the dominant elites, while the Franciscans preached to the poor and made thousands of conversions.

Once Japanese political power had been consolidated, the Japanese government grew suspicious of a movement that appeared to encourage dissent and was mobilizing a large part of society in a nontraditional way. Meanwhile, the Franciscans and the Jesuits undermined each other before Japanese authorities. This situation was further complicated by the arrival of the Dutch. The Dutch were Protestants with little concern for large-scale conversion. They also kept religion and commercial policy separate and were enemies of the Portuguese and Spaniards. They did everything they could to discredit the Catholic missionaries and, more specifically, the Portuguese merchants whom they aspired to displace.

The new Shogunate, meanwhile, was consolidating its authority. To do so, Hideoshi's successor, Tokugawa Ieyasu (1542–1616, Shogun, 1598–1616) made concessions to the traditional aristocracy that had just been defeated in order to forestall uprisings that might renew the civil war. This traditional elite, and Ieyasu himself, regarded Christianity with deep suspicion, because competing groups of European missionaries, and their Christianized Japanese followers, could not resist meddling in Japanese politics. In 1614 Ieyasu banned Christianity in Japan, and in 1616 he restricted all Europeans to a few cities. By the 1640s only Dutch and Chinese ships were allowed to trade with Japan, and they were confined to a closely supervised small island near Nagasaki. At the same time, Ieyasu brutally suppressed Japanese Christianity, slaughtering many converts and forcing others to make symbolically powerful renunciations of their faith. By the 1630s the Christian movement had nearly been wiped out and Japan had entered an era of calculated isolation that lasted until the nineteenth century.

## THE JESUIT INITIATIVE IN CHINA

The third fascinating episode of global expansion drawn to Asia was a remarkable attempt to Christianize the Chinese Empire from above. It was an ambitious experiment in religiously motivated expansion based on the efforts of a few dozen dedicated men. As in India and Japan, the missionary effort in China involved a number of Catholic religious groups, most notably the Jesuits and Franciscans. The main story is that of the Jesuits, and the outcome was quite different from that in Japan.

Recognized by the papacy in 1540, the Jesuit order was dedicated to recovering Protestant countries for Catholicism and to converting non-Christians. The Jesuits equipped themselves with formidable intellectual skills, language training, and scholarly and administrative abilities. They used these skills not to engage in popular conversion, but to insert themselves into the governing circles of the countries they hoped to convert. Along with other religious orders, the Jesuits sent missionaries all over the world. They were seen Christianizing Amerindians in Paraguay and Baja California; they recovered Bohemia, Poland, and much of Hungary for Catholicism; and they appeared at royal courts in India, Southeast Asia, and Japan in addition to China. The story of their activities in China is thus of interest in itself and as an example of the noncommercial cultural contacts that were proliferating around the world.

Reflecting a European conviction that there was a necessary parallel between the religion of a country's ruler and that of his subjects, the Jesuits sought to become the respected confidants of the rulers whom they hoped to convert. They invested years in absorbing the language, religion, and culture of target societies and looked for ways to minimize the differences between Catholicism and local beliefs. They hoped that in this way they could convince non-Christian rulers to take what looked like a relatively easy leap of faith, convert to Christianity, and then convert their subjects.

The strengths and weaknesses of this approach are illustrated by the Chinese case. After initial frustrations in the 1540s and 1550s, in 1583 a small group of Jesuits was permitted to reside at court. (See Illustration 6.3.) By the early 1700s, when the experiment failed, dozens of remarkable men had been engaged in the enterprise. The best known is Matteo Ricci, but he is only the most accessible to the modern reader. Spanish, Portuguese, French, German, and Italian, these men survived years of training, travelled thousands of miles, and lived for decades immersed in Chinese culture.

Their principal weapons were highly intellectual. First, they set themselves to understand China and the sophisticated Confucian tradition that legitimized imperial authority. They did this in part because they were looking for parallels between Confucian beliefs and Christianity. They also did it because it gained them admission to court. Some Jesuits quite literally became scholar-bureaucrats themselves and held important positions in the Chinese government. In this way, they were able to engage in complex debates with the intellectual elite that controlled China.

Their other intellectual weapon was European science and technology. Sixteenth-century China was in many ways more sophisticated and intellectually tolerant than Europe, but in certain areas Europe had developed skills that greatly interested the Chinese. Europe had become much more advanced in gunnery, gunpowder manufacture, and the metallurgy of cannon founding. Military skills were not highly regarded by China's scholar-gentry elite, but they became important in the 1600s as the Ming government confronted nomadic military pressure from the north. When the Ming were replaced by the warlike Manchus, the Jesuits were for a time appreciated because of this military technology.

More important from the perspective of Jesuit strategy, however, was the fact that by 1600 Europe had made considerable strides in optics,

**ILLUSTRATION 6.3**
*A JESUIT IN CHINESE DRESS.*
*Beginning in the late 1500s the Jesuits worked hard to establish their influence at the Chinese court. They presented themselves as Christian Mandarins and used European science to make Christianity intellectually respectable to the educated Mandarin elite. Here we see Adam Schaal, one such Jesuit, depicted in Chinese dress with Western scientific instruments.*
Source: The Granger Collection, New York.

astronomy, and mechanical timekeeping. These skills fascinated Chinese scholars, not because of their economic or navigational applications, but because they spoke to the neo-Confucian concern for ritual connections between celestial and earthly harmony. As we saw, that connection was part of scholar-gentry strategy for control of the emperor. From the Chinese viewpoint, therefore, the goal was to borrow tools that perfected their own way of understanding religion, politics, and the world around them.

The Jesuit goal was to make European intellectual accomplishments respectable in Chinese eyes, so that Christian theology would be seen as worthy of consideration. To a remarkable degree the Jesuits achieved some of their goals. From shortly after 1606 until well into the nineteenth century, European Jesuits held the position of Imperial Astronomer, and China's royal observatory was the most sophisticated on earth. At the same time, the Chinese government showed little anxiety about Christian mission activity, and by 1700 there were 300,000 Christians in China.

This remarkable Jesuit project collapsed, not because of Chinese resistance, but because of controversy within the Catholic Church. While they used European science to make European ideas respectable to the Chinese, the Jesuits also tried to reconcile Christian and Confucian religious concepts. This effort culminated in what is called the Chinese Rites controversy. Because Confucianism emphasized moral and ethical behavior without insisting on the divinity of its founder, it gave the Jesuits some interesting philosophical tools. They tried to define Confucian reverence for ancestors and for the emperor as private and nonreligious forms of civic deference. The Jesuits also pointed out that many Confucian moral and ethical teachings were the same as those of Christianity. They maintained that, because Confucianism did not claim divine inspiration, or attribute divinity to its founder, its rites were gestures of civic loyalty and paternal respect. The Jesuits also minimized aspects of Christianity that were difficult for Confucian intellectuals to accept, particularly Christ's virgin birth and the concept of the Trinity. This approach allowed the Jesuits to assert that there was enough common ground between the two religions to justify the idea that Confucius had been inspired by God. Thus, they thought, it was possible to create a Chinese version of Catholicism that did not violate Christian precepts, but which would permit the scholar-gentry elite to convert without abandoning Confucian values.

Similar compromises had been found between Catholicism and distinctive Christian communities in eastern Europe and the middle East, but the Jesuit proposal for a Chinese Rite was too audacious for the religious politics of Rome. The proposal was attacked by conservative theologians in Europe and undermined by the jealousy of other missionary movements. In 1705 the pope sent a papal legate (ambassador) to Beijing to lecture the Jesuits publicly about the dubious nature of their theology. In 1743 the papacy definitively rejected the proposed Chinese Rite. The rejection of the Jesuits' European intellectual system by other Europeans, whose logic was obviously defective in Chinese eyes, destroyed the Jesuits' intellectual status at the Chinese court and the scholar-gentry courtiers lost interest in them.

In contrast to Japan, however, this loss of favor did not result in the suppression of Christianity in China. The Jesuits remained at court and continued to provide imperial astronomers for another century. Chinese officials simply lost interest in the Jesuits' intellectual project and marginalized them. The same thing happened to the large Christian community in China. Because Confucianism legitimated the Emperor without claiming divine authority, the Chinese government usually was not concerned about the religious convictions of its subjects. All the Empire asked of its subjects was an essentially civic acknowledgment of the emperor's authority. Only when religion involved a challenge to imperial authority did the government attack a religious community. The most striking case was the partial suppression of Buddhism in the 800s C.E. Despite the failure of the Jesuits' attempt to create a Chinese Rite, therefore, Christianity in China survived to become yet another religion alongside Confucianism, Taoism, Buddhism, and Islam.

# THE COMPLEXITIES OF EXPANSION IN EAST ASIA

Thus the age of expansion (1200–1700) in the Far East contains many ambiguities. Ultimately the two most obvious focal points were China and Europe. Despite the apparently introspective nature of imperial China, she dominated the region by her very presence and size. Undeniably the Chinese government withdrew officially from the maritime world of southeast Asia after 1435. Nevertheless, only a century before both the Mongol Yuan dynasty, and then the first Ming emperors, had demonstrated that China was fully capable of establishing a powerful presence across a very large part of the world. While the later Ming dynasty assumed a defensive geopolitical position between 1433 and 1644, China's potential for political and military expansion was reaffirmed after 1650. The new Manchu rulers quickly revitalized the administrative and military institutions of the Empire. Moreover, while they did not renew earlier naval initiatives, between 1650 and 1790 they nearly doubled the size of the mainland area of the Chinese Empire. (See Map 6.2.) At the time of the American Declaration of Independence in 1776, Chinese rule extended into Korea, Manchuria, Mongolia, central Asia, Vietnam, and Burma. Chinese control was not firmly established in many of these areas, but as of 1800 China was the largest pre-modern empire in history.

At the same time, the sheer size and growth of the Chinese economy after 1400 made it the motor that drove the maritime world of Southeast Asia. China was a wealthy market with an insatiable demand for raw materials, spices, and monetary metals. Whether carried on by Indonesian, Japanese, Portuguese, Spanish, or Dutch merchants and officials, most economic and political initiatives in the region were shaped by the reality of China. Moreover, many of the contacts between other countries and China were mediated by the Chinese themselves. Despite the official withdrawal of China from Southeast Asia after 1433, thousands of Chinese merchants, sailors, and settlers created a Chinese diaspora throughout the region. The influence of that diaspora is seen from the role of the Chinese merchant community in Spanish Manila to the emulation of Chinese bureaucracy in Vietnam and the influence of Chinese culture on the ruling elite in Siam.

Only where local politics were fragmented and local states small and commercially pragmatic did Europeans make much headway before 1700. Under those conditions they could play a decisive role in local affairs despite their limited resources. By 1700 Europeans had been active in the

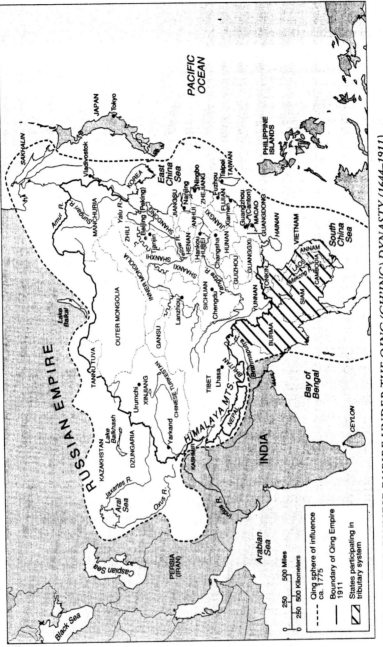

**MAP 6.2** THE CHINESE EMPIRE UNDER THE QING (CH'ING) DYNASTY (1644–1911).
*In 1644 the Manchu seized control of the Empire and took the dynastic name of Qing. This map shows the extent of Chinese influence at the time of American independence in 1775.*

Far East for almost two centuries. They sailed under Portuguese and Spanish flags in the 1500s, while in the 1600s the Dutch and the English were the most prominent Europeans.

The Portuguese presence in the Far East was by far the oldest European example, and was geographically the most ambitious. From 1498 they used techniques perfected by the Italians in the Mediterranean and modified by Portuguese experience with west African kingdoms to establish fortified bases in Malacca, Indonesia, Macao, Taiwan, and Japan. The last fragments of that Portuguese diaspora are still seen in the ongoing crisis in Timor, where the people of Portuguese East Timor have been repressed by the Indonesian government, and by the island of Macao, which returned to Chinese control in 1999, in the wake of the British departure from Hong Kong in 1996.

As of the 1600s, the Portuguese "empire" was really a diaspora of Portuguese communities scattered across the African and Asian world. All Portuguese in Asia were nominally subjects of their king, but in an era when it took three years to send a letter to Lisbon and get a reply, many Portuguese (and other Europeans) acted with a great deal of autonomy. It was in such circumstances that in 1511 the Portuguese seized Malacca, a small but strategic city-state. This allowed them to monitor trade between the Indian Ocean and the western Pacific. Their next concern was to penetrate Indonesia, where a number of islands produced spices that were valuable in Europe (and also in the Near East, India, and China). The Portuguese were never strong enough to control production, but in an Indonesia composed of many small Muslim sheikdoms, the Portuguese could use the divide-and-conquer tactics that they (and other Europeans) had used elsewhere.

The Spaniards did not become a permanent presence until the later 1500s, when they established themselves in the Philippine Islands with the same strategies they had used in the Canary Islands, the Caribbean, and mainland America. The fact that they encountered a world of small and weak political units allowed them to establish their authority despite limited resources. Intervention in local disputes, occasional use of force, missionary activity, and a flexible balance between colonial authority and local elites allowed the Spaniards to develop Manila as a doorway to the China trade. Constrained by the Spanish crown's desire to direct American silver toward Europe, by the riskiness of trans-Pacific shipping, and by the concerns of the merchants in Mexico and Seville, trade between America, Manila, and China was restricted to a limited exchange of Chinese luxuries for American silver. The limited scope of the Spanish presence also reflected the results of Habsburg dynastic successes in Europe. Since the King of Spain was also the King of Portugal between 1580 and 1640, they saw no point in expanding a Spanish presence into areas already open to the Portuguese.

The Portuguese and the Spaniards entered an environment of open trade in which Muslims, Chinese, Hindus, and Indonesians all took part in a diversified network not easily controlled by anyone. They were successful in Southeast Asia because they found places that were weak enough for them to dominate with limited resources. The Portuguese then used a combination of threat and protection to sell licenses that shielded Asian ships from Portuguese harassment. The situation encouraged independent action by Portuguese colonists. As a result, much of the "Portuguese" trade in Asia was independent of Portuguese royal control. Practically speaking, it was like other commerce between Asian markets. Many of the Portuguese who participated in this intra-Asia trade were expatriates who had "gone native." Most of them married Asian women and not a few converted to Islam, the religion of most commercial communities in the Indian Ocean. After 1600, however, the Portuguese empire increasingly confronted strong Asian governments in Persia, India, and Southeast Asia, as well as competition from the Dutch and English, and their fortified strongholds were lost or marginalized.

If a politically fragmented Indonesia encouraged individual commercial initiatives by the Portuguese and then the Dutch, the situation in China and Japan had the reverse effect. Equipped with well-organized governments, China and Japan (after about 1590) easily controlled European initiatives, both commercial and military. The agents of the Portuguese king and his *Estado do India* quickly discovered that they had to negotiate in good faith with the Chinese empire on a diplomatic level. Only as a result of government-to-government negotiations were the Portuguese allowed regular trade in China and Japan and permitted to send in Christian missionaries. As we saw with the Japanese expulsion of Europeans in the seventeenth century, this kind of commerce was vulnerable to changes in Japanese or Chinese policy. (See Illustration 6.4.)

European expansion into Asia sought not only political influence and profit, but also the conversion of local populations to Christianity. Here, European missionaries had some success in places where they did not encounter Islam or confront systematic government resistance. On the western coast of South India, in the Philippines, and in Japan before the completion of unity, they found niches open to missionary activity, and converted many people to Christianity. When the missionaries and Christianity were seen as a political threat in Japan, however, the missionaries were efficiently expelled and Christianity was brutally suppressed. The story was rather different in China. There, the Jesuit vanguard of Christianity gained access to the imperial court because it was seen as potentially useful and interesting within the Chinese worldview. The more populist Franciscans also gained entry into China and made many converts. When, in the early 1700s, the Jesuit program in China was sabotaged by other Europeans, the Jesuits were marginalized, Christianity was allowed to coexist with other religions.

The picture changed only slightly when Dutch Europeans arrived in the Asian Pacific. The Dutch East India Company, as we saw in Chapter 5, had more resources than its Portuguese competitor. As did the Portuguese, the Dutch focused first on the Indonesian spice trade. To avoid Portuguese strongholds in East Africa, Goa, and Malacca, the Dutch sailed across the empty southern Indian Ocean toward Australia, then headed north to the straits between Sumatra and Java. On Java, the Dutch

**ILLUSTRATION 6.4**
*DISARMED EUROPEAN SHIP IN A CHINESE PORT.*
*Chinese authorities were suspicious of European motives. This eighteenth-century Chinese painting shows a European ship in a Chinese port. Before being allowed to begin trade activities, the ship had first to unload its cannon, which are seen in the shed at the right side of the picture. Well into the eighteenth century, Europeans traded in China on Chinese terms.*

Source: Carlo Cipolla, *Guns, Sails and Empires: Technological Innovation and the Early Phases of European Expansion, 1400–1700* (New York: Minerva Press, 1965), facing p. 97. Cipolla's acknowledgement: Dr. F. Dahl, who kindly brought to my attention this painting at the University Library of Lund, Sweden.

exploited local conflicts to gain control of the port of Batavia (now Jakarta). From there they moved into the Spice Islands and, with more military resources than the Portuguese could muster, the Dutch gained control of both the marketing of spices and a large part of actual production. They were unable to force the Portuguese out of the China trade, but they did obtain a monopoly on European trade with Japan. After 1614 the Japanese Shoguns suppressed Christianity and expelled most foreigners. They did not cut off outside contact entirely, but ejected all

Europeans except the Dutch. Foreign trade was restricted to a small island near Nagasaki, and only Chinese and Dutch ships were allowed to enter. The Dutch, who were not concerned with spreading Christianity, were less of a risk for the Japanese government than other Europeans, and the Dutch replaced the Portuguese as middlemen for part of Japan's foreign trade.

It should be noted that Japanese "isolation" was not so extreme as it sometimes appears. Japanese merchants and ship owners had long maintained an active foreign trade of their own. Despite new restrictions, they continued to carry on trade with Indonesia, Manila, and Vietnam. Members of the Japanese governing elite followed world affairs and paid attention to developments in European military technology. The story is not so much one of isolation as one of a supervised, limited borrowing of cultural material when it was useful within Japan.

---

### READING 6.6

*Japan has a reputation for being isolated after the 1630s, but adapted to modernity very quickly after the middle of the nineteenth century. Their isolation was in fact selective. The Dutch continued a regular trade with Japan, and educated Japanese read books imported by the Dutch. The following illustration of ongoing openness to European knowledge was written by Sugita Gempaku, an eighteenth-century Japanese.*

Ryotaku, Junan, and I returned [from the autopsy] together. We remarked to each other how amazing the autopsy had been, and how inexcusable it had been for us to be ignorant of the anatomical structure of the human body. . . . I suggested that we should perhaps translate a portion of *Tafel Anatomi* [an eighteenth-century Dutch anatomy textbook], which would clarify facts about the human body, both internally and externally, and would really make a great contribution to medicine. . . . We agreed that it would be simply impossible to start translating sections dealing with the intestines first. Since the book opened with the pictures of the front and back views of the human body, and since they dealt with the external parts whose names were known to all of us in Japanese, we decided that the easiest way to start would be to relate each explanation in Dutch to its corresponding part in the pictures. This part of the work later became the morphological index to *Kaitai hinsho [the New Book on Anatomy*, published in Japan in 1771–1775].

To be sure there were so many words we simply were unable to understand . . . [that] we made it a rule to mark such words, which hopefully we would someday be able to translate, with an encircled cross, and used to nickname unknown words as "kutsuwa jumonji" [an encircled cross]. . . . Yet we kept telling ourselves that we would be rewarded in the end and went on meeting and toiling six or seven times a month. And after about a year we gradually enriched our Dutch vocabulary and came to understand things about that country. We were able to translate ten or even more lines a day if the sentences were not too crowded. To be sure, we put questions to the translators every spring when they came up to Yedo for the annual homage. Also we attended autopsies and dissected various animals to clarify uncertain parts.

---

This passage comes from *Rangaku kotohajime*, Iwanami edition (Tokyo, 1930), trans. M. Iriye, pp. 54–58, in McNeill and Iriye, *Modern Asia and Africa*, pp. 137–140.

On balance, therefore, the era of expansion in the western Pacific is marked by a few key observations. China was the largest and most dynamic society in the region, and throughout East Asia commercial and political trends were shaped by developments in that country. Japan moved from disunity to a politically united Shogunate, and the new government reduced outside contacts in order to simplify management of internal affairs. Europeans, specifically the Portuguese, Spanish, and Dutch, became permanent participants in East Asian affairs, but they were less important in Asian affairs than traditional views of "European expansion" infer.

We have evidence that Europeans played an important role as middlemen between Japan and China as Japan was being unified, but it is far from clear that the outcome in Japan would have been different without them. Indeed, in the absence of the Portuguese, the Japanese might well have established stronger commercial ties with Vietnam, Indonesia, and the Philippines. Economic expansion in China was probably assisted by the silver and copper that arrived in European ships, but Chinese economic expansion was self-generated. Without silver imports, China would have found other ways of expanding its money supply. After all, it was Song China that first successfully used paper currency centuries before 1500. At the same time, Chinese intellectuals found the European science brought by the Jesuits interesting. Ultimately, however, they used it in ways that fitted their own vision of the world, rejecting the assumptions that had produced the science that they were borrowing.

# 7

# OUTCOMES AND PORTENTS

The interplay of political, cultural, religious, and economic expansion that created an interconnected world after about 1200 C.E. is marked by three major traits. At least by implication, this view of the era 1200–1700 also raises questions about the role of western civilization in the world during the nineteenth and twentieth centuries and about global developments in the twenty-first century. The main features of world history during 1200–1700 are important here because they help us understand events in that period. Because those features have persisted to the present, however, perhaps they will also help us to understand the coming decades.

Three traits stand out after 1200. One is the emergence of two prominent, if very different, reference points for world history, China and Europe. By 1700 these two civilizations played major roles in shaping the global exchanges that were the heart of world history. The second prominent trait of the era was (and remains) the persistent strength and adaptability of local culture and institutions. This strength can be seen wherever one culture expanded into the territory of another, but it is especially important to keep it in mind when we read accounts of European expansion that are written by Europeans. The significance of European expansion before 1700 has often been misunderstood and overstated, as historians unconsciously project the European dominance of the nineteenth century backward to earlier times. The third key feature of world history that surfaced by 1700—and this may seem to contradict the previous point—was the global reach of European trade, credit, and market connections. There is controversy over what allowed Europeans to build such a worldwide network of trade and finance, and its implications were just beginning to appear in 1700. This global reach became central to world trends only in the nineteenth and twentieth centuries, and it is now being challenged. Let us address these points in more detail.

## THE DUAL FOCUS OF GLOBAL DYNAMISM

The expansiveness of world cultures that marks the modern world began to gain momentum after about 1000 C.E. and was well established by the 1200s. As we saw, it was in part set in motion by the warming of the global climate between 800 and 1200, which encouraged the expansion of both nomadic and sedentary societies. The reversal of the climatic trend after 1200 worsened the tension between the two societies, and produced a wave of nomadic invasions into settled agricultural zones from China to Mexico. The situation was further altered by the transfer of disease between areas with very different epidemiological histories and accumulated resistances. The bubonic plague produced important demographic power vacuums that encouraged expansion. The result was the widespread political expansion of the migrating militarized elites of Asia, Africa, the Mediterranean, the Middle East, and the Americas.

By the 1400s, the empires and kingdoms that emerged from this process were being reinforced by general population growth. Throughout Asia, Europe, and much of Africa the worst effects of the bubonic plague were fading and populations were starting to rebuild. While America experienced a different chronology, most of the world saw steady population growth until after 1600, and in many areas it continues today. This demographic trend brought long-term expansion of the labor force, agriculture, commerce, and tax revenues. These factors made it easier to construct large economic and political systems.

Gradually, however, two focal areas emerged, based on two quite different civilizations. China has been the economic and cultural center of East Asian developments since the Han Dynasty, before the time of Christ. Although China was not openly aggressive overseas after 1430, her large and growing population, sophisticated industries, intensive agriculture, and appetite for imports made China an enormous magnet for international trade and politics. In addition to that social and economic dynamism, China had a remarkable tradition of effective central government. China has not always been unified, but her imperial tradition has been constant and most of modern China has been under one government since the Mongol Yuan Dynasty took over in the later 1200s. It is useful to remember that, at the time of the American Declaration of Independence in 1776, China was the largest centrally governed country that the world had ever known, with two to three times as many inhabitants as the entire continent of Europe. Moreover, then, as now, Chinese emigrants and cultural influence extended far beyond those boundaries.

The second focal point for global developments that was emerging by 1700 was Europe. Unlike China, Europe has never been politically unified, despite important common patterns of religion, political traditions, and family structure. Indeed, Europe was almost constantly torn by internal wars until 1945. Until after 1700 Europe was also a relatively backward region compared with China or India. Its population was relatively small, most of its industrial products were crude to Indian or Chinese eyes, and it produced only modest amounts of monetary metals within its own territories.

By 1700, Europeans were present almost everywhere, usually in small numbers, but only in the Atlantic islands and the Americas did they control the political and economic high ground (see Map 7.1). European successes were defined by two factors. One was the limited resources available to European governments and to the adventurers who spearheaded the European form of expansion. As we saw in Chapter 2, European governments were weakly organized and had difficulty controlling resources. Constantly at war inside Europe, little of what they collected could be spared to support expansion outside of Europe. This meant that early expansion was funded by a haphazard combination of royal assistance and high-risk venture capital. As a result, early European expeditions consisted of small numbers of marginal adventurers with limited resources. Few in number, once away from Europe they were often over a year's sailing time from home and reinforcements. This meant that they tended to use tactics that reflected both desperation and ruthlessness. Only after 1600, with the organization of the Dutch East India Company, and after 1650, with the reorganization of the English East India Company, did this begin to change. With both government backing and large-scale capitalization, these two enterprises began to lay the foundation for a more substantial European presence in Asia. Even these developments, however, were hints of future European power rather than signs of European control in the 1600s.

The second factor that shaped European success was the political situation they found in Africa, the Indian Ocean, and East Asia. Where they found countries with effective governments, as they did in Turkey, Persia, China, India, and Japan after unification, Europeans had little choice but to abide by local laws and trade on locally established terms. When they resisted, as in their first contacts with China and Japan, they were promptly sent packing. Alternatively, Asian governments used them as diplomatic or commercial pawns in their own affairs. Nothing is more striking than the pictures of European ships forced to store their cannon on shore before they could do business in China (Illustration 6.4). Only where parts of Africa and Asia were organized into competing city-states and principalities, as was much of Italy in Europe, could Europeans create permanent strongholds and impose their own terms of trade. It is no accident that the Portuguese and Dutch had their biggest initial successes in coastal Africa, the south Indian coast, and Indonesia. At the time that the Europeans arrived, those parts of Afro–Asia consisted of a complex network of small, interdependent countries. Some of them were small enough so that the limited military potential of small European expeditions could play a crucial role in local disputes.

If limited European resources and the local accidents of Afro–Asian politics defined and limited European successes before 1700, another factor helps explain their ability to enter into distant economies as well as they did. That factor was American silver. Before the 1700s Europe produced few things that interested Asian consumers, while Asia produced a great many things that Europeans wanted to own. This meant that on its own, Europe could not earn the foreign exchange it needed to buy Asian exports. This is one reason why the Portuguese, Dutch, and English worked so hard to provide shipping services between Asian countries.

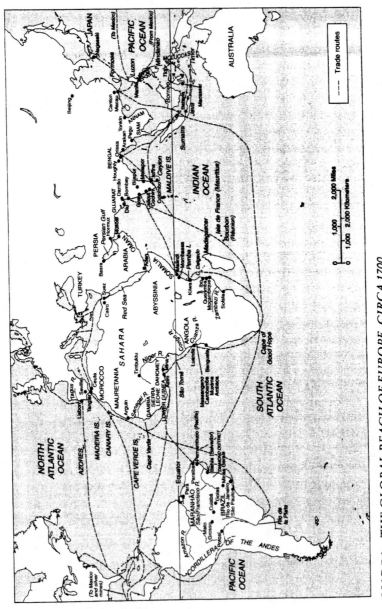

**MAP 7.1** *THE GLOBAL REACH OF EUROPE, CIRCA 1700.*
*While Asian trade stayed within its own areas, Europeans built a commercial network that spanned the globe. As the*
*world became more interdependent, the Europeans' global network gave them a strategic advantage.*

The profits from those services were an important source of the capital needed to buy Asian goods for sale in Europe.

After 1560 Mexican and Peruvian silver, channeled through Seville in Europe and Manila in Asia, began to flood the world economy. Silver, which is scarce, is a valuable metal for luxury use, and was used to coin money all over Europe and Asia. The expanding Asian economies presented a strong demand for money in order to keep their economies expansive. As a result, a given quantity of silver bought more goods in Asia than in Europe or America. Silver was cheap and plentiful in America, and also in Europe (and in Japan). It is no accident that China and Japan agreed to allow European trade after 1550.

This is a controversial point. There is general agreement that American silver made possible European trade with Asia well into the 1700s. It was not that the European economy itself was more productive or sophisticated than that of Mughal India or Ming and Manchu (Qing) China; it was simply that Europeans could now provide something that sold very profitably in Asian markets.

The controversy arises not over the fact of silver, but over its impact on the Asian economies that imported it. This essay takes the position that the Ottoman, Safavid, Mughal, and Chinese Empires needed an expanding money supply to provide for the needs of expanding economies. For that reason, they were ready to trade goods for silver at an exchange rate that let Europeans sell those goods profitably at home. Thus Europe's "success" was a function of the weakness of indigenous politics in America (which allowed Europeans to exploit American mines) and of the demands of a dynamic market economy in Asia.

The alternative interpretation is that such silver "flooded" the economies that received it and precipitated monetary inflation that undermined Asian economies and societies. This parallels a similar argument about inflation in Europe. In Europe, however, there is little agreement on the actual amount and impact of inflation, and considerable support for the idea that without American silver, other forms of money would have evolved. Silver thus was a symptom of an economic trend, not its cause. There is little reason to think that the same argument does not also apply to the bigger and more complex economies of China and India.

It may seem a technical matter, but it has an important point. If European silver inflated Asian prices and undermined Asian political institutions, it is possible to argue that European activities were undermining Asian autonomy as early as 1600. If European silver was attracted to Asia by the strong demand for money in expanding Asian economies, Europe's position in Asia was due to the strength of the Asian world, not its supposed weaknesses. In that case, as this book argues, Europe's impact on Asia remains quite modest until well after 1700.

The real portent on the European side was not its power in the larger world, but the changes that contact with the world was precipitating within Europe. In the cultural realm, encountering the world created intellectual currents that intersected with the challenge to traditional religious authority represented by the Renaissance and the Protestant Reformation. This contributed to a steady secularization of the ways in which Europeans dealt with their world. One outcome of this trend was the scientific revolution. Another result of world contact was the beginnings of cultural relativism. By this we must understand that Europeans consciously began to study other cultures and to grant them an autonomous validity. However imperfectly this has spread through the West, it is one of the more hopeful legacies of the era 1200–1700.

At the same time, the politically chaotic society housed in Europe was, after about 1650, evolving a remarkable pattern of expanding demand, increasing individual wealth, risk-sharing and capital-accumulating commercial techniques, and a receptiveness to the potential of new technologies. In effect, the European counterpart to the massive, gradually expanding, and resilient Chinese tradition of Asia was the self-reinforcing engine of trade that took shape in the European Atlantic by the end of the 1600s. As of 1700 that Atlantic economy was still far from matching that of China or India in size. It had, however, achieved a pattern of sustained, self-reinforcing growth based in part on the trade being financed by American silver. This economic growth was to give Europe a dominant role in the world during the century and a half after 1800.

# THE STRENGTH OF LOCAL CULTURES

Although the emergence of China and Europe as the two most prominent centers of world expansion is important, so too is the remarkable degree to which societies everywhere resisted, adapted, and borrowed selectively from the various alien missionaries, soldiers, and merchants who arrived in their midst. Even the forceful expansion of a powerful military empire like China under the Mongol Yuan dynasty could be stopped, as their abortive invasions of Japan and Indonesia demonstrated. Similarly, when Europeans arrived in Africa or Asia, they had little luck at imposing themselves on well-organized states. The first European empires in Asia were possible because large parts of the continent were organized into small states with correspondingly small-scale local conflicts. This allowed Europeans with very limited resources to influence local affairs and establish permanent bases. As we saw with the Portuguese, however, the development of strong governments in Persia, India, Siam, and Burma played an important role in their eventual marginalization in Asia. Where Europeans met strong governments, as in Russia, Japan, India, and China, they had to accept the conditions for doing business established by local authorities. Furthermore, many African and Asian societies were more adept at assimilating and adapting new methods and technologies to their own needs than western textbooks often admit. Even in the Americas and the Atlantic, where European authority was more effective sooner than in Asia, it had definite limits. The African slave trade was only possible because some (but not all) African states collaborated in the trade. The Spanish empire in America survived because the Spaniards accepted numerous compromises with Amerindian culture and left large spheres of autonomy to indigenous communities.

# THE GLOBALIZATION OF EUROPEAN ECONOMIC ACTIVITY

As of 1500, European commercial techniques were not much different from those of the rest of the world, and their maritime technology had only recently become competitive with that of the Indian Ocean or China. In 1700 this equilibrium was shifting, although the change was still far from obvious. European capitalism had learned to organize private, large-scale, sustained commercial and manufacturing enterprises, which were new in Europe and which were to prove increasingly effective elsewhere. Europeans had also figured out how to channel wealth into long-term investments that allowed investors to leave management to professional entrepreneurs. The development of the joint stock company, forerunner of the modern corporation, was crucial. It allowed small investors to own a part of a company in the form of standardized, saleable shares, while separating them from the task of management. The English and Dutch East Indian Companies, two of many similar enterprises, exemplify this capability.

Out of this situation evolved something genuinely new: a network of trade and credit that was entirely in European hands and literally stretched around the world. (See Map 7.1.) An individual in any important city in the world could now invest in business on a global scale. It was possible for a widow in Copenhagen or Barcelona to invest in a sequence of commercial transactions that would take her money around the globe and deliver the profits to her nearby banker. The money that the widow in Copenhagen gave to her London or Amsterdam merchant-banker could have bought European goods or American silver for shipment to a European agent in a place like Bombay. The sale of those commodities in India could have funded the purchase of Indian textiles to be delivered by a Dutch or Portuguese ship to customers in China. The proceeds from that transaction could be used to buy Chinese porcelains for delivery by Chinese ships to Manila, and then by Spanish ships to Acapulco, where the porcelain and silk would probably have been exchanged for American silver on the way to Cadiz in Spain. In Cadiz, other commercial agents would have exchanged it for Spanish wine, wool, or olive oil, which found ready markets in Amsterdam or London. The accumulated profits finally would end up in the hands of the merchant banker in London or Amsterdam to whom the widow had entrusted her investment. There they would wait for the widow in Copenhagen to draw on them with promissory notes payable through a commercial agent in her hometown.

Whether that particular example ever happened, it illustrates that a worldwide network of European credit and trade had been created. The network operated on European concepts of contract, credit, and trust, and it touched every important society. This system interacted freely with local counterparts everywhere in the world, and a Malay or Mughal widow could have done the same thing as the widow in Copenhagen. Nevertheless, the system was uniquely European and increasingly was at the service of the expanding European economy.

As long as Asian, African, and European societies dealt with each other as peers, the impact of European expansion was not particularly strong. By 1700, however, significant trends were appearing. Europeans had already created lopsided exchanges such as the American silver mining industry and the African slave trade. They had encouraged whole districts in India to become dependent upon exports to unstable markets in Europe. They were taking over much of the shipping industry between Asian countries. In parts of Indonesia they seized direct control of production and introduced slave labor. Although insignificant in the world picture of 1700, such developments, combined with an impersonal network of global credit and capital, would later produce unintended and unhappy consequences.

As westerners, it is hard for us to avoid talking extensively about Europe and its heritage. But to understand the world of 1200–1700, or that of today, we have to remember that unique and politically powerful cultures also existed in China, Japan, Africa, India, Southeast Asia, Turkey, and Iran (to name a few). It is easy to write a world history in which both large and small local cultures around the world have been dominated and exploited by Europeans (and later the United States) in the two and a half centuries since 1700. Since World War II, however, we have had to recognize the incompleteness of that perception. Other cultures have continued to follow their own paths to the future, more often than not borrowing from each other on their own terms rather than on western ones.

In the currently bewildering transition from the twentieth century to the twenty-first, the West finds itself confronted by the same unique and powerful cultures that it confronted before 1700. The fact that China, like an elephant found standing in the parlor, remains an enormous and uncertain reality reminds us of the underlying global dualism that surfaced between 1200 and 1700. The fact that societies all over the "non-European" and Latin American world have learned how to develop and use the technologies and capitalist techniques we think of as western intellectual property reminds us again that until after 1700, Europe was marginal to most of the world. When Europeans first encountered these dynamic societies in the 1400s and 1500s, they did not readily think of them as partners, but often had to treat them as such. Europeans (and now European–Americans) must again learn to deal with other cultures as partners.

# SUGGESTED READINGS

The most interesting books on world history are often hard to classify according to region or period. Thus a good part of this suggested list of additional readings consists of books that seem general in their focus. They are supplemented by suggestions relevant to specific areas or continents.

One wide-ranging set of important articles, edited by Felipe Fernández-Armesto, is *The Global Opportunity* (Brookfield, Vt.: Variorum, 1995). Jerry Bentley, *Old World Encounters: Cross-Cultural Contacts and Exchanges in Pre-Modern Times* (New York: Oxford University Press, 1993) has a similar focus and is availiable in an inexpensive paperback. The ecological dimension of the relative success and failure of European colonization is laid out in Alfred Crosby, *Ecological Imperialism: The Biological Expansion of Europe, 900–1900* (Cambridge: Cambridge University Press, 1986). One of the more stimulating examples of global history, although many of the findings have been incorporated into Crosby's book, is William H. McNeill, *Plagues and Peoples* (New York: Doubleday, 1976). McNeill not only documents the impact of the bubonic plague of the 1300s, but places the whole problem of disease and epidemics in the context of world history. McNeill also addresses the use of gunnery and the development of empires in *The Pursuit of Power* (Chicago: University of Chicago Press, 1982). This topic is also approached from a broader perspective in Geoffrey Parker, *The Military Revolution: Military Innovation and the Rise of the West* (Cambridge: Cambridge University Press, 1988). Alfred Crosby offers a suggestive approach to views of reality in *The Measure of Reality: Quantification and Western Society, 1250–1600* (Cambridge: Cambridge University Press, 1998). The problem of changing climate can be approached by looking at H. H. Lamb, *Climate Present, Past, and Future*, Vol. II (London: Methuen, 1977), and T. M. L. Wigley, M. J. Ingram, and G. Farmer (eds.), *Climate and History: Studies in Past Climates and Their Impact on Man* (Cambridge: Cambridge University Press, 1981). There is an ongoing discussion of the degree to which the interaction between parts of the world made up an interactive system from very early times. One of the most recent is Andre Gunder Frank, *ReOrient: Global Economy in the Asian Age* (Berkeley: University of

California Press, 1998). Frank provides a full introduction to the numerous analyses of large-scale, interactive global issues and their authors.

One of the more interesting attempts to categorize different kinds of encounters between Europeans and others, and to explain the differing outcomes, is found in Urs Bitterli, *Cultures in Conflict: Encounters Between European and Non-European Cultures, 1492–1800* (Stanford: Stanford University Press, 1989). The chronic problem of perception and misperception in cross-cultural encounters is approached by several papers in Stuart Schwartz (ed.), *Implicit Understandings: Observing, Reporting, and Reflecting on the Encounters Between Europeans and Other Peoples in the Early Modern Era* (New York: Cambridge University Press, 1994). The most interesting model for long-distance trade over the centuries, and one that touches many corners of the globe, is Philip Curtin, *Cross-Cultural Trade in World History* (Cambridge: Cambridge University Press, 1984). An older attempt at world history, from the perspective of the emergence of European economic dominance, is in Fernand Braudel, *Civilization and Capitalism, 15th–18th Century*, especially Vol. III, *The Perspective of the World*, Sian Reynolds (trans.), (New York: Harper and Row, 1979). Eric Wolf's *Europe and the People Without History* (Berkeley: University of California Press, 1982) also has an impressive global sweep while using a Marxist model of modes of production to frame the interaction between Europeans and other peoples. Carlo Cipolla's *Guns, Sails and Empires: Technological Innovation and the Early Phases of European Expansion, 1400–1700* (New York: Minerva Press, 1965) is titled with reference to Europe, but has fascinating chapters on the comparative use of widely known Eurasian technologies connected with ship building and gunnery. For a good summary of the themes in this book cast in terms of European expansion, see G. V. Scammel, *The First Imperial Age: European Overseas Expansion, c. 1400–1715* (London: Unwin Hyman, 1989). For a view of this as a problem in cultural interaction, see Anthony Pagden, *European Encounters with the New World* (New Haven: Yale University Press, 1993).

The earlier counterpart to these histories is the rise of the Mongol Empire, which is best approached through David Morgan's *The Mongols* (Oxford: Blackwell, 1987), which is a good antidote to Paul Ratchnevsky's *Genghis Khan: His Life and Legacy* (Oxford: Blackwell, 1991) and J. J. Saunders, *The History of the Mongol Conquests* (London: Routledge, 1971). For a descriptive overview of both the Mongol Empire and the other Islamic regions of the 1300s, see Ross E. Dunn, *The Adventures of Ibn Battuta: A Muslim Traveler of the 14th Century* (Berkeley: University of California Press, 1986). Dunn uses Ibn Battuta's writings to construct a vivid picture of the regions visited by that author. The last major sequel to the Mongol invasions, that of Tamerlane, is recounted in Beatrice Forbes Manz, *The Rise and Rule of Tamerlane* (Cambridge: Cambridge University Press, 1989).

The Mediterranean and Ottoman traditions are dealt with in a variety of sources. A comparative perspective on the three great Mediterranean powers is available through the eyes of the Venetian ambassadors of the later sixteenth century, as edited by James C. Davis, *Pursuit of Power: Venetian Ambassadors' Reports on Spain, Turkey, and France in the Age of Philip II, 1560–1600* (New York: Harper & Row, 1970). One of the most important books since World War II on the Mediterranean in the sixteenth century is Fernand Braudel's *The Mediterranean and the Mediterranean World in the Time of Philip II* (New York: Harper and Row, 1972–1973). This massive book surveys all of the actors in the region, shows the underlying dynamic that brought the main contenders together, and provides an excellent narrative of the conflict between the Spaniards and the Ottomans. Two of the standard accounts of the rise of the Spanish Empire in Europe are J. H. Elliott, *Imperial Spain, 1469–1716* (London: Penguin, 1970, first published 1963), and Henry Kamen, *Spain, 1469–1714: A Society of Conflict* (London: Longman, 1983). Elliott's version is more nuanced but somewhat dated; Kamen's version is considerably more up to date.

The most recent and one of the more accessible treatments of the Ottoman Empire is in Jason Goodwin, *Lords of the Horizon: A History of the Ottoman Empire* (Henry Holt & Co., 1999). One of the classic general histories of the rise of the Ottoman Empire is in Franz Babinger, *Mehmed the Conqueror and His Time*, edited by William Hickman and translated by Ralph Manheim (Princeton: Princeton University Press, 1978). A more general history of the empire is found in Stanford Shaw, *History of the Ottoman Empire and Modern Turkey, Vol. I: Empire of the Gazis: The Rise and Decline of the Ottoman Empire, 1280–1808* (Cambridge: Cambridge University Press, 1991, first published, 1976). An alternative book with a narrower chronological focus is Halil Inalcik, *The Ottoman Empire: The Classical Age, 1300–1600* (London: Weidenfeld & Nicolson, 1973). For a more recent and more broadly focused collection of essays, see Halil Inalcik and David Quataert (eds.), *The Economic and Social History of the Ottoman Empire, 1300–1914* (Cambridge: Cambridge University Press, 1994). A brief introduction to Ottoman themes is available in Norman Itzkowitz, *Ottoman Empire and Islamic Tradition* (New York: Alfred A. Knopf, 1972). Gulru Necipoglu, *Architecture, Ceremonial, and Power: The Topkapi Palace in the Fifteenth and Sixteenth Centuries* (Cambridge: The MIT Press, 1991) provides a fascinating and beautifully illustrated analysis of the structure and role of the Ottoman royal palace in the 1400s and 1500s. The administrative workings of the empire and the development of the provincial bureaucracy can be explored in I. Metin Kunt, *The Sultan's Servants: The Transformation of Ottoman Provincial Government, 1550–1650* (New York: Columbia University Press, 1983).

A more general and accessible picture of the texture of the Ottoman world is available in Raphaela Lewis, *Everyday Life in Ottoman Turkey* (London: B. T. Batsford, 1971). The openness of the Ottoman system to ethnic and religious minorities is well illustrated in Avigdor Levy, *The Sephardim in the Ottoman Empire* (Princeton: Darwin Press, 1992). For a fascinating sense of how the Ottomans perceived Europe in the early modern period, see Fatma Muge Gocek, *East Encounters West: France and the Ottoman Empire in the Eighteenth Century* (New York: Oxford University Press, 1987). Gocek's account is based on the reports of the Ottoman ambassador to France in 1720–1721. The 1990s have again reminded us of the complex heritage of the Balkans, and one can find an extensive survey of the situation there before the era of Ottoman rule in John Fines's *The Late Medieval Balkans: A Critical Survey from the Late Twelfth Century to the Ottoman Conquest* (Ann Arbor: University of Michigan Press, 1994). Palmira Brummett, *Ottoman Seapower and Levantine Diplomacy in the Age of Discovery* (Albany: SUNY Press, 1994), offers an excellent understanding of Ottoman policies during the years when the Ottomans conquered the Mameluk Empire, subordinated Venice to Ottoman commercial goals, and extended Ottoman influence into the Indian Ocean.

Various books deal with early European expansion into the Atlantic, the most basic of which is probably J. H. Parry, *The Age of Reconnaissance* (Berkeley: University of California Press, 1981, first published 1963). It has been considerably updated in several respects by Felipe Fernández-Armesto's *Before Columbus: Exploration and Colonization from the Mediterranean to the Atlantic, 1229–1492* (London: MacMillan Education, 1987) and his *Columbus* (Oxford: Oxford University Press, 1992), possibly the best modern biography of Columbus. The best older treatment of early activities in the Caribbean remains that of Carl Ortwin Sauer, *The Early Spanish Main* (Berkeley: University of California Press, 1969). Marvin Lunenfeld has taken a rather distinctive approach in his *1492: Discovery, Invasion, Encounter: Sources and Interpretations* (Lexington: D. C. Heath, 1991), which combines modern interpretations with primary sources in an intriguing way. The classic statement about the impact of America on Europe is J. H. Elliott, *The Old World and the New, 1492–1650* (Cambridge: Cambridge University Press, 1972). A newer and more broadly focused discussion of the same topic is in Roger Schlesinger, *In the Wake of Columbus: The Impact of the New World on Europe, 1492–1650* (Wheeling, Ill.: Harlan Davidson, 1996), which offers a concise summary of the ways in which interaction with America affected European culture and politics. One of the fundamental surveys of Spain in America is J. H. Parry, *The Spanish Seaborne Empire* (New York: Knopf, 1966). James Lang's *Conquest and Commerce: Spain and England in the Americas* (New York: Academic Press, 1975) offers a direct comparison of the two varieties of Atlantic expansion mentioned in the title. This book says little about the interaction between Europeans and Amerindians in what became the United States and Canada, but two collections of documents and articles offer an introduction to that topic: Francis Jennings, *The Invasion of America: Indians, Colonialism, and the Cant of Conquest* (New York: Norton, 1976), and Alan L. Karras and J. R. McNeill (eds.), *Atlantic American Societies from Columbus through Abolition, 1492–1888* (London: Routledge, 1992). On the bigger issue of the expansion of the European economy to the point where it drew distant regions into dependence on European markets and merchants and was ready to launch an Industrial Revolution, the classic account is in Ralph Davis, *The Rise of the Atlantic Economies* (Ithaca: Cornell University Press, 1986; first published 1973). The conceptual framework for the discussion of the plantation-based world of the maritime fringes of the Atlantic is taken largely from Philip Curtin, *The Rise and Fall of the Plantation Complex: Essays in Atlantic History* (Cambridge: Cambridge University Press, 1990), reinforced by the excellent work of John Thornton, *Africa and Africans in the Making of the Atlantic World, 1400–1680* (Cambridge: Cambridge University Press, 1992).

A vast number of books deal with Pre-Columbian America and the establishment of Spanish authority there. Among those that have been suggestive for this book is Geoffrey Conrad and Arthur Demarest's *Religion and Empire: The Dynamics of Aztec and Inca Expansionism* (Cambridge: Cambridge University Press, 1990), which gives a good initial interpretation of the dynamics of the two great Amerindian Empires that preceded the Spanish Empire. J. H. Elliott has edited an excellent collection of articles as an introduction to Spanish America in an elaborate volume with extensive illustrations. See Elliott's *The Spanish World: Civilization and Empire, Europe and the Americas, Past and Present* (New York: Harry Abrams, 1991). A recent introduction to the Aztec world is found in Inga Clendinnen, *Aztecs: An Interpretation* (Cambridge: Cambridge University Press, 1993). A shorter analysis that looks at most aspects of Aztec–Mexica society is found in Frances F. Berdan, *The Aztecs of Central Mexico: An Imperial Society* (Fort Worth: Holt, Rinehart and Winston, 1982). Clendinnen's *Ambivalent Conquests: Maya and Spaniard in Yucatan, 1517–1570* (Cambridge: Cambridge University Press, 1987) is a concise exercise in cross-cultural history. Two rather different attempts to understand Inca culture can be found in Irene Silverblatt, *Moon, Sun, and Witches: Gender Ideologies and Class in Inca and Colonial Peru* (Princeton: Princeton University Press, 1987), and Rolena Adorno, *Guaman Poma: Writing and Resistance in Colonial Peru* (Austin: University of Texas Press, 1986). For a classic overview of the Inca world as part of the Spanish Empire and modern Latin America, see Magnus Morner, *The Andean Past: Land, Societies, and Conflicts* (New York: Columbia University Press, 1986). Colin MacLachlan provides an interesting and thoughtful discussion of the entire Spanish heritage in America in his *Spain's Empire in the New World: The Role of Ideas in Institutional and Social Change* (Berkeley: University of California Press, 1988).

The vast area that includes the Muslim world and much of the Indian Ocean can be approached from several perspectives. One of the most thorough general books is Ira Lapidus's *A History of Islamic Societies* (Cambridge: Cambridge University Press, 1988). For a shorter and somewhat impressionistic account of Islam and Islamic culture, see Alfred Guillaume, *Islam* (London: Penguin, 1954). On the three great Muslim empires of the Middle East and South Asia (Ottoman, Safavid, and Mughal), read Marshall G. S. Hodgson, *The Gunpowder Empires and Modern Times* (Chicago: University of Chicago Press, 1972). The early sophistication of Arab shipping and navigation is set out in George F. Hourani's entertaining *Arab Seafaring in the Indian Ocean in Ancient and Early Medieval Times,* as expanded by John Carswell (Princeton: Princeton University Press, 1995, first published 1951). The complexities of the Indian Ocean world are best seen in such books as K. N. Chaudhuri, *Trade and Civilization in the Indian Ocean: An Economic History from the Rise of Islam to 1750* (Cambridge: Cambridge University Press, 1989). An older account that is also important for understanding parts of Africa and Brazil is found in C. R. Boxer, *The Portuguese Seaborne Empire, 1415–1825* (New York: Knopf, 1969). The same comment is true of Boxer's companion volume, *The Dutch Seaborne Empire, 1600–1800* (London: Penguin, 1990, first published 1965). On the same topic, see Sanjay Subrahmanyam's *The Portuguese Empire in Asia, 1500–1700: A Political and Economic History* (London: Longman, 1993), which is much more up to date and less Eurocentric in its perspective.

For a closer look at both Portuguese and Indian contexts for the arrival of Europeans in India, see two recent books: Sanjay Subrahmanyam, *The Career and Legend of Vasco da Gama* (Cambridge: Cambridge University Press, 1998) and Luc Cuyvers, *Into the Rising Sun: Vasco da Gama and the Search for the Sea Route to the East* (New York: TV Books, Inc., 1998). As for the Mughal Empire, Waldemar Hansen's *The Peacock Throne: The Drama of Mogul India* (New York: Holt, Rinehart and Winston, 1972) is a readable general history of the empire. A. S. Basham's *A Cultural History of India* (Oxford: Clarendon Press, 1975) covers the entire Muslim period in India, while J. M. Shelat's *Akbar* (Bombay: Bharatiya Vidge Bhavan, 1959, republished in 1967) is a good biography of the greatest Mughal emperor. A more recent account of Mughal India is in John F. Richards, *The Mughal Empire* (Cambridge: Cambridge University Press, 1993), while a succinct political narrative can be found in Stanley Wolpert's *A New History of India* (5th edition, New York: Oxford University Press, 1997). An eyewitness description of Akbar's court can be found in Pierre du Jarric, *Akbar and the Jesuits, an Account of the Jesuit Missions to the Court of Akbar,* translated by C. H. Payne (New York: Harper and Brothers, 1926, republished, New Dehli: Tulsi Publishing House, 1979). On the consolidation of the smaller Southeast Asian countries, see Victor Lieberman, *Burmese Administrative Cycles: Anarchy and Conquest, c. 1580–1760* (Princeton: Princeton University Press, 1984); David K. Wyate, *Thailand: A Short History* (New Haven: Yale University Press, 1982); David Chandler, *A History of Cambodia* (Boulder: Westview Press, 1992); and Alexander Woodside, *Vietnam and the Chinese Model* (Cambridge: Harvard University Press, 1971). The gradual increase in the relative importance of European oceanic trade in Asia and the decline of the overland alternative routes is laid out in Niels Steensgaard, *The Asian Trade Revolution of the Seventeenth Century: The East India Companies and the Decline of the Caravan Trade* (Chicago: University of Chicago Press, 1974). A detailed discussion of Southeast Asia is in Anthony Reid, *Southeast Asia in the Age of Commerce, 1450–1680* (2 vols.; New Haven: Yale University Press, 1988, 1993).

Africa and its projection into America is not as well studied, but several readable books are available, some of them from perspectives that would not occur at first to many readers. Among the latter is Graham Connah, *African Civilizations: Precolonial Cities and States in Tropical Africa: An Archaeological Perspective* (Cambridge: Cambridge University Press, 1987), which offers matter-of-fact archaeological evidence for a remarkably rich pre-European, sub-Saharan African world. Philip Curtin has provided a very readable discussion of important parts of west Africa before European control in his *Economic Change in Precolonial Africa: Senegambia in the Era of the Slave Trade* (Madison: University of Wisconsin Press, 1975). Other histories of particular African kingdoms include L. W. Henderson, *Angola: Five Centuries of Conflict* (1979), and A. F. Ryder, *Benin and the Europeans, 1485–1897* (1969). Here, too, it is worth mentioning again John Thorton, *Africa and the Africans*.

One of the more accessible discussions of the slave trade, which puts it into African as well as European and American perspective, is Edward Reynolds, *Stand the Storm: A History of the Atlantic Slave Trade* (London: Allison & Busby, 1989). This can be compared with Basil Davidson, *The African Slave Trade: Precolonial History, 1450–1850* (Boston: Little, Brown, 1961; first published as *Black Mother* in hardcover) and the very much older discussion of the slave trade first published in England in 1920 by E. D. Morel, *The Black Man's Burden: The White Man in Africa from the Fifteenth Century to World War I* (New York: Modern Reader Paperbacks, 1969). The massive scope of the slave trade, in terms of the numbers, sources, and destination on forced African migration is suggested by Philip Curtin, *The African Slave Trade: A Census* (Madison: University of Wisconsin Press, 1969).

One can find a useful general introduction to East Asia, and the major sedentary civilizations of Asia in general, in Rhoads Murphey, *A History of Asia* (New York: HarperCollins, 1996). This is a general Asian history textbook, but is also a good first introduction to China, Japan, and India, and offers good summaries of many local narratives that could not be fitted into a book the size of this one. C. Schirokauer, *A Brief History of Chinese and Japanese Civilization* (New York: Harcourt, Brace, Jovanovich, 1989), is also helpful in this connection. For a thoughtful starting point for an understanding of premodern China, one should look up Mark Elvin, *The Pattern of the Chinese Past* (Stanford: Stanford University Press, 1973). The underlying fact of ongoing demographic and agricultural expansion that is central to understanding China is touched on in Dwight H. Perkins, *Agricultural Development in China, 1368–1968* (Chicago: University of Chicago Press, 1969). For a good introduction to the 2000-year-old interaction between China and the nomadic communities on her inland frontiers, see Thomas J. Barfield, *The Perilous Frontier:*

*Nomadic Empires and China, 221 B.C. to A.D. 1757* (Oxford: Blackwell, 1989). The history of the Mongol or Yuan dynasty is well illustrated in Morris Rossabi, *Khubilai Khan: His Life and Times* (Berkeley: University of California Press, 1988). A good counterpart to this is Marco Polo himself, available as *The Travels of Marco Polo* (Wadsworth Editions, 1997). One of the remarkable institutions of traditional China was the scholar-gentry bureaucracy. A good insight into this aspect of Chinese society is in I. Miyazaki, *China's Examination Hell: The Civil Service Examinations of Imperial China* (New Haven: Yale University Press, 1981, previously published in 1964). A discussion of the role of the Confucian literati in the formation of the Ming state is available in John Dardess, *Confucianism and Autocracy: Professional Elites and the Founding of the Ming Dynasty* (Berkeley: University of California Press, 1983). On the threats to stability in Ming China, see Chang and Chang, *Crisis and Transformation in Seventeenth-Century China* (Ann Arbor: University of Michigan Press, 1998). The idea that Asians were unable to resist European intrusions is exploded in an older but still valuable collection of essays edited by Joseph R. Levenson, *European Expansion and the Counter-Example of Asia, 1300–1600* (Englewood Cliffs: Prentice-Hall, 1967). The Chinese initiatives into the Indian Ocean in the early 1400s are well presented in Louise Levathes, *When China Ruled the Seas: The Treasure Fleet of the Dragon Throne, 1400–1433* (New York: Simon and Schuster, 1994). The larger issue of Chinese expansion can be explored in Wang Gungwu, *China and the Chinese Overseas* (Singapore: Times Academic Press, 1991).

For a glimpse of the richness of Chinese culture, and for endless images of medieval and early modern China, one can start with the sumptuous exhibition catalogue of the treasures of the National Palace Museum in Taipei, Wen C. Fong and James C. Y. Watt (eds.), *Possessing the Past: Treasures from the National Palace Museum, Taipei* (New York: Harry Adams, 1996). Among his various books on China, Jonathan Spence has published two particularly fascinating cross-cultural perceptions of China and Europe. One is *The Memory Palace of Matteo Ricci* (New York: Viking Penguin, 1984), which is built upon the career and reports of the Jesuit Matteo Ricci in China; the other is *The Question of Hu* (New York: Vintage, 1989). The latter recounts the story of a Chinese convert brought to France in the early eighteenth century and the mutual incomprehension that developed between Hu and his French sponsors.

To begin incorporating Japan into the picture, one can consult G. B. Sansom, *The Western World and Japan: A Study in the Interaction of European and Asiatic Cultures* (Tokyo and Rutland, VT: Charles E. Tuttle Company, 1987; first published in 1950). This places early modern Japan in an Asian context, but is sometimes dated in its vocabulary and stereotypes. For a more modern survey of Japanese history, see E. Reischauer, *Japan: The Story of a Nation* (New York: McGraw Hill, 1990, first published 1970). On the period touched on in this book, see also Conrad Totman, *Early Modern Japan* (Berkeley: University of California Press,

1993). The Japan of the 1500s and 1600s is also seen through Mary Elizabeth Berry's biography of *Hideyoshi* (Cambridge: Harvard University Press, 1982), one of the central figures in the unification of Japan. For eyewitness views of Japan in the same era, see Michael Cooper, *They Came to Japan: An Anthology of European Reports on Japan, 1543–1640* (Berkeley: University of California Press, 1965). The reverse perception is available in Donald Keene, *The Japanese Discovery of Europe* (Stanford: Stanford University Press, 1969). The more recent vision of Tokugawa Japan after unification, which challenges the old isolation model, is discussed in Chie Nakane and Shinzaburo Oishi (eds.), Conrad Totman (trans.), *Tokugawa Japan: The Social and Economic Antecedents of Modern Japan* (Tokyo: University of Tokyo Press, 1991). The internal balance of power between central government and local society is discussed in Philip C. Brown, *Central Authority and Local Autonomy in the Formation of Early Modern Japan* (Stanford: Stanford University Press, 1993).

# ACKNOWLEDGMENTS

The author wishes to acknowledge the use of material taken from the following publications:

Adler, Elkan Nathan (ed.), *Jewish Travellers in the Middle Ages: 10 Firsthand Accounts* (New York: Dover, 1987), pages 43–44, 69, 159–160, 162, 166, 169–170.

Davis, James C. (ed. and trans.), *Pursuit of Power: Venetian Ambassadors' Reports on Spain, Turkey, and France in the Age of Philip II, 1560–1600* (New York: Harper & Row, 1970), pages 120, 122, 127–133.

Ebrey, Patricia (ed.), *Chinese Civilization: A Sourcebook* (2nd ed., New York: Free Press, 1993), pages 216–218.

Johnson, Oliver A. (ed.), *Sources of World Civilization, Vol. I: To 1500; Vol. II: Since 1500* (Englewood Cliffs, N.J.: Prentice Hall, 1994), Vol. I, pages 354, 429, 431–432; Vol. II, pages 141, 144–145, 148–149.

Kirshner, Julius, and Karl F. Morrison (eds.), *Readings in Western Civilization: Vol. 4. Medieval Europe* (Chicago: University of Chicago Press, 1986), pages 449–451.

Kishlansky, Mark (ed.), *Sources of World History: Readings for World Civilization* (2 vols., New York: HarperCollins, 1995), Vol. I, pages 166–167, 242–243, 269–272, 283–284; Vol. II, page 9.

Kishlansky, Mark, Patrick Geary, Patricia O'Brien, and R. Bin Wong. *Societies and Cultures in World History, Vol. A: To 1500, Vol. B: 1300–1800* (New York: HarperCollins, 1995), Vol. A, page 215, Vol. B, page 456.

Lunenfeld, Marvin (ed.), *1492: Discovery, Invasion, Encounter: Sources and Interpretations* (Lexington, Mass.: D. C. Heath, 1991), pages 21–22, 189–190, 283, 312–313.

McNeill, William, and Mitsuko Iriye (eds.), *Modern Asia and Africa* (New York: Oxford University Press, 1971), pages 20, 29–30, 137–140.

McNeill, William, and Jean W. Sedlar (eds.), *China, India, and Japan: The Middle Period* (New York: Oxford University Press, 1971), pages 147–149, 154–157.

McNeill, William, and Marilyn Waldman (eds.), *The Islamic World* (Chicago: University of Chicago Press, 1973), pages 113–116, 249–251, 264–266.

Reilly, Kevin (ed.), *Readings in World Civilizations, Vol. 2: The Development of the Modern World* (3rd ed., New York: St. Martin's, 1995), pages 65–66, 81–82, 85.

Reynolds, Edward, *Stand the Storm: A History of the Atlantic Slave Trade* (London: Allison & Busby, 1989), page 45.

Schwartz, Stuart, Linda Wimmer, and Robert Wolff (eds.), *The Global Experience: Readings in World History, Volume II* (New York: Longman, 1997), pages 5–6, 16, 57–59, 73–75, 91–92.

Wiesner, Merry, Julius Ruff, and William Wheeler (eds.), *Discovering the Western Past: A Look at the Evidence. Vol. I: To 1715* (Boston: Houghton Mifflin, 1989), pages 273–274.

## MAP CREDITS

### MAP 1.1 THE MONGOL EMPIRES IN THE THIRTEENTH CENTURY.
Source: Ira Lapidus, *A History of Islamic Societies* (Cambridge: Cambridge University Press, 1988), p. 277.

### MAP 1.2 NOMADIC MIGRATION PATTERNS IN ASIA, AFRICA, AND EUROPE.
Source: Based on K. N. Chaudhuri, *Trade and Civilization in the Indian Ocean: An Economic History from the Rise of Islam to 1750* (Cambridge: Cambridge University Press, 1989), p. 41. Conceptual material from Eric Wolf, *Europe and the People Without History* (Berkeley: University of California Press, 1982), pp. 25–30.

### MAP 1.3 ISLAMIC EXPANSION TO 1700, WITH PRINCIPAL LONG-DISTANCE TRADE ROUTES BEFORE 1500.
Source: Ira Lapidus, *A History of Islamic Societies* (Cambridge: Cambridge University Press, 1988), p. 242. Trade routes as shown in John Mckay, Bennett Hill, and John Buckler, *A History of World Societies, Vol. A: From Antiquity Through the Middle Ages* (Boston: Houghton Mifflin, 1988), pp. 263 and 470.

### MAP 1.4 AFRO-EURASIAN TRADE CIRCUITS PRIOR TO 1500.
Source: Robert Strayer, *The Making of the Modern World: Connected Histories, Divergent Paths, 1500 to the Present* (2nd ed., New York: St. Martin's. 1995), p. 111, which is derived from Janet Abu-Lughod, *Before European Hegemony* (New York: Oxford University Press, 1989), p. 37.

### MAP 2.1 EUROPE AND THE EMPIRE OF CHARLES V ABOUT 1550.
Source: Stanley Chodorow, Hans Gatzke, and Conrad Schirokauer, *A History of the World, Vol. I* (San Diego: Harcourt Brace Jovanovich, 1986), p. 511.

### MAP 2.2 THE OTTOMAN EMPIRE AT ITS GREATEST EXTENT IN 1683.
Source: Robert Strayer, *The Making of the Modern World: Connected Histories, Divergent Paths, 1500 to the Present* (New York: St. Martin's, 1995), p. 223.

### MAP 3.1 WEST AFRICA, THE MALI EMPIRE, AND MAIN AFRICAN TRADE ROUTES BETWEEN 1300 AND 1500.
Source: Adapted from Mark Kishlanky, et al, *Societies and Cultures in World History, Vol. A: To 1500* (New York: HarperCollins, 1995), p. 212, with additions.

### MAP 3.2 ATLANTIC TRADE ABOUT 1700.
Source: Robert Strayer, *The Making of the Modern World: Connected Histories, Divergent Paths, 1500 to the Present* (2nd ed., New York: St. Martin's, 1995), p. 116.

### MAP 4.1 AMERINDIAN EMPIRES ON THE EVE OF THE SPANISH CONQUEST.
Source: Leften S. Stavrianos, *The World Since 1500: A Global History* (Englewood Cliffs: Prentice-Hall, 1982), p. 262.

### MAP 4.2 THE SPANISH EMPIRE IN AMERICA ABOUT 1600.
Source: Marvin Lunenfeld (ed.), *1492: Discovery, Invasion, Encounter: Sources and Interpretations* (Lexington: D. C. Heath, 1991), p. xl, with dates from Robert Strayer, *The Mak-

ing of the Modern World: Connected Histories, Divergent Paths, 1500 to the Present (2nd. ed., New York: St. Martin's, 1995), p. 4.

## MAP 5.1 THE FOUR GREAT ASIAN EMPIRES OF THE PERIOD 1600–1700.

Source: William McNeill, *A World History* (New York: Oxford University Press, 1971), p. 333.

## MAP 5.2 THE RISE OF THE MUGHAL EMPIRE TO ITS HEIGHT IN 1707.

Source: Ira Lapidus, *A History of Islamic Societies* (Cambridge: Cambridge University Press, 1988), Map 19, p. 453.

## MAP 5.3 THE INDIAN OCEAN IN THE 1600s.

Source: K. N. Chadhuri, *Trade and Civilization in the Indian Ocean: An Economic History from the Rise of Islam to 1750* (Cambridge: Cambridge University Press, 1989), p. 96, with additional details.

## MAP 6.1 THE CHINESE EMPIRE UNDER THE MING DYNASTY (1368–1644).

Source: Philip J. Adler, *World Civilizations, Vol. II* (Minneapolis: West Publishing, 1996), p. 503.

## MAP 6.2 THE CHINESE EMPIRE UNDER THE QING (CH'ING) DYNASTY (1644–1911).

Source: Stanley Chodorow, Hans W. Gatzke, and Conrad Schirokauer, *A History of the World, Vol. I* (San Diego: Harcourt Brace Jovanovich, 1986), p. 545.

## MAP 7.1 THE GLOBAL REACH OF EUROPE, CIRCA 1700.

Source: C. R. Boxer, *The Portuguese Seaborne Empire, 1415–1825* (New York: Knopf, 1969), fold-out map inside rear flyleaf, with routes added.

## TEXT CREDITS

The following works from which substantial portions are quoted in this book, are protected by the copyright law of the United States and international copyright laws.

1. *Jewish Travellers in the Middle Ages*, Elkan Nathan Adler, editor, pp. 43, 44, 69, 159–170. Copyright © 1987 Dover Publications. Reprinted by permission.

2. *The History of India as Told by Its Own Historians*, H. M. Elliot and John Dowson, eds. (London: Trubner & Co., 1871)

3. *The Life and Works of Jahiz*, translator. D. M. Hawkes, Charles Pellat ed., 1969, Routledge & Kegan Paul, excerpted from pp. 91–97, 106–8, 195–97, 239–43, 251, 257–58, 265–67.

4. *A Literary History of Persia*, Edward G. Browne, editor, Vol. 2, pp. 427–431, 1902. Reprinted with permission of Cambridge University Press.

5. *The History of the World Conqueror* by 'Ala-ad-Din 'Ata-Malik Juvaini, translated from the text of Mirza Muhammad Qazvini by John Andrew Boyle, Vol. I, pp. 23–24, 153, 159–164, 201–207. Copyright © 1958 Manchester University Press. Reprinted by permission.

6. *Sundiata*, D. T. Niane, editor, G. D. Pickett, translator. Copyright © 1965 Longman Group, Ltd. Reprinted by permission.

7. *Readings in Western Civilization*: Vol. 4, Medieval Europe, edited by Julius Krishner and Karl F. Morrison, pp. 449–451 (#70 Matteo Villani). Copyright © 1987 University of Chicago Press. Reprinted by permission.

8. *Translations and Reprints from the Original Sources of European History,* Vol. III, No. 6, (Philadelphia: Department of History of the University of Pennsylvania, 1912).

9. From *The Prince*: A Norton Critical Edition, Second Edition by Niccolo Machiavelli, translated by Robert M. Adams. Copyright © 1992, 1977 by W. W. Norton & Company, Inc. Used by permission of W. W. Norton & Company, Inc.

10. *A Defense of Liberty Against Tyrants* by Philippe Duplessis-Mornay.

11. Excerpt from *The Pursuit of Power: Venetian Ambassadors' Reports,* edited and translated by James C. Davis. English translation copyright © 1970 by James C. Davis. Reprinted by permission of HarperCollins Publishers, Inc.

12. *The Turkish Letters of Ogier Ghiselin De Busbecq, Imperial Ambassador at Constantinople,* 1554–1562, translated by Edward S. Foster, 1927, pp. 58–62, 65–66, 109–114, by permission of Oxford University Press, Ltd.

13. Reprinted with the permission of Simon & Schuster from *The Muslim World on the Eve of Europe's Expansion,* edited by John J. Saunders. Copyright © 1966 by Prentice-Hall, Inc., renewed 1994 by John J. Saunders.

14. From *Ibn Battuta in Black Africa* by Sassiol Harndren and Noel Q. Kish, eds. and translators, (Princeton, NJ: Markus Wiener Publishers, 1994, p. 315)

15. From Andreoni's *Cultura e opulencia do brasil, por suas drogas e minas,* Andree Mansuy, editor, translator Linda Wimmer (Paris: Institut des Hautes Etudes, 1968), pp. 165–167, 183–187, excerpted from Stuart Schwartz, Linda Wimmer and Robert Wolff, *The Global Experience,* Vol. II. Copyright © 1998 Addison Wesley Longman. Reprinted by permission of Addison Wesley Educational Publishers, Inc.

16. From *Monumenta Missionaria Africana,* Antonio Brasio, editor, Linda Wimmer translator (Lisboa: Agencia Geral do Ultramar, 1952), Vol. 10, pp. 294–95, 335, 404, 470, 488. Excerpted from Stuart Schwartz, Linda Wimmer and Robert Wolff, *The Global Experience,* Vol. II. Copyright © 1998 Addison Wesley Longman. Reprinted by permission of Addison Wesley Educational Publishers, Inc.

17. *Interesting Narrative of the Life of Olaudah Equianao, or Gustavus Vassa, the African,* by Olaudah Equiano, published in 1789.

18. *Captain Cano, or Twenty Years of an African Slaver* by Theodore Canot, (London: Richard Bentley, 1854).

19. *New and Accurate Description of the Coast of Guinea,* (London: J. Knapton, 1705; 2/e, 1721).

20. *History of the Incan Empire* by father Bernabe Cobo, translated and edited by Roland Hamilton. Copyright © 1979 University of Texas Press.

21. From C. R. Markham, editor and translator, *The Letters of Amerigo Vespucci,* pp. 27–28, (London: Hakluyt Society, 1894)

22. From Michele de Cuneo's Letter on the Second Voyage, 28 October 1495 in *Journals and Other Documents in the Life and Voyages of Christopher Columbus,* translated and edited by S. E. Morison, (New York: The Heritage Press, 1963), p. 212.

23. From *The Spanish Conquest in America and Its Relation to the History of Slavery and to the Government of the Colonies,* Vol. I, pp. 264–267, by Arthur Helps (London: J. W. Parker & Sons, 1855–1861).

24. From *The Broken Spears* by Miguel Leon-Portilla. Copyright © 1962, 1990 by Miguel Leon-Portilla. Expanded and Updated Edition © 1992 by Miguel Leon-Portilla. Reprinted by permission of Beacon Press, Inc.

25. *The Annals of the Cakchiquels,* pp. 115, 119, 129–33, 143–144. Translated by Adrian Recinos and Delia Goetz. Copyright © 1953, 1981 by the University of Oklahoma Press. Reprinted by permission.

26. *The History of India as Told by its Own Historians* by H. M. Elliot and John Dowson, editors, pp. 374–388. (London: Trubner & Co., 1871).

27. Al-Badaoni, *Muntakhabu-T-Tawarikh.* Translated by W. H. Lower, (New York: Reed, 1973). Excerpted from Stuart Schwartz, Linda Wimmer and Robert Wolff, *The Global Experience,* Vol. II. Copyright © 1998 Addison Wesley Longman. Reprinted by permission of Addison Wesley Educational Publishers, Inc.

28. *A Journal of the First Voyage of Vasco Da Gama,* edited and translated by E. G. Raven-stein, (London: Hakluyt Society, 1898), pp. 77–79.

29. *Southeast Asia in the Age of Commerce,* Vol. 1: The Lands Below the Winds by Anthony Reid. Copyright © 1988 Yale University Press. Reprinted by permission of the publisher.

30. From *Memoirs of a Malayan Family:* Written by Themselves. Translated by W. Mars-den, pp. 1–7, 14–33, (London: Oriental Translation Fund, 1830).

31. From *Sources of Chinese Tradition,* compiled by Wm. Theodore de Bary, Wing-tsit Chan and Burton Watson. Copyright © 1960 Columbia University Press, NY NY. Reprinted with permission of the publisher.

32. From *China in the Sixteenth Century* by Matthew Ricci, translated by Louis J. Gal-lagher, S. J. Copyright © 1942 and renewed 1970 by Louis J. Gallagher, S. J. Reprinted by permission of Random House, Inc.

33. Reprinted with the permission of The Free Press, a Division of Simon & Schuster, from *Chinese Civilization: A Sourcebook,* 2/e by Patricia Buckley Ebrey. Copyright © 1993 by Patricia Buckley Ebrey.

34. *The Life and Letters of St. Francis Xavier,* edited by Henry James Coleridge, 2/e, (London: Burns and Oates, 1890).

35. From *Modern Asia and Africa,* edited by William H. McNeill and Mitsuko Iriye, trans-lated by Mitsuko Iriye. Copyright © 1971 by Oxford University Press, Inc. Used by permission of Oxford University Press, Inc.

# Index

*Index*